D0586347

HOMEWORK FOR GROWN-UPS QUIZ BOOK

Also by E. Foley & B. Coates

HOMEWORK FOR GROWN-UPS

ADVANCED HOMEWORK FOR GROWN-UPS

HOMEWORK FOR GROWN-UPS QUIZ BOOK

Fiendishly Fun Questions
to
Test Your Old-school Knowledge

E. Foley & B. Coates

SQUARE PEG

For Iris and Joe

Published by Square Peg 2011

2 4 6 8 10 9 7 5 3 1

First published in Great Britain in 2011 by
Square Peg
Random House, 20 Vauxhall Bridge Road,
London SW1V 2SA

www.randomhouse.co.uk

Addresses for companies within The Random House Group Limited can be found at:
www.randomhouse.co.uk/offices.htm

The Random House Group Limited Reg. No. 954009

A CIP catalogue record for this book
is available from the British Library

ISBN 9780224095204

The Random House Group Limited supports The Forest Stewardship Council (FSC®), the leading international forest certification organisation. Our books carrying the FSC label are printed on FSC® certified paper. FSC is the only forest certification scheme endorsed by the leading environmental organisations, including Greenpeace. Our paper procurement policy can be found at www.randomhouse.co.uk/environment

Text designed by Peter Ward
Typeset in Bembo by Palimpsest Book Production Limited, Falkirk, Stirlingshire
Printed in Great Britain by Clays Ltd, St Ives plc

CONTENTS

INTRODUCTION

Whether your idea of fun is an evening spent with friends and family basking in the glow of twinkly Christmas tree lights while you take the opportunity to probe the most cob-webbed corners of your intellect, or if the joy of good, old-fashioned competitive spirit is what sets your pulse racing, this book is your perfect fix. The *Homework for Grown-ups Quiz Book* will test your knowledge and prove once and for all who knows best. It's full of fiendishly fun questions to stimulate the grey matter and promises to provide the perfect framework for hours spent bettering yourself and your loved ones.

Do the simplest questions have you scratching your head, or are you the one who shouts out the answers to the bioluminescence section of *University Challenge*? Either way, the *Homework for Grown-ups Quiz Book* will be a treat. Here you will find intellectual interrogations (both highbrow and a little lower) with an eye towards the traditional educational systems of the past – mining the old favourites of Maths, English, Science, Geography, History, Physical Education, Classics, the Arts (Art, Drama, Dance, Music, Film Studies), Home Economics, Religious Education and Break Time. You'll find verbal reasoning, brain teasers, riddles, word searches and crosswords to fox and fascinate, to tease and tantalise. And pay close attention to the answers too, which are dazzling in their detail – so you can still learn while enjoying thrashing your granny at general knowledge.

So have your pencils ready, and your competitive spirit cresting: it's time to get puzzling.

ENGLISH LANGUAGE AND LITERATURE

Cry God for Harry, England and Saint George, it's time to test your literary and linguistic learning. From the delights of the dictionary to the great novels of the past, you will soon find yourself teased and tested on the glories of our language and our unparalleled cultural heritage.

Age cannot wither our mother tongue, nor custom stale her infinite variety: in fact, the English language grows more powerful every day as she spreads her charms across the globe via the inescapable tentacles of the internet. The array of topics covered in this chapter stands as a testament to the endless treasure trove of enjoyment and enlightenment that the study of English can bring to your life. How well do you know your verbs and adverbs? How intimate are you with the Romantic poets? Can you guess the next lines of the great Bard's most famous soliloquies? Below you will find your grammar goaded, your bookshelves badgered and your reading rated. There's even a spelling test lying in wait for you.

1. For a modestly sized island in a chilly grey sea, Britain has had several significant foreign invasions, from the Romans and Angles and Saxons to the Vikings and Normans, all seeking out our excellent weather and reputation for customer service. We have also been responsible for more than our own fair share of invading and international meddling. This eventful history and the onetime reach of the British Empire mean that our language has been greatly enriched by other tongues, and some of the least exotic-seeming words in our repertoire have surprising roots. Match up the following words with their language of origin:

a) Chipmunk	Old Persian
b) Jackal	Irish
c) Pistachio	Turkish
d) Tomato	Dutch
e) Platinum	Arabic
f) Spectacles	German
g) Abyss	Spanish
h) Giraffe	Nahuatl
i) Tycoon	Khoikhoi
j) Tyke	Mandarin
k) Cot	Japanese
l) Gnu	Old Norse
m) Drab	Ojibwe
n) Sauna	Old French
o) Abseil	Finnish
p) Slob	Hebrew
q) Maven	Ancient Greek
r) Ukulele	Hindi
s) Holster	Hawaiian
t) Tea	Latin

2. Which wonderful and morally edifying epic work from the early days of our national literature is set in the Malvern Hills?

a) *Piers Plowman*
b) *Paradise Lost*
c) *Beowulf*
d) *Angel Uncovered*

3. As a wise man once said, 'Poets are the unacknowledged legislators of the world.' That wise man was in fact a poet himself, Percy Bysshe Shelley (husband of the author of *Frankenstein*), but we won't hold that against him. In his honour, seek out the fifteen poets' surnames hidden in the word search below:

H	A	K	B	C	U	R	I	L	K
R	E	E	U	O	G	T	C	A	Y
O	L	A	R	W	U	I	L	R	P
S	I	T	N	P	B	L	A	K	E
S	O	S	S	E	B	T	R	I	R
E	T	W	D	R	Y	D	E	N	P
T	E	H	E	R	R	I	C	K	O
T	F	I	V	N	O	N	M	M	P
I	C	D	O	N	N	E	L	J	E
W	O	R	D	S	W	O	R	T	H

4. We can't continue for a second longer without testing you on the rich oeuvre belonging to the king of English literature, the Immortal Bard. Identify the Shakespeare play in which the following, somewhat emotional, quotation appears:

Needs must I like it well: I weep for joy
To stand upon my kingdom once again.
Dear earth, I do salute thee with my hand,
Though rebels wound thee with their
  horses' hoofs:
As a long-parted mother with her child
Plays fondly with her tears and smiles in
  meeting,
So, weeping, smiling, greet I thee, my
  earth,
And do thee favours with my royal
  hands.

5. Most people think of the saucy *Lady Chatterley's Lover* when David Herbert Lawrence is mentioned. However, he was also the author of numerous other novels, essays, plays and poems. Have a look at the beautiful stanzas of 'A Baby Running Barefoot' below and answer the following questions.

> When the bare feet of the baby beat across the grass
> The little white feet nod like white flowers in the wind,
> They poise and run like ripples lapping across the water;
> And the sight of their white play among the grass
> Is like a little robin's song, winsome,
> Or as two white butterflies settle in the cup of one flower
> For a moment, then away with a flutter of wings.
>
> I long for the baby to wander hither to me
> Like a wind-shadow wandering over the water,
> So that she can stand on my knee
> With her little bare feet in my hands,
> Cool like syringa buds,
> Firm and silken like pink young peony flowers.

a) How many similes are there in this poem?
b) Which letter does Lawrence use alliteratively most often?
c) Name the term which describes the repeated sound in 'butterflies', 'settle' and 'flutter' in the last two lines of the first verse?
d) Name the term which describes the repeated sound in 'butterflies', 'cup' and 'flutter'?

6. Over the course of history various famous, and infamous, personages have donated their names to the English language. Which of the following words are derived from historical figures' names?

Pepper
Pansy
Biro
Moustache
Ribbon
Quisling
Boycott
Methane

Dahlia
Gopher
Nicotine
Banjo
Naff
Proffer
Volt
Sideburns

7. Here's a test of your powers of retention. The great novels of the Victorian age are weighty in both senses of the word: do you stay hooked right up to page 832 or do you doze off just before the final, usually morally uplifting, pay-off? Match the following famous last lines to the classics of English literature from which they come:

a) 'I lingered round them, under that benign sky: watched the moths fluttering among the heath and harebells, listened to the soft wind breathing through the grass, and wondered how any one could ever imagine unquiet slumbers for the sleepers in that quiet earth.'
b) '"She may swear that on her knees to the holy cross upon her necklace till she's hoarse, but it won't be true!" said Arabella. "She's never found peace since she left his arms, and never will again till she's as he is now!"'
c) '"It is a far, far better thing that I do, than I have ever done; it is a far, far better rest that I go to than I have ever known."'
d) 'But the effect of her being on those around her was incalculably diffusive: for the growing good of the world is partly dependent on unhistoric acts; and that things are not so ill with you and me as they might have been, is half owing to the number who lived faithfully a hidden life, and rest in unvisited tombs.'

8. When Swedish dynamite-inventor Alfred Nobel set up his famous prizes he stipulated that one should be given for 'the most outstanding work of an idealistic tendency' published in a given year. The Nobel Prize in Literature (don't make a fool of yourself by calling it the Nobel Prize *for* Literature) has been awarded 103 times since 1901 – name four British winners.

9. This question will examine your English Comprehension skills. Read the opening paragraph from Jane Austen's novel *Northanger Abbey* and answer the questions below:

> No one who had ever seen Catherine Morland in her infancy would have supposed her born to be an heroine. Her situation in life, the character of her father and mother, her own person and disposition, were all equally against her. Her father was a clergyman, without being neglected, or poor, and a very respectable man, though his name was Richard – and he had

never been handsome. He had a considerable independence besides two good livings – and he was not in the least addicted to locking up his daughters. Her mother was a woman of useful plain sense, with a good temper, and, what is more remarkable, with a good constitution. She had three sons before Catherine was born; and instead of dying in bringing the latter into the world, as anybody might expect, she still lived on – lived to have six children more – to see them growing up around her, and to enjoy excellent health herself.

a) How many different adjectives are there in this passage?
b) How many different proper nouns are there?
c) Would you identify the tone of these lines as tragic, ironic, suspenseful, erotic or sombre?
d) Why does Austen suggest that Catherine should really have an abusive father and dead mother in order to qualify as a heroine?

10. The literary landscape would be a far less exciting place without those intrepid writers willing to sit down and imagine what it might be like to strangle a woman or hunt down a murderous suspect for our edification and amusement. Crime writers through the ages have cast sharp eyes over our definitions of morality, revealed the hypocrisies of corrupt societies and, of course, scared us all silly. Match up the following criminal investigators from the murky world of crime fiction with the villains they pursue and the authors of their stories:

Philip Marlowe	James Sheppard	Edgar Allan Poe
Sherlock Holmes	Casper Gutman	Wilkie Collins
C. Auguste Dupin	Eddie Mars	Raymond Chandler
Hercule Poirot	Godfrey Ablewhite	Dashiell Hammett
Sam Spade	James Moriarty	Agatha Christie
Sergeant Cuff	an orangutan	Arthur Conan Doyle

11. The poet and onetime soldier and Controller of the Customs of Hides, Skins and Wools in the port of London, Geoffrey Chaucer, took a mighty step forward for English literature when he began to write his poems in the English vernacular rather than in the more usual official languages of French and Latin. In 1387 he began his masterpiece, *The Canterbury Tales*, an account of a group of pilgrims travelling to the shrine of Thomas

Becket in Canterbury and telling each other stories along the way in the hope of winning the prize of a pub lunch. Chaucer's original plan was to write 120 tales but he only managed to get to twenty-four. Which of the following are NOT genuine Canterbury tales?

The Knight's Tale
The Rosicrucian's Tale
The Miller's Tale
The Wife of Bath's Tale
The Landlord's Tale
The Pardoner's Tale
The Nun's Priest's Tale
The Reeve's Tale
The Man at Arms' Tale
The Skivvy's Tale
The Cook's Tale
The Man of Law's Tale
The Friar's Tale
The Summoner's Tale
The Clerk's Tale
The Model's Tale
The Parson's Tale
The Merchant's Tale
The Squire's Tale
The Minstrel's Tale
The Fishwife's Tale
The Franklin's Tale
The Physician's Tale
The Pardoner's Tale
The Shipman's Tale
The Soldier's Tale
The Prioress's Tale
The Monk's Tale
The Milner's Tale
The Second Nun's Tale
The Canon's Yeoman's Tale
The Stablelad's Tale
The Manciple's Tale
The Chandler's Tale

12. Mr Deasy, Gabriel Conroy and Robert Hand are all characters from works by which author?

13. Identify the play the following quotation comes from and the feisty and ill-fated playwright responsible for it:

I count religion but a childish toy,
And hold there is no sin but ignorance.
Birds of the air will tell of murders past!
I am ashamed to hear such fooleries.
Many will talk of title to a crown:
What right had Caesar to the empery?
Might first made kings, and laws were then most sure
When like the Draco's, they were writ in blood.

14. Fill in the crossword below on the subject of the accomplished aesthete, peerless playwright and world-class wit, Oscar Wilde.

ACROSS

3. *The Picture of Dorian* ____ (4)
5. Wilde's play involving characters called Jokanaan and Herod Antipas (6)
6. '____, I am dying beyond my means' (4)
9. Wilde's friend and lover who commissioned Jacob Epstein to create Wilde's tomb at Père Lachaise cemetery in Paris (4)
11. *The Importance of Being* ____ (7)
13. The ____ of Queensberry, who was responsible for Wilde's prosecution (8)

DOWN

1. *Lady Windermere's* ____ (3)
2. *A Woman of* ____ *Importance* (2)
3. 'I have nothing to declare but my ____' (6)
4. The colour of the book Lord Henry sends to Dorian in the novel in 3 across (6)
7. The receptacle Ernest Worthing is placed in as a baby in the play in 11 across (7)
8. *The Ballad of Reading* ____ (4)

10. *The* ____ *of Man under Socialism* (4)
12. ____ *Profundis* (2)
14. 'I am ____ clever that sometimes I don't understand a single word of what I am saying' (2)

15. If you aren't particularly pernickety about vocabulary yourself, then use your powers of imagination to put yourself in a pedant's shoes to answer this question. According to traditional grammatical guidelines, a person who is unconcerned about a particular matter should be described as:

a) Disinterested
b) Uninterested
c) Deinterested

16. The two dark masters of American literature, William Faulkner (1897–1962) and Ernest Hemingway (1899–1961), were almost exact contemporaries. Both of them won the Nobel Prize in Literature and the works of each of them are considered stalwarts of the American literary canon. These similarities did not make them pals, however, and they criticised each others' work publicly. This is unsurprising as they were very different writers, Hemingway being celebrated for his terse, plain style and Faulkner for his ornate, poetic vision. Enthusiasts often get riled up and feisty when comparing the two and hardcore fans believe that you have to pick sides between Papa and William Cuthbert – you can't possibly appreciate both. If you haven't chosen your man yet then the books below should help you make up your mind. Match the book titles up with the relevant author.

The Torrents of Spring
Pylon
Intruder in the Dust
In Our Time
Mosquitoes
Men Without Women
True at First Light
The Town
As I Lay Dying
Islands in the Stream

17. These days, as we dash off hundreds of emails and texts every day, we seem to go for a little less punctuation and a little more action in our missives. However, it is important for sense and style to have a firm grasp of where those tiny but significant marks should be placed. Punctuate the following passage from Charles Dickens' *Bleak House* correctly:

> The raw afternoon is rawest and the dense fog is densest and the muddy streets are muddiest near that leaden headed old obstruction appropriate ornament for the threshold of a leaden headed old corporation temple bar and hard by temple bar in lincolns inn hall at the very heart of the fog sits the lord high chancellor in his high court of chancery

18. The first exposure many of us have to narratives depicting the chaotic nature of the universe is through nursery rhymes and their often eccentric characters and plots. Many are the parents who have scratched their heads and wondered what exactly has happened to the weasel and what it has to do with treacle, and why the mice were chasing the farmer's wife in the first place. Unscramble the anagrammed nursery rhyme characters below:

a) Hard Humbled Robot
b) Leftist Elf Summit
c) A Paschal Babe Bake
d) Cello Dog Ink
e) Duty Myth Pump
f) Cork In Cob
g) Hero Toe Smog
h) Soy Garden Goes Gooey
i) My War Raged
j) Timbered Lichen
k) A Detached Filth Dent
l) Picket Itchy Key

19. If a man were to knock on your door desperate to use your phone because his companion was 'parturient' – whom would he most likely be wishing to call?

a) The police
b) The fire brigade
c) His stockbroker
d) The hospital

20. Identify the classics of British and American literature that are being referred to by the following newspaper headlines:

a) SCHOOLBOYS RESCUED FROM DESERT ISLAND! SEVERAL STILL MISSING
b) DRIFTER KILLED IN STRUGGLE AFTER MURDERING RANCHER'S WIFE
c) HAYSLOPE INFANTICIDE ESCAPES DEATH SENTENCE!
d) COKETOWN SCHOOLTEACHER'S SON FLEES COUNTRY AFTER ROBBERY!
e) YOUNG WOMAN SUSTAINS SERIOUS HEAD INJURY ON LYME COBB
f) ALABAMA MAN ACCIDENTALLY STABS SELF TO DEATH!

21. Pick out three grammatical errors in the following sentence. For a bonus point, identify the work of English literature the sentence refers to.

> George and myself are keen to have our eagerly-anticipiated wedding in October.

22. We all have our spelling weak spots: even when we know that 'weird' is spelled 'weird' we can end up making the same mistake again and again. Even the most grammatically aware among us sometimes shame themselves with a 'you're' for 'your' or 'their' for 'they're' when writing in haste. Which of the following tricky words have been mispelled?

Aerial
Amendment
Broccoli
Ceiling
Complementary (meaning 'free')
Conoisseur
Deceive
Feasible
Haemorhage
Indite
Knowledgable
Lieutenant
Liquify
Miscellaneous
Phlegm
Priviledge
Seige
Supersede
Twelfth
Withold

23. If a man were to knock on your door desperate to use your phone because his companion was 'conflagrant' – whom would he most likely be wishing to call?

a) The police
b) The fire brigade
c) His stockbroker
d) The hospital

24. Time to brush up your knowledge of poetic forms here. From sestinas to sonnets and haikus to heroic couplets, the study of poetry has a mellifluous vocabulary to describe its various shapes and sizes. Which of the following is the definition of a villanelle?

a) Five stanzas of tercets followed by one quatrain, using only two rhymes
b) Six sestets followed by one tercet with lines ending in set patterns of repeated words
c) Sets of tercets where the middle line of each tercet rhymes with the first and last lines of the following tercet
d) Octaves of iambic pentameters with the rhyme scheme ABABABCC

25. Language is constantly evolving and one of the latest new dialects to emerge among 'the youth' is that of 'text speak'. Translate the following passages into standard English and see if you can guess the characters from classic English novels who might have written the messages.

a) 'Omg, boss cnt c. Yf strtd fyr lk b4. G2g'
b) 'So mbrsd. Sis hs run off w soulja. Lil f%l. Nytmare.'
c) 'Soz wl b l8. Gloves 404. Wl b w u asap.'
d) 'W@ a mstake. Cougar h%kd ^ w n pub wz my mum'

26. Which best-selling collection of poetry features characters called Bustopher Jones, Gus and Old Deuteronomy?

27. If someone disdainfully describes a friend's cat as 'glabrous', what breed is the poor maligned moggy most likely to be?

a) British Blue
b) Sphynx
c) Abyssinian
d) Scottish Fold

28. If a man were to knock on your door desperate to use your phone because his companion was 'felonious' – whom would he most likely be wishing to call?

a) The police
b) The fire brigade
c) His stockbroker
d) The hospital

29. A useful adjunct to the Roman alphabet used for the English language is the NATO Phonetic Alphabet. This is a 'radio alphabet' used for spelling out words with complete clarity in situations, such as air traffic control, where it's very important that no errors are made. It is also very useful for spelling your name out to call-centre operatives so they don't end up loading you on to their systems as Mr Fnyth rather than Mr Smith.

Using your knowledge of the NATO Phonetic Alphabet, give the name of the novel referred to below. (Clue: the author's surname was originally Korzeniowski.)

The capital of a South American country

The first name of a renowned Irish writer (clue: see question 14)

The name of a Shakespearean hero

The triangular mouth of a river

The name of a Shakespearean heroine

The seventh-largest country in the world

The short version of the name of the archangel who fights the dragon in Revelations

30. What meter is Samuel Taylor Coleridge's intoxicating poem 'Kubla Khan' written in? To help you on your way, the first lines are given below.

a) Iambic tetrameter
b) Anapaestic tetrameter
c) Iambic pentameter
d) Trochaic pentameter

In Xanadu did Kubla Khan
A stately pleasure-dome decree:
Where Alph, the sacred river, ran
Through caverns measureless to man
Down to a sunless sea.

31. Do you often find yourself describing people as 'nice'? It's good to try to be more creative with your everyday speech and one easy way to jazz up your conversation is to throw in the odd fancy adjective. Guess the meanings of the following zoological words, and then try to use at least one of them in normal discourse today:

a) Pavonine
b) Corvine
c) Ursine
d) Leporine

32. 'She dwells with Beauty – Beauty that must die . . .' You know you're in for a good time after a cheery opener like that. Look at the following stanza and answer the questions that follow:

She dwells with Beauty – Beauty that must die;
And Joy, whose hand is ever at his lips
Bidding adieu; and aching Pleasure nigh,

Turning to poison while the bee-mouth sips:
Ay, in the very temple of Delight
Veiled Melancholy has her sovran shrine,
Though seen of none save him whose strenuous tongue
Can burst Joy's grape against his palate fine:
His soul shall taste the sadness of her might,
And be among her cloudy trophies hung.

a) Which tragically short-lived poet wrote this poem?
b) What is the title of the poem?
c) What metre is the poem written in?
d) What is the rhyme scheme of the poem?

33. There are some poetic works that stir the heart and bring a tear to the eye whenever they are recited, winning them consistently high scores in competitions to find the nation's favourite poem. Much like traditional hymns or the stations on your train's commute, you might feel confident that you can remember the next lines of scripts that are so familiar, but it's often harder than you think when you aren't reciting alongside the rest of the congregation or the velvet tones of the station announcer. See if you can remember the next lines of the following famous poems:

a) Rudyard Kipling's 'If'

> If you can keep your head when all about you
> Are losing theirs and blaming it on you;
> If you can trust yourself when all men doubt you,
> But make allowance for their doubting too;
> If you can wait and not be tired by waiting,
> Or being lied about, don't deal in lies,
> Or being hated, don't give way to hating
> ....

b) William Wordsworth's 'Daffodils'

> I wander'd lonely as a cloud
> That floats on high o'er vales and hills,
> When all at once I saw a crowd,

A host, of golden daffodils;
Beside the lake, beneath the trees,
....

c) Alfred, Lord Tennyson's 'The Lady of Shallot'

On either side the river lie
Long fields of barley and of rye,
That clothe the wold and meet the sky;
And thro' the field the road runs by
To many-tower'd Camelot;
And up and down the people go,
Gazing where the lilies blow
Round an island there below,
....

d) Rupert Brooke's 'The Soldier'

If I should die, think only this of me:
That there's some corner of a foreign field
That is for ever England. There shall be
In that rich earth a richer dust concealed;
A dust whom England bore, shaped, made aware,
Gave, once, her flowers to love, her ways to roam,
A body of England's, breathing English air,
....

34. Which epic Elizabethan English poem takes the form of six books describing the complex allegorical adventures of various knights? (Clue:The poem is written in stanzas of nine lines rhyming ABABBCBCC, with the first eight lines made up of ten syllables and the last made up of twelve.)

35. In the mid-twentieth century a group of English writers including Kingsley Amis, Philip Larkin, Elizabeth Jennings, John Wain, Robert Conquest and Thom Gunn were grouped together under which of the following names:

a) The New Romantics
b) The Formalists

c) The Movement
d) The Tribe of Ben

36. Was Shakespeare a feminist? What would a Marxist interpretation of *Pride and Prejudice* uncover? Thank heavens there are boffins aplenty raring to make careers out of poring over literary texts in great detail in order to reveal different ways of interpreting and appreciating them. Literary theorists come in many different flavours and often passionately disagree with other schools of thought. The school of literary theory which developed in the mid-twentieth century and focussed on the text of a literary work itself rather than the author's motivations is known as:

a) Marxist Literary Criticism
b) Structuralism
c) New Criticism
d) Literary Darwinism

37. Again, we have a test of memory for you here. If anyone's work is worth memorising it is of course Mr Shakespeare's. Hopefully you will already know the next lines of the following famous speeches by our greatest-ever dramatist. If not, then spend no time wallowing in the inevitable hot shame, but turn to the plays immediately and commit your favourite pieces to heart. Fill in the next lines of these quotations:

a) *Antony and Cleopatra*
MARK ANTONY: Friends, Romans, countrymen, lend me your ears;
....
b) *Henry V*
HENRY: We few, we happy few, we band of brothers;
For he to-day that sheds his blood with me
Shall be my brother; be he ne'er so vile,
....
c) *Macbeth*
MACBETH: Is this a dagger which I see before me,

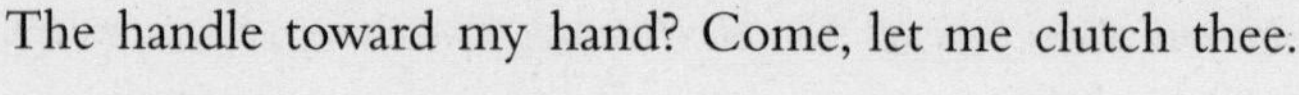
The handle toward my hand? Come, let me clutch thee.

....

d) *The Merchant of Venice*
SHYLOCK: Fair sir, you spit on me on Wednesday last;
You spurn'd me such a day; another time
You call'd me dog; and for these courtesies

....

38. We humans love to break the world and its history down into manageable chunks, to make it easier to feel a sense of control over the terrifying maelstrom that is time and experience. The study of English literature has its own chronological periods, where works of similar themes or styles were being produced or where certain historical events happened to bind a span of years together. When was the Augustan Age of English Literature?

a) 27 BCE–14 CE
b) 1700–1750
c) 1750–1800
d) 1800–1850

39. In Shakespeare's *The Tempest*, what is the name of Caliban's mother?

a) Hecate
b) Charybdis
c) Ariel
d) Sycorax

40. Sometimes the most experimental works of literature can surprise us by having been written far ahead of their time. Equally some modern writers choose to hark back to older, traditional models for their own aesthetic purposes. This can make it hard to date the books that make up our canon, but here we will ask you to give it your best shot. Put the following works in chronological order:

The Life and Opinions of Tristram Shandy, Gentleman (Volumes I and II) by Laurence Sterne
The Honorary Consul by Graham Greene
Decline and Fall by Evelyn Waugh
Heart of Darkness by Joseph Conrad
Barchester Towers by Anthony Trollope
The Prime of Miss Jean Brodie by Muriel Spark
A Passage to India by E. M. Forster
Wise Children by Angela Carter
The Waves by Virginia Woolf
Clarissa by Samuel Richardson
Sir Gawain and the Green Knight by the Gawain Poet
The Rivals by Richard Brinsley Sheridan
Adonaïs by Percy Bysshe Shelley
Endgame by Samuel Beckett
Death of a Naturalist by Seamus Heaney
Volpone by Ben Jonson
Under Milk Wood by Dylan Thomas
Mrs Warren's Profession by George Bernard Shaw
Brave New World by Aldous Huxley
The Arcadia by Philip Sidney

41. Identify the metaphysical author of the following poem. (Clue: As well as being a prominent poet the author was also a sailor, MP, diplomat and Dean of St Paul's Cathedral – although not all at once.)

For my first twenty years, since yesterday,
I scarce believed thou couldst be gone away;
For forty more I fed on favours past,
And forty on hopes that thou wouldst they might last;
Tears drown'd one hundred, and sighs blew out two;
A thousand, I did neither think nor do,
Or not divide, all being one thought of you;
Or in a thousand more, forgot that too.
Yet call not this long life; but think that I
Am, by being dead, immortal; can ghosts die?

42. The molossus is:

a) A poetic form related to the Malaysian pantoum
b) A metric foot consisting of three stressed syllables
c) A dramatic monologue on the subject of death
d) A prehistoric aquatic creature

43. As well as serving as a one-line summary of Shakespeare's great tragedy *King Lear*, the sentence below is also an opportunity for another examination of your grammatical acumen. Gather up your parsing prowess and identify the nouns, verbs, adjectives, adverbs, pronouns and articles in the following sentence:

The foolish king cruelly rejected his only decent daughter.

44. If a man were to knock on your door desperate to use your phone because his companion was 'penurious' – whom would he most likely be wishing to call?

a) The police
b) The fire brigade
c) His stockbroker
d) The hospital

45. Here's a dictionary-based brainteaser to test your vocabulary and your powers of deduction: Which word is an antonym of huge, includes three of the five vowels, and derives from the Latin word for 'less'?

46. One way to stun the other bibliophiles at your book group is occasionally to slip a few swish critical terms into your chitchat. Match up the following ideas from literary theory with the correct definitions:

a) objective correlative	Roland Barthes' theory that the reader creates the meaning of a text rather than the writer.

b) collective unconscious	Harold Bloom's theory that poets struggle to escape the shadow of their predecessors to create something new.
c) anxiety of influence	T. S. Eliot's theory that in order to express an emotion writers have to describe a set of objects, situations or chain of events that creates that emotion in the reader or audience.
d) death of the author	Carl Jung's theory that all cultures share common thoughts and experiences and that literature is the expression of these.

47. What is the name of the genre of theatre which encompasses works by Thomas Kyd, Christopher Marlowe, William Shakespeare, Thomas Middleton and John Webster and which draws many of its archetypal ingredients from the work of the Roman writer Seneca?

48. Life would be terribly boring if we all just communicated in straightforward factual sentences like robots. Figures of speech aren't just used in poetry and self-consciously literary writing, we also use them in everyday contexts as well. The following sentences are all examples of which rhetorical device?

> 'The City objects to government reforms.'
> 'The rebels swore loyalty to the Crown.'
> 'He preferred to use his mother tongue.'

49. Book titles are a critical part of a literary work. They can be purely informative, lyrically atmospheric or hint at deeper thematic concerns. The latest winner of the *Bookseller* Diagram Prize for Oddest Title of the Year, *Crocheting Adventures with Hyperbolic Planes*, could be said to do all three. Insert the correct colours to complete the following well-known book titles:

a) *The Color* .... by Alice Walker
b) .... *Dog* by Martin Amis
c) *The* .... *Letter* by Nathaniel Hawthorne
d) .... *Fang* by Jack London
e) *A Pair of* .... *Eyes* by Thomas Hardy
f) *On the* .... *Hill* by Bruce Chatwin
g) *A Clockwork* .... by Anthony Burgess
h) *How* .... *Was My Valley* by Richard Llewellyn

50. The study of English literature is usually just 'words, words, words', as Hamlet wearily says, so to jazz things up a bit we have a picture puzzle for you here. The following illustrative clues refer to the work of which twentieth-century British writer?

ENGLISH LANGUAGE AND LITERATURE ANSWERS

1.

a) 'Chipmunk' comes from the Ojibwe (a Native American language) '*atchitamon*'.
b) 'Jackal' comes from the Turkish '*çakal*'.
c) 'Pistachio' comes from the Old Persian '*pistah*'.
d) 'Tomato' comes from the Nahuatl (the language of the Aztecs) '*tomatl*'.
e) 'Platinum' comes from the Spanish '*plata*' meaning 'silver'.
f) 'Spectacles' comes from the Latin '*specere*' meaning 'to look'.
g) 'Abyss' comes from the ancient Greek '*abussos*' meaning 'bottomless'.
h) 'Giraffe' comes from the Arabic '*zarāfa*'.
i) 'Tycoon' comes from the Japanese '*taikun*' meaning 'great lord'.
j) 'Tyke' comes from the Old Norse '*tik*' meaning 'bitch'.
k) 'Cot' comes from the Hindi '*khāt*' meaning 'hammock'.
l) 'Gnu' comes from the Khoikhoi (a southern African language) '*i-ngu*'.
m) 'Drab' comes from the Old French '*drap*' meaning 'cloth'.
n) 'Sauna' comes from the Finnish '*sauna*'.
o) 'Abseil' comes from the German '*ab*' meaning 'down' and '*seil*' meaning 'rope'.
p) 'Slob' comes from the Irish '*slab*' meaning 'mud'.
q) 'Maven' comes from the Hebrew '*mevin*' meaning 'understanding'.
r) 'Ukulele' comes from the Hawaiian '*ukulele*' meaning 'jumping flea'.
s) 'Holster' comes from the Dutch '*holster*'.
t) 'Tea' comes from the Mandarin '*chá*'.

2. a) *Piers Plowman*, also known as *Piers the Ploughman* and the less snappy *The Vision of William concerning Piers the Plowman,* is an epic Middle English poem that was written by William Langland in the late 1360s. Several different manuscript sources survive, and the longest version stands at an impressive 2,567 lines. The poem describes the dream-vision experienced by the narrator, Will, after he falls asleep in the Malvern Hills and dreams of various elaborate allegorical situations concerning medieval society, Christianity and the search for salvation. It knocks those dreams about losing your teeth or turning up at work with no clothes on into a cocked hat. Impress yourself with your instinctive knack for Middle English by reading the opening lines below aloud:

In a somer sesun, whon softe was the sonne,
I schop me into a shroud, as I a scheep were;
In habite as an hermite unholy of werkes
Wente I wyde in this world wondres to here;
Bote in a Mayes morwnynge on Malverne hulles
Me bifel a ferly, of fairie, me-thoughte.

3.

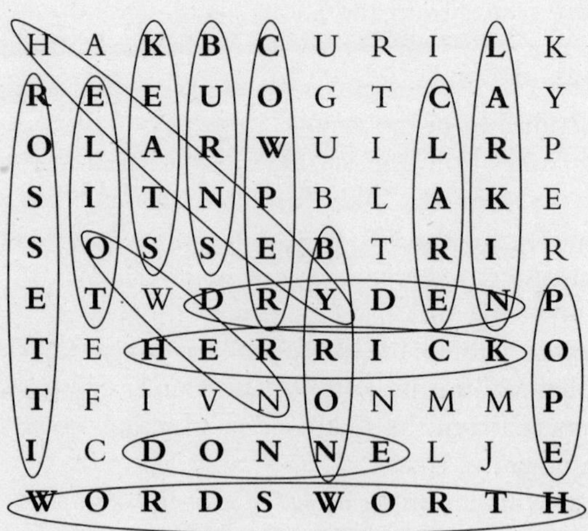

Burns, Byron, Clare, Cowper, Donne, Dryden, Eliot, Heaney, Herrick, Keats, Larkin, Owen, Pope, Rossetti, Wordsworth.

4. *Richard II.* (The eagle-eyed among you will have spotted the clues in the question: 'We can't continue for a **second** longer without testing you on the **rich** oeuvre belonging to the **king** of English literature, the Immortal Bard.')

This speech comes in Act III, Scene 2 as Richard arrives back in Britain after a trip away from his kingdom. He returns to find his authority threatened by the pushy young upstart, and (unbeknownst to Richard, obviously) future King Henry IV, Bolingbroke. This scene sees the troubled monarch beginning to lose heart at what awaits him and he soon works himself into such a slough of despond that he sighs to his companions: 'For God's sake, let us sit upon the ground / And tell sad stories of the death of kings.' What a fun night.

5.

a) 7. A simile is a figure of speech where one thing is compared to another using the words 'like' or 'as'. The seven examples in this poem are 'like white flowers in the wind', 'like ripples lapping across the water', 'like a little robin's song', 'as two white butterflies', 'Like a wind-shadow wandering over the water', 'like syringa buds', 'like pink young peony flowers'.

b) W.

c) Consonance. Consonance is the repetition of consonants – in this instance the letter 't'.

d) Assonance. Assonance is the repetition of vowel sounds – in this instance the letter 'u'.

6. Biro, quisling, boycott, dahlia, nicotine, volt, sideburns.

Biro is a brand name that has come to be used much more widely, in the same way people of lax meticulosity talk about hoovering even though they are not using a Hoover-brand vacuum cleaner. Biro, meaning a particular type of ballpoint pen, comes from the name of its Hungarian inventor, László József Biró (1899–1985), who came up with the design with his brother Georg and patented it in 1938. Biró's work as a journalist introduced him to the thick, smudge-free ink used in newspaper printing and inspired him to use it in writing implements. His invention's popularity was ensured by the RAF, who ordered large quantities due to the pen's superior ability to write at altitude.

Quisling, meaning 'traitor', comes from the name of the Norwegian Second World War Major Vidkun Quisling (1887–1945) who collaborated with the Nazis during the occupation. He was executed for treason at the end of the war but his name lives on – albeit not in the manner in which his mother might have hoped.

Boycott, meaning 'avoid dealings with in protest', comes from the name of Captain Charles Cunningham Boycott (1832–1897) who was an English land agent working on the Anglo-Irish Earl Erne's estate (score a bonus point if you can say this five times without any slips of the tongue) in County Mayo in Ireland. In 1880 Boycott resisted the Irish Land League's efforts to campaign for the rights of tenant farmers and as a result was ostracised by the local community – the postman wouldn't even deliver letters to him. He left Ireland that same year for the less challenging environs of Suffolk.

The pulchritudinous perennial, the **Dahlia**, was named in honour of the eighteenth-century Swedish botanist, and student of top-notch taxonomist Linnaeus, Andreas Dahl (1751–1789).

The notoriously moreish ingredient of cigarettes, **nicotine**, is named after Jacques Nicot (c.1530–1600), the diplomat who brought tobacco to France after being introduced to its supposed health-giving powers by a friend in Lisbon. It was considered particularly good for headaches, syphilis and asthma.

The SI unit of electromotive force, the **volt**, is named after the Italian physicist Alessandro Volta (1745–1827) who invented the forerunner of the battery and discovered methane gas. Napoleon made him a count in 1810 in honour of his achievements. All this was achieved after a slow start that would have had modern parents despairing of his developmental milestones, as apparently little Alessandro didn't speak until he was four years old.

Sideburns are named after the American civil war soldier General Ambrose Burnside (1824–1881) who little knew, as he lost the Battle of Fredericksburg with over 10,000 casualties, that he'd be remembered for his moustache-to-hairline 'do'.

7.

a) *Wuthering Heights* by Emily Brontë
b) *Jude the Obscure* by Thomas Hardy
c) *A Tale of Two Cities* by Charles Dickens
d) *Middlemarch* by George Eliot

8. Any four of the following: Doris Lessing, Harold Pinter, William Golding, Elias Canetti (yes, despite having an Italian name and being born in Germany, Canetti was granted British citizenship in 1952), Sir Winston Churchill, Bertrand Russell, T.S. Eliot, John Galsworthy, Rudyard Kipling and V. S. Naipaul (Trinidadian-British).

9.

a) 11 ('good' appears three times): neglected, poor, respectable, handsome, considerable, good, useful, plain, remarkable, latter, excellent.
b) 2 – Catherine Morland and Richard.
c) Ironic. Jane Austen is considered the queen of irony – you can imagine her perfectly arched eyebrow and wry smile as she jotted down this passage.
d) *Northanger Abbey* satirises the gothic and romantic novels popular at the time of its composition in the late 1790s. These books contained many literary stereotypes such as the idea that a romantic heroine needed to have a difficult or tragic background.

10.

Philip Marlowe uncovers the misdeeds of Eddie Mars in Raymond Chandler's *The Big Sleep*.

Sherlock Holmes wrangles with James Moriarty in several of Arthur Conan Doyle's stories.

C. Auguste Dupin points the finger at an orangutan in Edgar Allan Poe's *The Murders in the Rue Morgue*.

Hercule Poirot nabs James Sheppard in Agatha Christie's *The Murder of Roger Ackroyd*.

Sam Spade gets embroiled with Casper Gutman in Dashiell Hammett's *The Maltese Falcon.*

Sergeant Cuff reveals Godfrey Ablewhite as the villain in Wilkie Collins' *The Moonstone.*

11.

The Rosicrucian's Tale
The Landlord's Tale
The Man at Arms' Tale
The Skivvy's Tale
The Model's Tale (we hope you got this one at the very least)
The Minstrel's Tale
The Fishwife's Tale
The Soldier's Tale
The Milner's Tale
The Stablelad's Tale
The Chandler's Tale

12. James Joyce. Mr Deasy appears in *Ulysses*, Gabriel Conroy in *Dubliners* and Robert Hand in the play *Exiles.*

13. This speech comes from *The Jew of Malta* by the brilliantly talented playwright Christopher Marlowe (1564–1593). Kit Marlowe was a controversial figure, not just in his writings, which dealt with the hot topics of religion, immorality and politics, but also in his personal life. He is believed to have held some sort of shady espionage position in the Elizabethan court and was arrested many times before ostensibly being murdered (by a knife to the eye) in a fight over who should pay the bill in a tavern. This speech forms part of the prologue of the play and is spoken by the character Machevill (a representation of the historical character Niccoló Machiavelli, author of the book *The Prince* which sets forth no-nonsense, ruthless rules for political power). Its purpose is to set up the cynical immorality of the title character Barabas, the Jew of Malta, whom Machevill mentions as a kindred spirit.

14.

	1 F		2 N		3 G	R	A	4 Y		
5 S	A	L	O	M	E			E		
	N				N		6 A	L	A	S
			7 H		I			L		
	8 G		A		U		9 R	O	S	10 S
11 E	A	R	N	E	S	T		W		O
	O		D							U
	L		B				12 D			L
		13 M	A	R	Q	U	E	S	14 S	
			G						O	

15. b) 'Disinterested' strictly means 'impartial' although it is increasingly used as a synonym for 'uninterested'.

16.

Faulkner: *Mosquitoes*, *As I Lay Dying*, *The Town*, *Intruder in the Dust*, *Pylon.*

Hemingway: *Islands in the Stream*, *In Our Time*, *Men Without Women*, *True at First Light*, *The Torrents of Spring.*

17. Here's how Dickens did it:

> The raw afternoon is rawest, and the dense fog is densest, and the muddy streets are muddiest near that leaden-headed old obstruction, appropriate ornament for the threshold of a leaden-headed old corporation, Temple Bar. And hard by Temple Bar, in Lincoln's Inn Hall, at the very heart of the fog, sits the Lord High Chancellor in his High Court of Chancery.

18.

a) Hard Humbled Robot	Old Mother Hubbard
b) Leftist Elf Summit	Little Miss Muffet
c) A Paschal Babe Bake	Baa Baa Black Sheep
d) Cello Dog Ink	Old King Cole
e) Duty Myth Pump	Humpty Dumpty
f) Cork In Cob	Cock Robin
g) Hero Toe Smog	Mother Goose
h) Soy Garden Goes Gooey	Goosey Goosey Gander
i) My War Raged	Margery Daw
j) Timbered Lichen	Three Blind Mice
k) A Detached Filth Dent	The Cat and the Fiddle
l) Picket Itchy Key	Hickety Pickety

19. d) 'Parturient' means 'in labour'.

20.

a) *Lord of the Flies* by William Golding
b) *Of Mice and Men* by John Steinbeck
c) *Adam Bede* by George Eliot
d) *Hard Times* by Charles Dickens
e) *Persuasion* by Jane Austen
f) *To Kill a Mockingbird* by Harper Lee

21. The sentence should read: 'George and I are keen to have our eagerly anticipated wedding in October.'

The first error is the use of 'myself'. 'Myself' is a reflexive pronoun and should be used when the subject and object of a sentence are the same. It should not be used as a substitute for 'I' or 'me'.

The second error is the hyphenation of 'eagerly anticipated'. When an adverb is used to qualify an adjective it is not hyphenated unless the sentence would be unclear without hyphenation e.g. 'the light-yellow dress' means something different to 'the light yellow dress'. As a general rule, adverbs ending in '-ly' should not be hyphenated.

The third error is the easiest to spot: 'anticipated' has been mispelled.

Bonus point: This sentence is written in the voice of Emma Woodhouse from Jane Austen's *Emma* and refers to the marriage of Emma and Mr George Knightley, which comes at the end of the novel, after various misadventures. The final chapter of the novel makes clear that their wedding takes place in October.

22. 'Complementary' should be spelled 'complimentary' in order to mean 'free'. ('Complementary' means 'combining to form a complete whole or enhance each other'.)
'Conoisseur' should be spelled 'connoisseur'.
'Haemorhage' should be spelled 'haemorrhage'. This word comes from the ancient Greek '*haema*' meaning '*blood*' and '*rhein*' meaning 'to flow'.
'Indite' should be spelled 'indict'. The confusion around this word often arises because it is pronounced 'indite'.
'Knowledgable' should be spelled 'knowledgeable'.
'Liquify' should be spelled 'liquefy'.
'Priviledge' should be spelled 'privilege'.
'Seige' should be spelled 'siege'.
'Withold' should be spelled 'withhold'. A useful one to remember for Scrabble when you end up with lots of 'h's to use up.

23. b) 'Conflagrant' means 'on fire'.

24. a) Incidentally, b) is the definition of a sestina, c) is the definition of terza rima and d) is the definition of ottava rima.

25.

a) A direct translation would be: 'Oh my god, boss can't see. Wife started fire like before. Got to go'. A less literal translation might read: 'Oh my goodness, my employer has lost his sight. His wife set fire to the house, as she has done on a previous occasion. I must go to him.'
This is a message from Charlotte Brontë's Jane Eyre regarding her beloved Rochester's blinding in the fire started by his mad wife Bertha Mason. This event leads to Bertha's death and Rochester and Jane's subsequent marriage.

b) A direct translation would be: 'So embarrassed. Sister has run off with soldier. Little fool. Nightmare'. A less literal translation might read: 'I am embarrassed to tell you that my sister has run off with a soldier. She is a little fool. This is a nightmarish situation.' This is a message from Elizabeth Bennet regarding her sister Lydia's elopement with Captain Wickham in *Pride and Prejudice*. Mr Darcy's involvement in averting a scandal after this event contributes to Elizabeth eventually agreeing to marry him.

c) A direct translation would be: 'Sorry, will be late. Gloves lost. Will be with you as soon as possible.' A less literal translation might read: 'I'm so sorry I will be late because I have mislaid my gloves. I will be with you as soon as possible.' This is a message from the White Rabbit in *Alice's Adventures in Wonderland*. Alice follows him down the rabbit hole as he is rushing to see the Duchess and later surprises him, causing him to drop his white gloves. '404' has come to mean 'lost' or 'mislaid' because on the internet 404 is the heart-sinking error code that means 'web page not found'.

d) A direct translation would be: 'What a mistake. Cougar I hooked up with in the pub was my mum'. A less literal translation might read: 'I've made a terrible mistake. The attractive older lady I had relations with after meeting her in the inn was my mother'. This text is from Henry Fielding's *Tom Jones*. On his amorous adventures around the south of England Tom has a liaison with a Mrs Waters, who is later revealed to be Jenny Jones, the woman who is believed to have given birth to Tom and abandoned him as a baby. Thankfully, in the end, this proves not to be the true story of Tom's lineage so he is spared any long-term Oedipus-style angst.

26. T. S. Eliot's *Old Possum's Book of Practical Cats*. The Andrew Lloyd Webber singy-dancy version of this marvellous work is one of the longest-running musicals of all time. All together: '*Mem*-ree . . .'

27. b) 'Glabrous' means 'hairless'. Sphynx cats appear to be hairless but in fact have a very short fine coat.

28. a) 'Felonious' comes from the noun 'felon' meaning 'criminal'.

29. Lima, Oscar, Romeo, Delta, Juliet, India, Mike. *Lord Jim* by Joseph Conrad. Conrad was born Józef Teodor Konrad Korzeniowski. He was Polish but became a British subject in 1886 and wrote his novels in English.

The full NATO Phonetic Alphabet is:

Alpha, Bravo, Charlie, Delta, Echo, Foxtrot, Golf, Hotel, India, Juliet, Kilo, Lima, Mike, November, Oscar, Papa, Quebec, Romeo, Sierra, Tango, Uniform, Victor, Whisky, X-ray, Yankee, Zulu.

30. a) Each line of the poem has four feet and each foot is made up of an iamb (one unstressed syllable followed by one stressed syllable).

31.

a) Like a peacock
b) Like a crow
c) Like a bear
d) Like a hare

32.

a) John Keats. Keats died from tuberculosis in 1821 at the age of twenty-five.
b) 'Fast Times at Ridgemont High'. No, not really, it's 'Ode on Melancholy'.
c) Iambic pentameter.
d) ABABCDEDCE.

33.

a) And yet don't look too good, nor talk too wise
b) Fluttering and dancing in the breeze
c) The island of Shallot
d) Washed by the rivers, blest by the suns of home

34. Edmund Spenser's *The Faerie Queene*. This ambitious work was originally intended, according to a letter from the author to Sir Walter Raleigh, to be composed of twelve parts but only six complete books were published: the first three in 1590 and the second three in 1596. The poem was written to praise Queen Elizabeth I who appears in it as Gloriana. The verse form used in the poem was invented by the author and is known as a Spenserian stanza.

Book I exemplifies the virtue of Holinesse through the adventures of the Redcrosse Knight.
Book II exemplifies the virtue of Temperance through the adventures of Guyon.
Book III exemplifies Chastity through the adventures of Britomart and Belphoebe.
Book IV exemplifies Friendship through the adventures of Triamond and Cambell.
Book V exemplifies Justice through the adventures of Artegall.
Book VI exemplifies Courtesy through the adventures of Calidore.

35. c)

36. c)

37.

a) I come to bury Caesar, not to praise him.
b) This day shall gentle his condition:
c) I have thee not, and yet I see thee still.
d) I'll lend you thus much moneys?

38. b) The Augustan Age was a period in English literature in which poets and writers looked back into the past to the Latin literary models of the rule of the Roman Emperor Augustus (27 BCE–14 CE). Alexander Pope, Joseph Addison, Jonathan Swift and Richard Steele are all considered Augustan writers.

39. d)

40.
Sir Gawain and the Green Knight by the Gawain Poet (c. 1375)
The Arcadia by Philip Sidney (1581)
Volpone by Ben Jonson (1606)
Clarissa by Samuel Richardson (1748)
The Life and Opinions of Tristram Shandy, Gentleman (Volumes I and II) by Laurence Sterne (1759)
The Rivals by Richard Brinsley Sheridan (1775)
Adonaïs by Percy Bysshe Shelley (1821)
Barchester Towers by Anthony Trollope (1857)
Mrs Warren's Profession by George Bernard Shaw (1893)
Heart of Darkness by Joseph Conrad (1902)
A Passage to India by E. M. Forster (1924)
Decline and Fall by Evelyn Waugh (1928)
The Waves by Virginia Woolf (1931)
Brave New World by Aldous Huxley (1932)
Under Milk Wood by Dylan Thomas (1954)
Endgame by Samuel Beckett (1957)
The Prime of Miss Jean Brodie by Muriel Spark (1961)
Death of a Naturalist by Seamus Heaney (1966)
The Honorary Consul by Graham Greene (1973)
Wise Children by Angela Carter (1991)

41. This poem is 'The Computation' by John Donne. Donne is considered the founder of the Metaphysical school of poets which included Andrew Marvell, George Herbert and Henry Vaughan. The Metaphysical poets used original and incongruous imagery and elaborate conceits in their works. They were prominent in the seventeenth century but fell out of favour for many years before T. S. Eliot and other modernists promoted a revival of interest in them in the early twentieth century.

42. b)

43.

Nouns: king, daughter
Verb: rejected
Adjectives: foolish, decent, only
Adverb: cruelly
Pronoun: his
Definite article: the

44. c) 'Penurious' means 'very poor'.

45. Minuscule.

46.

a) The objective correlative is T. S. Eliot's theory that in order to express an emotion writers have to describe a set of objects, situations or chain of events – the objective correlative – that creates that emotion in the reader or audience.
b) The collective unconscious is Carl Jung's theory that all cultures share common thoughts and experiences and that literature is the expression of these.
c) The anxiety of influence is Harold Bloom's theory, from his 1973 book of the same name, that poets struggle to escape the shadow of their predecessors to create something new.
d) The death of the author is Roland Barthes' theory that the reader creates the meaning of a text rather than the writer.

47. Revenge Tragedy is the name given to the Jacobean and Elizabethan genre of tragic plays that includes Kyd's hugely popular *The Spanish Tragedy*, Marlowe's *The Jew of Malta* and Shakespeare's *Hamlet.* A distant ancestor of modern-day 'torture-porn films', revenge tragedies often involved wrathful heroes inspired to vengeance by the ghosts of their dead relatives, insanity, disguise, extreme physical violence and a bloodbath finale. The violence is often wonderfully inventive: victims die from kissing poisoned Bibles or skulls as well as suffering the more pedestrian stabbings and strangulations.

48. These sentences all include examples of metonymy. Metonymy is where one word, is subsituted for another word to which it is closely related. In the first example, 'The City' is used to stand in for 'the financial and commercial institutions situated in the City of London'. 'Crown' stands in for 'monarchy' and 'tongue' for 'language'.

49.

a) Purple
b) Yellow
c) Scarlet
d) White
e) Blue
f) Black
g) Orange
h) Green

50. These pictures represent the novels of George Orwell in chronological order.

Burmese Days (1934) is represented by the leopard that the main character Flory shoots on an expedition with the woman he later seeks, unsuccessfully, to marry.

A Clergyman's Daughter (1935) is represented by the hare as the protagonist's name is Dorothy Hare.

Keep the Aspidistra Flying (1936) is represented by the mouse because the would-be poet Gordon Comstock's only published work is entitled *Mice*.

Coming Up for Air (1939) is represented by the carp because when George Bowling revisits the village he grew up in he is particularly keen to find the pond where, as a young boy, he intended to catch a huge carp.

Animal Farm (1945) is represented by a pig because the pigs are the main characters in the book.

Nineteen Eighty-four (1949) is represented by the rat because of the horrifying fate that waits for Winston Smith in Room 101.

MATHEMATICS

Fair mathematics, the crest of all knowledge, the Handmaiden of all the Sciences, has been driving us potty since the dawn of time. Fret not if memories of Mr Appleton's treacherous trigonometry tests in 6A have you breaking out in a cold sweat: take solace in the stark truth that we humans have been grappling with the concepts of mathematics for many thousands of years. In fact, one of the earliest evidences of our attempts at counting lies in the Lebombo Bone, an early form of tallying involving notches cut into a baboon's fibula, which scientists have dated back an extraordinary 37,000 years. But, in truth, mathematics is all around us, and whether we know it or not we all use it every day: from assessing how long that roast chicken will need in the oven to crisp up to perfection, to making sure we haven't been overpaying HMRC, mathematics touches all our lives in myriad ways. And it can help us achieve the most extraordinary, beautiful, and even poetic pinnacles: without mathematics there would be no space travel, no astronomy, no computers, no iPods – so it really does pay to have a handle on the basics. Below we'll show you the delights of divisibility, test how familiar you are with fractions, and probe whether your proficiency with pie charts has stood the test of time.

1. Begin exercising that numerical nous by matching these mathematical key words to the correct definitions.

mixed number, integer, acute angle, trapezium, prime number, factors, lowest term, obtuse angle, icosagon, parallelogram

a) An angle that is less than a right angle.
b) A two-dimensional shape with 20 straight sides.

c) The smallest you can make a fraction).
d) An angle that is more than 90° and not more than 180°.
e) A positive or negative whole number, e.g. -4, 0, 9.
f) A four-sided shape that has all its opposite sides equal and parallel.
g) A number that contains a whole number and a fraction.
h) A four-sided shape that has only one pair of opposite parallel sides.
i) The numbers that divide into a number (e.g. 1, 2, 4, and 8 are .... of 8).
j) Any number that can be divided only by itself and 1.

2. Continue warming up with this simple mental arithmetic which you should be able to answer in a flash. No calculators please . . .

a) A typist averages 14 words to a line and 30 lines to a page. How many pages will be needed for 38,406 words?
b) Pencils cost a stationer £1.80 for a packet of 10. How many can she buy with £36.00?
c) Robert accidentally divides by 8 instead of multiplying by 8 and gets an answer of 564. What should his original answer have been?
d) The temperature in Sheffield is -6°C. It rises by 15°C, then falls by 20°C. What is the new temperature?

3. If all the numbers involved in the enjoyment of mathematics make you dizzy you'll be happy to see that this question is about letters instead – albeit letters used in the service of working out numerical problems. Which recognised mnemonic acronyms express the order of mathematical operations?

a) BEDMAS
b) PEDMAS
c) BODMAS
d) None of the above
e) All of the above

4. The Romans were active in trade and commerce and invented a way of indicating numbers that lasted for many centuries and still sees some specialised use today. Can you complete the following Roman numeral sums?

a) V + X – IX = ?
b) XVI + XXXV – VIII = ?
c) C ÷ II + IX x VIII = ?
d) MMMMMI + DI + XLI = ?

5. Pictured below are the petrol gauges of three cars.

A.

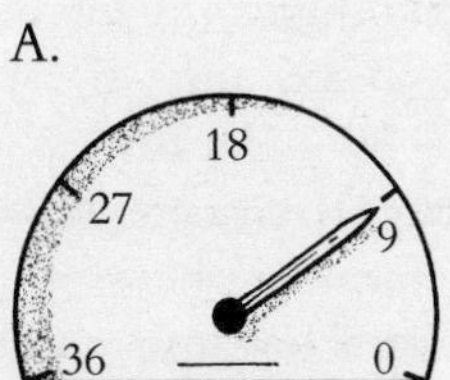

B.

C.

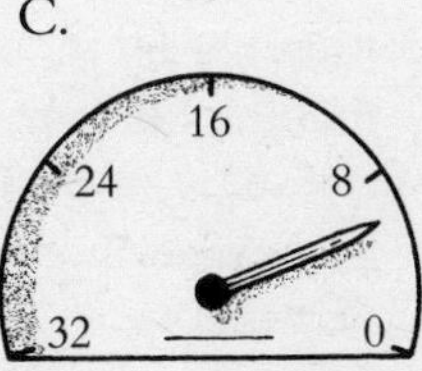

If petrol costs 69p per litre, in order to fill up their tanks . . .

a) Car A would need ____ litres. This would cost ____.
b) Car B would need ____ litres. This would cost ____.
c) Car C would need ____ litres. This would cost ____.
d) The cost of filling up all three cars would be ____.

6. True or false?

a) The number zero is not an integer.
b) In the number 10,897, '8' is the 'hundreds digit'.
c) 2 x -2 = -4
d) Odd and even numbers are the same as positive and negative numbers.

7. Which of the following numbers are NOT prime numbers?

0, 2, 3, 5, 7, 8, 11, 13, 17, 19, 21, 23, 29

8. Fill in the blanks with the words below and rediscover some of the rules of divisibility.

last, 0, both, 3, either, 6, 12, units, 2, 6, sum

An integer is divisible by 2 if its units digit is divisible by ____. (For example, we know just by glancing at it that 598,447,896 is divisible by 2 because the units digit ____ is divisible by 2.) An integer is divisible by ____ if the sum of its digits is divisible by 3 (so 2,145 is divisible by 3 because 2 + 1 + 4 + 5 = 12, and ____ is divisible by 3). An integer is divisible by 4 if its ____ two digits form a number that's divisible by 4. (For example 712 is divisible by 4 because 12 is divisible by 4.) An integer is divisible by 5 if its units digit is ____ 5 or ____. An integer is divisible by ____ if it's divisible by ____ 2 and 3. An integer is divisible by 9 if the ____ of its digits is divisible by 9. An integer is divisible by 10 if its ____ digit is 0.

9. One lucky contest winner receives ¼ of his winnings in cash, and is given four more prizes, each worth ¼ of the balance. If the cash and one of the prizes are worth a combined total of £35,000, what is the total value of his winnings?

a) £70,000
b) £75,000
c) £80,000
d) £140,000

10. $\frac{4}{5}$ as a percentage is:

a) 20%
b) 45%
c) 80%
d) 10%

11. A mathematical square to test your arithmetical acumen. Can you fill in the missing numbers? Use the numbers 1 to 9 to complete the equations and use each number only once. Fiendishly, each row is a maths equation and each column is also a maths equation. And BEDMAS/BODMAS/PEDMAS should of course be observed!

	-		+		14
-	■	×	■	÷	
	-		×		-5
+	■	-	■	×	
	×		-		39
13		-3		12	

12. Which famous Greek mathematician is reported (by Plutarch) to have run through the streets naked, shouting 'Eureka!' ('I have found it!') after discovering that a body immersed in a fluid is buoyed up by a force equal to the weight of the displaced fluid?

a) Euclid
b) Apollonius of Perga
c) Archimedes
d) Pythagoras

13. Pick at random a four-digit number (number a) in which each digit is different. Then jumble up the digits at random and write down the new number (number b). Which is smaller, a or b? Subtract whichever is smaller from whichever is larger. Now you should have another four-digit number (number c). Add the four digits of number c together which should give you a two-digit number (number d). Now add the two digits together from number d (number e). What number (if the steps above are followed correctly) will number e always be, no matter what four digits are chosen as number a?

a) 0
b) 7
c) 2
d) 9

14. A famous tennis star has his lucrative marketing contracts slashed after a series of lurid allegations reveal him to be less than his 'family man image'. If his yearly income from marketing stands at £3.4 million and he loses 70% of that, what will our 'unfortunate' chap still stand to earn?

a) 1.02 million
b) 1.82 million
c) 2.12 million
d) 2.42 million

15. What does this elegant and terribly special maths symbol $\sqrt{}$ mean? And what is it called?

16. On the grid below, can you:

a) Plot the points:

A (-2, 3)
B (1, 3)
C (3, 1)
D (-4, 1)

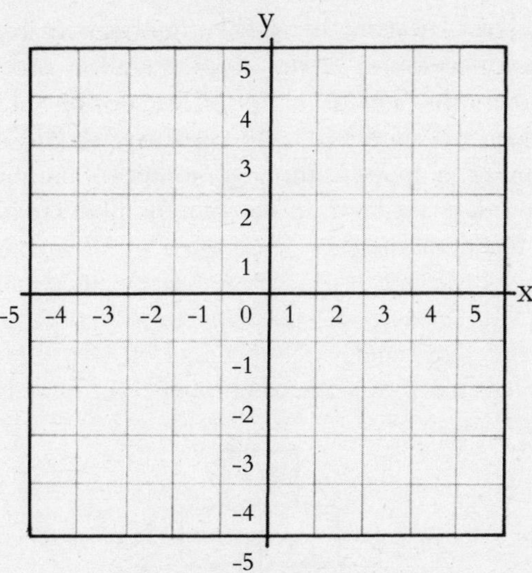

b) Find the area of ABCD.

17. What we referred to as the 'grid' in the question above is technically called a 'co-ordinate system'. The horizontal line is known as the x-axis and the vertical line as the y-axis. What are the four areas formed by the intersection of these axes called? And what is the name of the point at which the axes intersect?

18. Take a deep breath and answer this quickfire test of your numerical nous:

a) How many digits does one million have?
b) What is 50% expressed as a fraction?
c) How many kilometres are there in 15 miles?
d) How many inches are there in 16 cm?
e) What is -17.7° Celsius in Fahrenheit?
f) Is 28 x 6 – 100 more, less or equal to 67 + 13 ÷ 2?
g) What is 25% of 92?
h) If a class has 18 girls and 12 boys, what is the ratio of girls to boys in the class?
i) What is x if $2x + 6 = 18$?

j) If A is the first letter in the alphabet and carries 1 point, and Z is the twenty-sixth and carries 26 points, what is the total 'word score' of the word 'PAIN'?
k) What is the next number in the sequence 64, 81, 100, 121 . . . ?
l) What number is opposite the 6 on a dice?
m) How many days are there in the months December, April, June and October combined?

19. Look at the sum builder below. Based on the information given, can you complete the mountain of numbers? (In your head . . . ?)

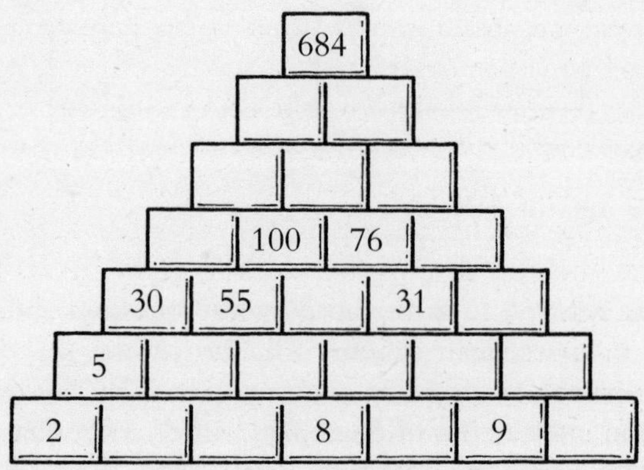

20. 'Sing a song of 6p a pocket full of rye, 4 + 20 blackbirds, baked in a π.' You must've guessed it was coming: It's pi time . . .

Pi is:

a) The theorem that in any right-angled triangle, the area of the square whose side is the hypotenuse (the side opposite the right angle) is equal to the sum of the areas of the squares whose sides are the two legs (the two sides other than the hypotenuse).
b) A geometric pattern or objects that have the same shapes at different scales.
c) The ratio of the circumference of a circle to its diameter.
d) The longest side of a right-angled triangle (the side opposite the right angle).

21. Using the words, terms and names below, can you fill in the blanks to create a plausible history of pi?

Sir Isaac Newton, infinite, 3.16045, ratio, 2010, circumference, π, so long, memorised, length, Babylonians, decimal, tedious, Greek, Egyptians, 3.141592, irrational, patience, 3.125, order, perimeter, Ahmes the Scribe

That the ____ of any circle is calculated by multiplying the ____ of the diameter by approximately ____ has been known for ____ that it is quite untraceable. The earliest known reference to pi comes from an Egyptian papyrus scroll, the Rhind papyrus (*c.* 1650 BCE) by ____, and indicates that ancient ____ used a value of 256/81 or about ____. We also know that the ____ (*c.* 2000 BCE) used ____ to approximate pi, a value they obtained by calculating the ____ of a hexagon inscribed within a circle. Archimedes (*c.* 250 BCE) devised a method to obtain pi to any desired accuracy given enough ____. Over the centuries, Chinese, Indian, and Arab mathematicians extended the number of ____ places known through ____ calculations, rather than improvements on Archimedes' method. By the end of the seventeenth-century, however, new methods of mathematical analysis in Europe provided improved ways of calculating pi involving infinite series. For example, ____ used his binomial theorem to calculate 16 decimal places quickly. In 1706, William Jones gave the ____ letter 'pi' its current mathematical definition and the symbol ____ was popularised by the Swiss mathematician Leonhard Euler to represent this ____. Because pi is ____ (not equal to the ratio of any two whole numbers), an approximation, such as 22/7, is often used for everyday calculations. Pi is a challenge to memorise because the number of digits in it is ____, and there's no discernible pattern anywhere to the ____ of the digits. The current unofficial world-record holder for the recitation of the greatest number of pi digits is Akira Haraguchi, who ____ 83,431. In January 2011 Shigeru Kondo, a Japanese businessman, was recognised as holding the official world record for calculating pi to five trillion digits, almost doubling the accuracy of the previous world record from ____ of 2.7 trillion digits.

22. Pi to the fifth decimal is:

a) 3.12414
b) 3.12159
c) 3.14159
d) 3.14152

23. Much of the time we spent 'learning' maths at school involved devising tricks and shortcuts that would enable us to come up with the correct answer without actually having to solve the problem or even understand what was being asked so that we could simply pass our tests and develop our intellect in other subjects. Can you guess at the answers to these questions without complicated mathematical workings?

Here are two quantities. Which of the following statements below the quantities is true?

A	B
$\frac{1}{16} + \frac{1}{7} + \frac{1}{4} =$	$\frac{1}{4} + \frac{1}{16} + \frac{1}{6} =$

a) The quantity of sum A is greater than the quantity of sum B.
b) The quantity of sum B is greater than the quantity of sum A.
c) The two quantities are equal.
d) The relationship between the two cannot be determined from the information given.

24. Here are another two quantities. Which of the following statements below is true of these exponents?

A	B
27^4	9^6

a) The quantity of A is greater than the quantity of B.
b) The quantity of B is greater than the quantity of A.
c) The two quantities are equal.
d) None of the above.

25. Say you are asked by a numerically illiterate friend to work out 30% of 50 for him and say that the answer choices are:

a) 5
b) 15
c) 30
d) 80
e) 150

Without doing any maths, can you eliminate two choices?

26. If, on Monday, you walked past the window of an exclusive sartorial boutique and saw that the divine but ridiculously expensive coat that you've had your eye on was reduced by 10% in a sale and then later that same week, during another promotion, it was reduced yet again by another 10%, what was the total percentage discount from the original price of the coat?

a) 15%
b) 19%
c) 20%
d) 21%
e) 25%

27. In *The Hitchhiker's Guide to the Galaxy*, Douglas Adams says that the number 42 is the ultimate answer to every possible question mankind can possibly have about every possible thing there can possibly be. Scores of people since have posited theories about the significance of the number 42; geeks have spent lifetimes trying to decipher what Adams meant. Which of the following true facts lies behind his anointment of 42 as the ultimate magic number?

a) Queen Victoria's husband Prince Albert died aged 42; they had 42 grandchildren and their great-grandson, Edward VIII, abdicated at the age of 42.
b) The *Titanic* was travelling at a speed equivalent to 42 km an hour when it collided with an iceberg.
c) The choice of the number was totally random.
d) Elvis Presley was 42 when he died.

28. What type of triangle is this?

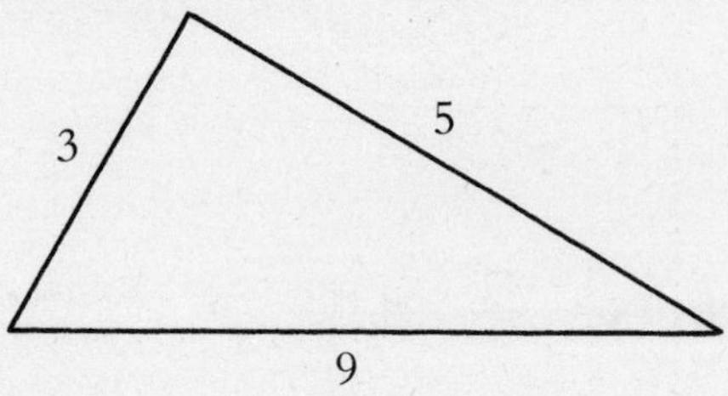

a) Equilateral
b) Isosceles
c) Right triangle
d) None of the above

29. In an ill-judged effort at home decoration Beatrice places 15 marbles in a bowl; some are red and all the others are blue. If the number of red marbles is one more than the number of blue marbles, what is the probability that a marble taken from the bowl is blue?

a) 1⁄15
b 2⁄15
c) 7⁄15
d) ½
e) 8⁄15

30. Six Degrees of Education: Which degree relates to what?

360°, 360°, 80°, 180°, 90°, 360°

a) A flat line is an ____ angle.
b) When two lines intersect, four angles are formed, the sum of which is ____.
c) When two lines are perpendicular to each other, their intersection forms four ____ angles.
d) The three angles inside a triangle add up to ____.
e) A circle contains ____.
f) The four angles inside any four-sided figure add up to ____.

31. Calculate the perimeter and the area of the rectangle shown below.

32. What are the names of the three kinds of triangles? (And we want trigonometrically correct answers rather than 'The Pyramids', 'Toblerones' and 'Dairy Lea'). And (aside from being triangles) what do they all have in common?

33. Identify the median, mode and range values in:

13, 5, 6, 3, 19, 14, 8, 3

34. In the rectangle below, what is the area of triangle *ABD*?

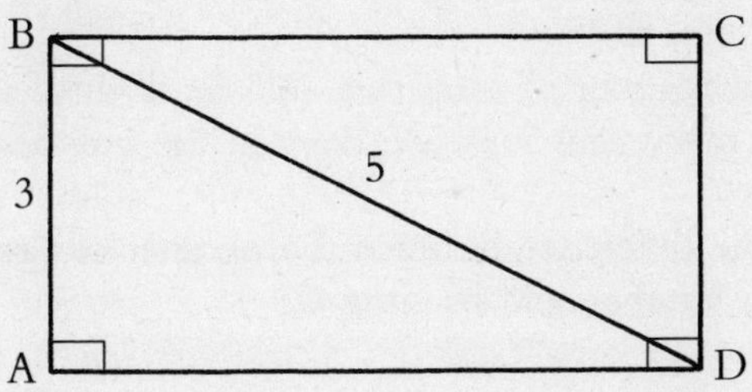

a) 6
b) 7.5
c) 10
d) 12
e) 15

35. It's time for a little light relief with some brain teasers. Ponder the following perplexing puzzles:

a) If you take 2 apples from 6, how many apples do you have?
b) What weighs more: a pound of lead, or a pound of feathers?
c) How many times can you subtract 4 from 30?
d) How many 9s are there between 1 and 100?
e) When do horses have 8 feet?

36. This pictograph shows the number of cans of curried parsnip soup sold by 3 different shops over the course of one week:

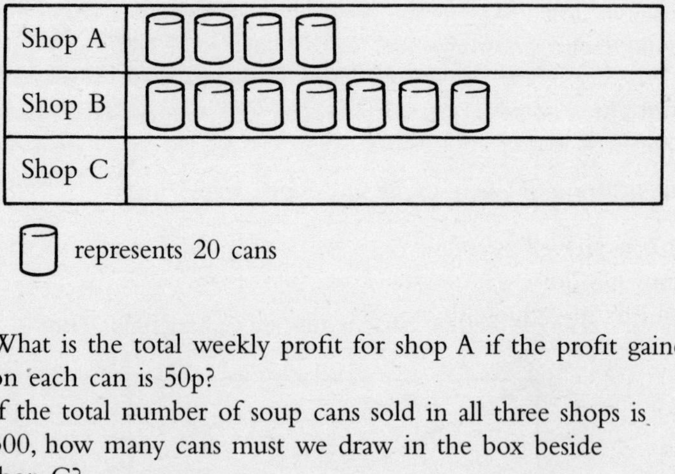

Shop A	
Shop B	
Shop C	

represents 20 cans

a) What is the total weekly profit for shop A if the profit gained on each can is 50p?
b) If the total number of soup cans sold in all three shops is 300, how many cans must we draw in the box beside shop C?
c) What is the difference between the number of cans sold by shop B and the number sold by shop C?

37. Remember 'pie charts'? Here is one that shows how Hannah spent £48 she won on the horses. Based on the information in the pie chart, work out the following:

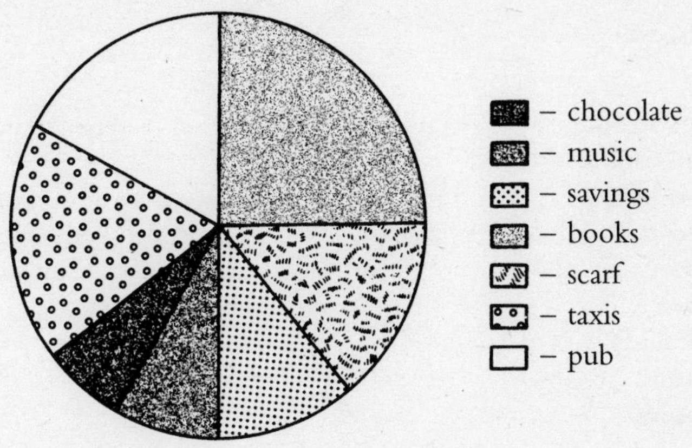

a) Hannah saved £ ____
b) The scarf cost £ ____
c) The taxis cost £ ____
d) The chocolates cost £ ____
e) The books cost £ ____
f) The music cost £ ____
g) Hannah spent £ ____ at the pub

38. If Oliver travels to New York on business and wishes to change £350 into US dollars, how much will he receive if the exchange rate of USDollars to GBPounds is 1.6?

a) £270
b) £389
c) £650
d) £560

39. The figure below is an example of a ____. How many a) faces b) vertices c) number of edges does it have?

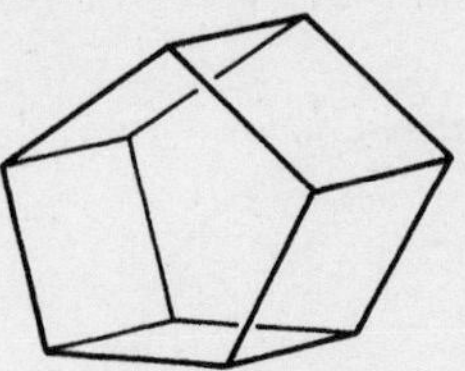

40. In order not to offend them with the wrong title, what would you call a person who uses an abacus?

a) Abaci
b) Abacause
c) Abacist
d) Abacin

41. Within the four branches of mathematics exist a plethora of other mathematical fields and functions. To mix our metaphors, place the field (or function) under the branch it derives from:

game theory, physics, matrices, transformations, fractions, group theory, trigonometry, factors, probability, perimeters, variables, statistics, square roots, inequalities, manifolds, co-ordinates, exponents, calculus, vectors, decimals

Arithmetic	**Algebra**	**Geometry**	**Analysis**

42. Which of the following assertions are true regarding Euclidean and non-Euclidean geometry?

a) Non-Euclidean geometry can only be taught to people who have mastered Euclidean geometry.
b) The essential difference between them concerns the nature of parallel lines.
c) Until the second half of the nineteenth century, all geometry was 'Euclidean'.
d) All of the above.

43. Which of the following depend on algorithms?

a) Computer programmes
b) Falling in love
c) Calculators
d) All of the above

44. It's time to grapple with graphs. We've made one which concerns the expenditure on metals by company X over the course of 15 years. Based on the data shown in the chart, can you answer the following questions? (Don't worry, we won't ask you to 'show your workings' as part of your answer.)

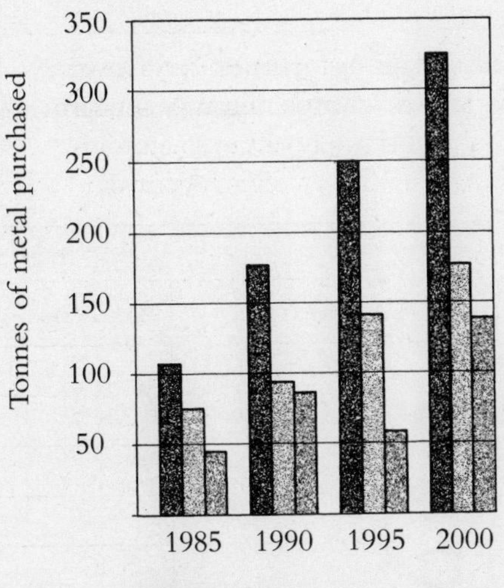

Year	Price at aluminium per tonne
1985	£1,900
1990	£2,200
1995	£2,700
2000	£3,400

i. Approximately how many tonnes of aluminium and copper combined were purchased in 1995?

a) 125
b) 255
c) 325
d) 375

ii. How much did Company X spend on aluminium in 1990?

a) £675,000
b) £385,000
c) £333,000
d) £165,000

iii. What was the approximate percentage increase in the price of aluminium from 1985 to 1995?

a) 8%
b) 16%
c) 30%
d) 42%

45. Broadly speaking, mathematics can be defined as the study of a) quantity, b) structure, c) space and d) change, through the principle branches of a _____, a _____, g ____ and a ____.

46. If the dashed line is the line of symmetry, how would you complete the shapes below?

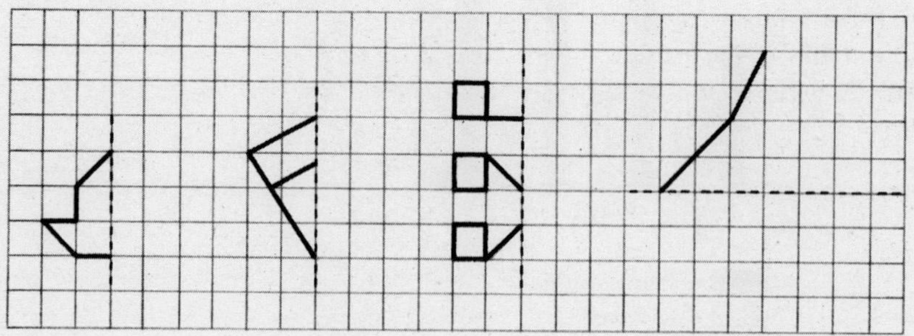

47. Comparing decimals is a wonderful way to pass a lazy Sunday afternoon . . . Which of the following is larger: 0.00099 or 0.001?

48. In the fractious world of fractions there are many opportunities for confusion; however, clarity can be gained in one area by remembering that dividing fractions is just like multiplying fractions, except for one crucial difference:

a) You have to turn the second fraction upside down before multiplying.
b) You have to alter the order of BEDMAS/PEDMAS/BODMAS operations and multiply before you divide.
c) You have to place the second fraction's denominator over its numerator before multiplying.
d) Both a and c.

49. What is $\frac{2}{3} \div \frac{4}{5}$?

50. 'To the nth degree', which means 'without limit', is not only the title of episode 19, season 4, of the *Star Trek* that aired in 1991, but also a phrase used with some regularity in everyday speech that entered the English lexicon through algebra. In algebra, the 'n' of nth degree stands for:

a) A variable with a known value.
b) An arbitrary number which is not a variable.
c) An arbitrary number which could be infinitely large and therefore never end.
d) A variable which is more than a million.

MATHEMATICS ANSWERS

1. a) Acute angle b) Icosagon c) Lowest term d) Obtuse angle e) Integer f) Parallelogram g) Mixed number h) Trapezium i) Factors j) Prime number

2. a) 92; b) 200; c) 36,096; d) -11°C (it rises to 9° and 9 – 20 is -11). Chilly.

3. e) BEDMAS = brackets, exponents, division, multiplication, addition, subtraction. PEDMAS = parenthesis, exponents, division, multiplication, addition, subtraction. BODMAS = brackets, order, division, multiplication, addition, subtraction. Weirdly, we've never come across PODMAS.

4. a) VI (5 + 10 – 9 = 6); b) XLIII (16 + 35 – 8 = 43); c) CDLXXII (100 ÷ 2 + 9 x 8 = 472); d) MMMMMDLI (5001 + 501 + 49 = 5551). The big differences between Roman and Arabic numerals (the ones we use today) are that Romans didn't have a symbol for zero, and that numeral placement within a number can sometimes indicate subtraction rather than addition. The Roman numbering system also lives on in our languages, which still use Latin word roots to express numerical ideas. A few examples: *unilateral, duo, quadricep, septuagenarian, decade, millilitre.*

5.

a) 27 (36 – 9), £18.63 (27 x 0.69)
b) 35 (40 – 5), £24.15 (35 x 0.69)
c) 28 (32 – 4), £19.32 (28 x 0.69)
d) £62.10 (27 + 35 + 28 x 0.69 = 62.1)

6.

a) False! Zero is a super, special little number and is also an integer (though it is neither positive nor negative).
b) True (remember units? tens, hundreds, thousands and ten thousands?).
c) True. When a positive number is multiplied by a negative number, the answer is always negative.
d) False. VERY false. An even number is any integer that can be divided evenly by 2; an odd number is any integer that can't. A positive number is an integer that is higher than zero, a negative number is an integer that is less than zero.

7. 0, 8, 21. Easy! Because you remember the definition of prime numbers from the very first question in this section. And did you also notice that the number 2 is the only even prime number on the list?

8. An integer is divisible by 2 if its units digit is divisible by **2**. (For example, we know just by glancing at it that 598,447,896 is divisible by 2 because the units digit **6** is divisible by 2.) An integer is divisible by **3** if the sum of its digits is divisible by 3 (so 2,145 is divisible by 3 because 2 + 1 + 4 + 5 = 12, and **12** is divisible by 3). An integer is divisible by 4 if its **last** two digits form a number that's divisible by 4. (For example, 712 is divisible by 4 because 12 is divisible by 4.) An integer is divisible by 5 if its units digit is **either** 5 or **0**. An integer is divisible by **6** if it's divisible by **both** 2 and 3. An integer is divisible by 9 if the **sum** of its digits is divisible by 9. An integer is divisible by 10 if its **units** digit is 0.

9.
c). One quarter of the winnings was in cash, so that's £20,000; the balance, therefore, would be £60,000 and he got 4 prizes worth a quarter of £60,000 (£15,000). Now, does the cash (£20,000) plus the value of one of the prizes (£15,000) equal £35,000, as the question requires? Yes!

10. c)

11.

7	-	1	+	8	14
-	■	×	■	÷	
3	-	2	×	4	4
+	■	-	■	×	
9	×	5	-	6	39
13		-3		12	

12. c) Archimedes (c. 287–212 BCE) was noted for his discovery of physical and geometrical principles and his mechanical inventions. His formulation of a hydrostatic principle is known as 'Archimedes' principle' and the 'Archimedes' screw', a machine he contrived for raising water, is still used in many developing countries.

13. d) The number 9 is a magic number! For every product of the 9 multiplication table, the sum of the digits in the product adds up to 9. For instance: 9 times 1 is equal to 9, 9 times 2 is equal to 18, 9 times 3 is equal to 27, and so on for 36, 45, 54, 63, 72, 81, and 90. When we add the digits of the product, such as 27, the sum *always* adds up to nine, i.e. 2 + 7 = 9. Now let's extend that thought. Could it be said that a number is evenly divisible by 9 if the digits of that number added up to nine? How about 673,218? The digits add up to 27, which add up to 9. And 673,218 divided by 9 is 74,802. Does this work every time? It appears so.

14. a)

15. It means square root, 'the number that, when multiplied by itself, gives a specified number' (so the square root of 9 is the number that has been multiplied by itself to get 9, which is 3, which would be represented as $\sqrt{9} = 3$). As early as the second millennium BCE, the clever Babylonians possessed effective methods for approximating square roots. As for the symbol itself, it's called the 'radical' and the number underneath the radical is known to its friends as the 'radicand'.

16. a)

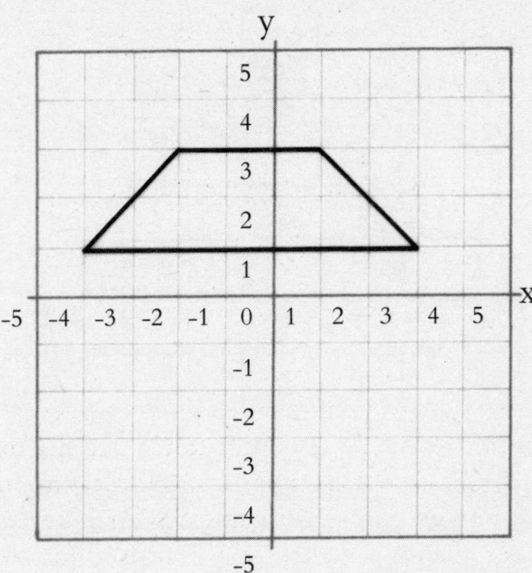

b) 10 cm^2

17. The four areas are called **quadrants** and the point where the axes meet is called the **origin**.

18.

a) 7
b) ½
c) 24
d) 6.3
e) 0°
f) More. 68 is more than 40
g) 23
h) 3:2
i) $x = 6$
j) 40
k) 144, the sequence is 8 x 8, 9 x 9, 10 x 10, 11 x 11, 12 x 12
l) 1
m) 122

19.

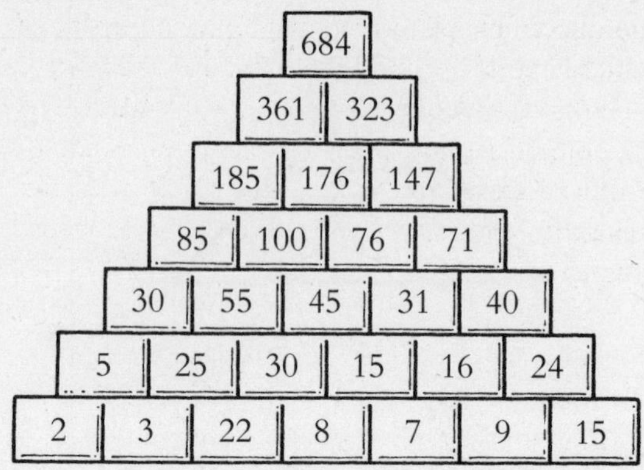

20. c) And do you know what definitions a), b) and d) are, respectively? Of course you do. They are the Pythagorean theorem, the definition of fractals and the definition of hypotenuse.

21. That the **circumference** of any circle is calculated by multiplying the **length** of the diameter by approximately **3.141592** has been known for **so long** that it is quite untraceable. the earliest known reference to pi comes from an Egyptian papyrus scroll, the Rhind papyrus (*c.* 1650 BCE) by **Ahmes the Scribe**, and indicates that ancient **Egyptians** used a value of 256/81 or about **3.16045**. We also know that the **Babylonians** (*c.* 2000 BCE) used **3.125** to approximate pi, a value they obtained by calculating the **perimeter** of a hexagon inscribed within a circle. Archimedes (*c.* 250 BCE) devised a method to obtain pi to any desired accuracy given enough **patience**. Over the centuries, Chinese, Indian, and Arab mathematicians extended the number of **decimal** places known through **tedious** calculations, rather than improvements on Archimedes' method. By the end of the seventeenth century, however, new methods of mathematical analysis in Europe provided improved ways of calculating pi involving infinite series. For example, **Sir Isaac Newton** used his binomial theorem to calculate 16 decimal places quickly. In 1706, William Jones gave the **Greek** letter 'pi' its current mathematical definition and the symbol π was popularised by the Swiss mathematician Leonhard Euler to represent this **ratio**. Because pi is **irrational** (not equal to the ratio of any two whole numbers), an approximation, such as 22/7, is often used for everyday calculations. Pi is a challenge to memorise because the number of digits in it is **infinite**, and there's no discernible pattern anywhere to the **order** of the digits. The current unofficial world-record holder for the recitation of the greatest number of pi digits is Akira Haraguchi, who **memorised** 83,431. In January 2011 Shigeru Kondo, a Japanese businessman, was recognised as holding the official world record for calculating pi to five trillion digits, almost doubling the accuracy of the previous world record from **2010** of 2.7 trillion digits.

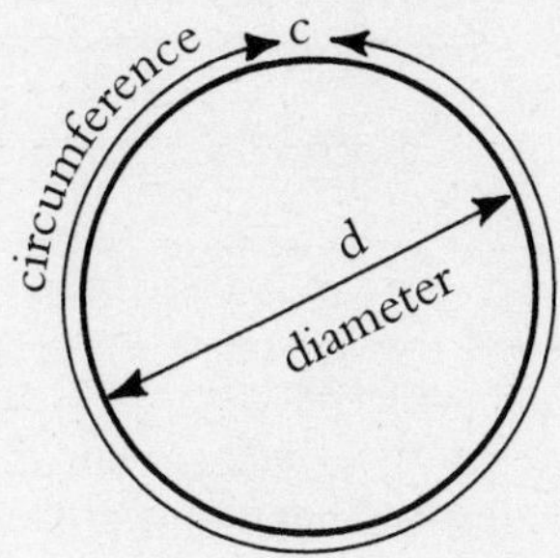

22. c)

23. b) This question wasn't terribly difficult, though if you answered it by crunching some heavy numbers, there is a much quicker way that doesn't involve any calculations. The first thing to do would be to eliminate option d). These are just numbers, so there *is* a solution. After that one can simplify by deleting any numbers that appear in both columns, as if they are both gone, they can't possibly make a difference to the outcome of trying to determine which quantity is greater. In this case, both $1/16$ and $1/4$ can be removed, leaving only $1/7$ in column A and $1/6$ in column B. Since there is no way $1/7$ and $1/6$ are equal, we can eliminate option c) and because we know you still know your fractions, you guessed correctly.

24. c) Again, you can answer this question by comparing and avoiding calculation. Obviously you eliminated d) because numerical values have to be either more than, less than or equal to one another. Both 27 and 9 are powers of 3. The number 27 is 3 x 3 x 3, so 27^4 is $(3 \times 3 \times 3)^4$. This equals (3 x 3 x 3) (3 x 3 x 3) (3 x 3 x 3) (3 x 3 x 3), also known as 3^{12}. In column B, 9 is 3 x 3, so 9^6 is $(3 \times 3)^6$. This equals (3 x 3) (3 x 3) (3 x 3) (3 x 3) (3 x 3) (3 x 3), also known as 3^{12}. So both are equal.

25. d) and e) can be got rid of instantly. Why? Well, think about it. Whatever 30% of 50 is, it must be less than 50, so any answer that is greater than 50 can't be right. That leaves a), b) or c) as the correct answer. Which is right? b) $^{50}/_{100}$ = 0.5 x 30 = 15

26. b) You didn't really think we would give you a question that you could solve simply by adding 10% plus 10%, did you? If the original price of the coat was £100, after a discount of 10% the price would be £90. And 10% of 90 is only 9, so in order to calculate the correct price, we add 10% plus 9% and get a 19% discount, leaving the final cost of the coat to be £81.

27. c) Adams always claimed the answer was very simple: it was a joke.

28. d) This is an 'impossible triangle' – a triangle that doesn't exist – because the length of any one side of a triangle is limited by the lengths of the other two sides, or the 'third-side rule' which states that: the length of any one side of a triangle must be less than the sum of the other two sides and greater than the difference between the other two sides.

29. c) We have 15 marbles and there is 1 more red than blue. That means there must be 8 red marbles and 7 blue marbles. Now we need the probability that we would pick a blue one, which would be 7 out of a possible 15, so the number of possible outcomes that satisfy the condition is 7 and the total number of possible outcomes is 15, which – expressed as a fraction – is ($^{7}/_{15}$). Easy!

30.

a) A flat line is an 80° angle.
b) When two lines intersect, four angles are formed, the sum of which is 360°.
c) When two lines are perpendicular to each other, their intersection forms four 90° angles.
d) The three angles inside a triangle add up to 180°.
e) A circle contains 360°.
f) The four angles inside any four-sided figure add up to 360°.

31. Calculating the perimeter of a rectangle must be one of the simplest of all maths problems as it's simply the sum of each of its sides. 4 + 8 + 4 + 8 = 24. Calculating the area is *moderately* more difficult: length times width (so 8 x 4 = 32).

32. Equilateral triangles, all three sides have equal length and (because all three sides are equal) all three angels are equal too. An **isosceles triangle** is a triangle in which two of the three sides are equal in length (which means two of the three angles are equal as well). **Right-angled triangles** are those in which one of the angles is a right angle (a 90° angle). As you already know from the answer to question 20, the longest side of a right-angled triangle (the side opposite the 90° angle) is called the hypotenuse. What every triangle in the universe has in common is that they all have three angles that add up to 180°.

33. The median can be found by arranging all the numbers in a set from the lowest to the highest and finding the one in the middle (so '8' is the median in our case). With an example of a set with an even number of numbers, the median would be the average of the two middle numbers, or a .5 number between them. The mode is the number or range of numbers in a set that occurs most frequently, so 3 is our mode. The range is the difference between the highest and the lowest numbers in a set, so 16 (19 – 3) is the range.

34. a) As you were told that this shape is a rectangle, you safely assumed that triangle *ABD* is a right-angled triangle. Not only that, but it's a 3-4-5 right-angled triangle, because it has a side of 3 and a hypotenuse of 5, with side *AD* = 4. So, the area of the triangle *ABD* is half the base (3) times the height (4). That's half of 12, otherwise known as 6.

35. a) 2; b) They both weigh the same (one pound); c) Only once. After the first time, it's no longer 30. . . ; d) 20; e) When there are two of them.

36. a) The total profit for shop A would be: 20 x 4 x 0.5 = £40; b) 4 cans must be drawn beside shop C (9 x 20 = 180); c) The difference between shop B and shop C = 20 x 3 = 60 cans.

37.

a) £12
b) £6
c) £8
d) £4
e) £6
f) £4
g) £8

38. d)

39. The shape is a pentagonal prism, a type of heptahedron, which has a) 7 faces (the polygons that make up its boundaries), b) 10 vertices (the points at which geometric shapes intersect), and c) 15 edges (the sides).

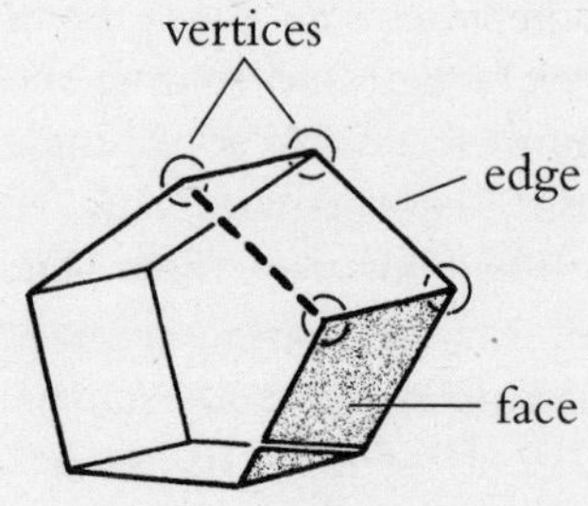

40. c) Abacist. Abaci is, obviously, simply the plural form of abacus.

41.

Arithmetic	**Algebra**	**Geometry**	**Analysis**
decimals	variables	transformations	probability
exponents	manifolds	perimeters	calculus
fractions	matrices	co-ordinates	game theory
square roots	inequalities	vectors	physics
factors	group theory	trigonometry	statistics

42. d) Believe it or not, we are all somewhat familiar with Euclidean geometry, as it's the geometry taught in secondary school. In essence, it's the study of plane and solid figures on the basis of the definitions of things like angles, circles and triangles, and axioms and theorems developed by the Greek mathematician Euclid (*c.* 300 BCE) and outlined in his great work the *Elements*. His five most common geometrical axioms are: 1. Given two points, there is a straight line that joins them. 2. A straight line segment can be prolonged indefinitely. 3. A circle can be constructed when a point for its centre and a distance for its radius are given. 4. All right angles are equal. 5. If a straight line falling on two straight lines makes the interior angles on the same side less than two right angles, the two straight lines, if produced indefinitely, will meet the side on which the angles are less than the two right angles. Non-Euclidean geometry is any geometry that is not Euclidean, but to be more specific, it is this fifth axiom about parallel lines (known as the 'Parallel Axiom') which caused debate among mathematicians. Put in layman's terms, in Euclidean geometry, given a point and a line there is exactly one line through the point that is in the same plane as the given line and never intersects it, so parallel lines remain at a constant distance from one another. The two most common non-Euclidean geometries are *spherical geometry* and *hyperbolic geometry*. In spherical geometry there are no such lines, only 'curves'. In hyperbolic geometry there are at least two distinct lines that pass through the point and are parallel to (in the same plane as and do not intersect) the given line and 'curve away' from another as outlined in the figure below.

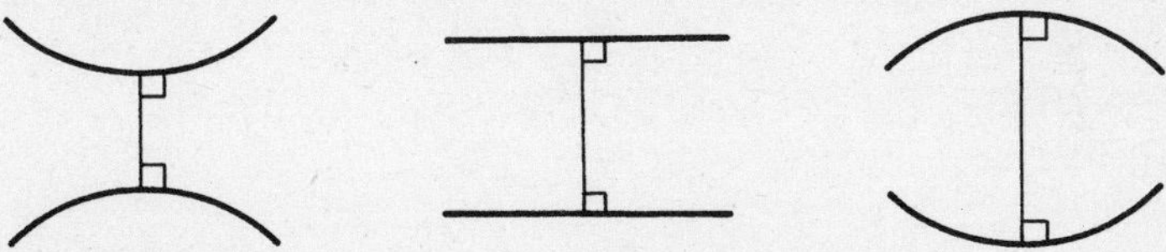

43. d) While the term 'algorithm' is most widely associated with calculations and the solving of mathematical problems, it simply denotes any system, process of rules or finite instructions that invariably leads to a particular outcome, so when a calculator is asked to multiply 9 x 7, it proceeds through a set of predetermined steps that it has been programmed to follow to arrive at the answer. 'Algorithm' derives from the Latin translation *Algoritmi de numero Indorum*, from the ninth-century Muslim mathematician al-Khwarizmi's arithmetic treatise 'Al-Khwarizmi Concerning the Hindu Art of Reckoning', which is perhaps why it's become almost exclusively a mathematical term. But as it really does just mean the process of rules required in order to arrive at a determined end, most conceptions of the brain (like the acquisition of food and indeed falling in love) are the result of complex algorithms.

44. i. d) As you can see from the graph the blue bar, representing aluminium, is at 250 in 1995, and the red bar (copper) is at approximately 125. As you will have noticed that the question says 'approximately', you knew that to answer the question correctly, you simply needed to add 250 to 125 (375).

ii. b) To answer this question you needed to find the number of tonnes of aluminium purchased in 1990 and simply multiply it by the price per tonne of aluminium in 1990. The graph tells us that 175 tonnes were purchased in 1990 and we know that aluminium cost £2,200 per tonne in the same year, so £385,000 is our answer.

iii. d) In 1985 the price of aluminium was £1,900 per tonne and in 1995, it was £2,700. As you know, percentage change is the difference ÷ by the original x 100. So 2,700 – 1,900 = 800. And 800 ÷ 1,900 x 100 can also be expressed as $\frac{8}{19}$ x 100 (with the two zeros cancelling each other out) which gives you $\frac{800}{19}$. And 800 ÷ 19 = 42.1.

45.

a) Arithmetic
b) Algebra
c) Geometry
d) Analysis

46.

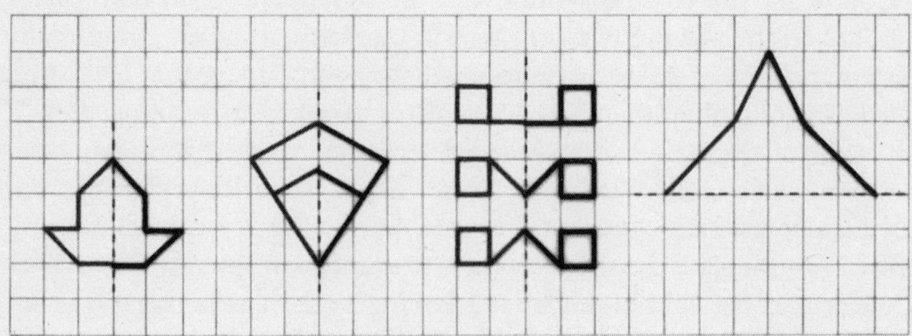

47. The number 0.001 is larger, but how did we arrive at that? Well, we didn't allow the number of digits in each decimal to inform our decision and we followed a little trick. Line up the two numbers by their decimal points:

0.00099
0.001

Then fill in the missing zeros:

0.00099
0.00100

Now that the numbers actually look the same, it's easy to see that since 100 is larger than 99, 0.001 is larger than 0.00099.

48. d) Denominator and numerator are just fancy ways of saying 'number on top' and 'number on bottom'.

49. $\frac{5}{6}$

To get this we flipped the denominator and numerator and multiplied:

$\frac{2}{3} \div \frac{4}{5} =$

$\frac{2}{3} \times \frac{5}{4} =$

$\frac{\overset{1}{\cancel{2}}}{3} \times \frac{5}{\underset{2}{\cancel{4}}} =$

$\frac{1}{3} \times \frac{5}{2} = \frac{5}{6}$

50. c)

GEOGRAPHY

We'd be lost without geography, both literally and metaphorically. It's true that our sense of the world around us, of its physical attributes as well as its resources, political divisions, its populations and climate has come on in leaps and bounds in the last thousand years (no one really believes the world is flat these days) but nevertheless horror stories have reached our ears of people having only the shakiest of grasp on location – in a recent survey of over 500 Americans, for example, nearly 47 per cent were unable to identify the Indian sub-continent on a map. But before we get too high-minded about our US cousins' cartographic challenges, we must ask ourselves how many of us could really pinpoint the county of Clackmannanshire on a map of the United Kingdom (answer: it's Scotland's smallest county, often nicknamed 'the Wee County', and it can be found nestling at the point where the River Forth joins the Firth of Forth, in Central Scotland). As citizens of a truly global village, it is essential that we know our place in the world, and so in this section prepare to reacquaint yourself with climate, currency and capital cities, as well as pondering the projection of Ptolemy, and speculating on the homeland of the spectacled bear.

1. Though you've probably never been there (we doubt very much that it's on any of Condé Nast's most exotic holiday-destination lists), what is the name of the Norwegian island, discovered in 1739 by the French navigator Jean-Baptiste-Charles Bouvet de Lozier (1705–86), that is considered to be one of the most isolated places on earth?

2. Since the introduction of the euro to our closest neighbouring countries, holidaying has become just a little less fun: goodbye lire, francs and Deutsche marks . . . but there are still over a hundred coinages across the world to charm and cheer us. Can you match the currency to the country?

Croatia	gourde
Latvia	birr
Slovenia	vatu
Armenia	kuna
Georgia	kip
Laos	lari
Myanmar (Burma)	metical
Thailand	euro
Ethiopia	sol
Mozambique	dobra
São Tomé and Príncipe	real
Vanuatu	baht
Haiti	kyat
Brazil	lats
Peru	dram

3. Which city is further north, Seattle or Montreal?

4. Latitude means:

a) The angular distance of a place east or west of a standard meridian.
b) The angular distance of a place north or south of the equator.
c) The angular distance of a place north or south of a standard meridian.
d) The angular distance of a place east or west of the equator.

5. Put the words below into the correct places to form a paragraph worthy of the most sophisticated NASA navigational system:

arcseconds, meridians, prime meridian, noon, circles, meridians, prime, Greenwich, Earth, dateline, hours, degrees

The ____ rotates on its polar axis once every 23.9345 ____. As an oblate sphere measuring a circumferential 360°, the Earth rotates through almost 15 angular ____ per hour. The Earth's lines of longitude (____) are great ____ that meet at the north and south polar axis. They are referenced by an east or west displacement from the ____. Accordingly, lines of longitude range from 0° E to 180° E and 0° W to 180° W. Degrees are further divided into arcminutes and ____. The prime meridian runs through ____ and the line of longitude displaced 180° E and 180° W from the prime meridian is termed the international ____. Standard ____ occur every 15° of longitudinal displacement from the ____ meridian (e.g., 15° W, 30° W, 45° W, etc.) and establish the local ____ for the time zone.

6. What are the nomadic tribes of Northern Africa called?

a) Zulus
b) Berbers
c) Maori
d) Kuba

7. A woman is taking a business trip from New York to Sydney, Australia. Leaving on 8 February at 6.04 a.m., she flies from New York to San Francisco, arriving at 9.30 a.m. At 11.51 a.m., she flies from San Francisco to Hong Kong, arriving at 6.40 p.m. the next day. The following morning she flies from Hong Kong to Sydney and arrives at 8.17 a.m. on 11 February. She has her meeting that afternoon and flies out from Sydney the next day at 11.50 a.m. on a flight back to New York with a two-hour and fifteen-minute stopover in Los Angeles. At what time, and on what day, does our doughty businesswoman return?

8. Unlock your inner Christopher Columbus with this quick crossword:

ACROSS

2. The only country, other than 1 down, that is not a member of the United Nations (6)
3. The most southerly capital (10)
5. The largest country (6)
7. The least densely populated country (8)
9. The most northerly capital city (9)
11. The language, other than English, spoken in Jamaica (6)
12. The highest national capital city (2, 3)
13. The capital of Fiji (4)
14. The largest national capital city (5)

DOWN

1. The smallest country (7, 4)
4. The language, other than English, spoken in Tonga (6)
6. The number of countries both China and the Russian Federation have borders with (8)
8. The most populous country (5)
10. The most densely populated country (6)

9. The suffix '-stan' derives its meaning from the Ancient Persian word for 'place of', and is so useful that over seven countries use it today. Can you name them all?

10. And which of these '-stan' countries were, until 1991, part of the Soviet Union?

11. Find FIVE countries that currently belong to the Commonwealth in the word search below:

12. Cloud conundrums. Can you identify the clouds from the lyrical descriptions below? (Scientific names, please . . .)

a) Carrying lots of moisture, my Latin name means 'heap';
I float fairly close to the ground on fair days
And I resemble a sheep.

b) Tall, dense, unstable and warm,
You'll find me near oceans;
I signify a storm.

c) Flat, featureless and greyish like smog,
I lie low in the sky
And bring drizzle and fog.

d) Thin and sheetlike I resemble a feather,
I'm see-through and high up;
I mean good weather.

e) Grey or blue-grey, I live in the middle of the sky;
I'm made of ice crystals and water droplets –
When I'm around, a storm is nigh!

13. Should you find yourself thirsty in the city of Reims, what beverage are you most likely to be served to slake that thirst?

a) Stella Artois
b) Sauvignon Blanc
c) Champagne
d) Medicinal Roman waters

14. Spelling test. Circle the correct spellings of these commonly misspelt/misspelled place names.

Philipines/Philippines
Madagascer/Madagascar
Oaxaca/Oxaca
Bordeaux/Bordeau
Mississipi/Mississippi
Saskatchawan/Saskatchewan
Llangollen/Llangollan
Upsala/Uppsala
Bolougna/Bologna
Azerbaijan/Azerbajian
Riyad/Riyadh
Bearing Sea/Bering Sea
Christchurch/Christ Church

Enniskillen/Eniskillen
Minsks/Minsk
Eritrea/Eritria
Columbia/Colombia
Zinjiang/Xinjiang
Antwerp/Antweerp
Schleswig-Holstein/Schleswiig-Holstein

15. The Juan de Fuca Strait, named after the maritime Greek pilot who discovered it (and yet had a completely different name that doesn't resemble anything Spanish), separates which two countries?

a) Bolivia and Paraguay
b) Bolivia and Peru
c) The United States and Canada
d) Spain and Portugal

16. Match the leaders to the place they were born:

Alexander Nevsky	Umtata
Nelson Mandela	Florence
Catherine de' Medici	Barry, Vale of Glamorgan
Dorgon	Stettin
John F. Kennedy	Shaoshan
Julia Gillard	Posen
Adolf Hitler	Rosario
Jânio da Silva Quadros	Allahabad
Benazir Bhutto	Kingston, New Brunswick
Mao Zedong	Pella
Léopold Senghor	Joal
Franklin D. Roosevelt	Brookline
Alexander the Great	Campo Grande
Paul von Hindenburg	Braunau am Inn
Sophie Friederike Auguste von Anhalt-Zerbst	Vladimir
Andrew Bonar Law	Hyde Park
Che Guevara	Karachi
Indira Gandhi	Yenden

17. Which of these is the odd one out?

a) Pacific Heights
b) Nob Hill
c) Tenderloin
d) Hillcrest Village

18. The English composer Gustav Holst was on to something when he wrote an entire orchestral suite in 1918 in honour of the planets. Though we don't know them, the planets are probably friendly and fun – the ultimate, untrodden, exotic holiday destinations – and they are even equipped with their own moons. Can you match the known number of moons to the planets (including the, erm, recently relegated dwarf planet) using the clues of some of the moons' names?

Venus	13, including Triton and Nereid
Mars	3, the largest of which is called Charon
Mercury	0
Jupiter	2, called Phobos and Deimos
Saturn	27, including Cordelia and Oberon
Uranus	1
Neptune	More than 60 with Titan as the largest
Earth	0
Pluto	More than 60 (the four brightest of which are called the Galilean satellites)

19. The Trans-Siberian railway is the longest single rail system in Russia, stretching from Moscow 5,726 miles (9,216 km) east. Conceived of by Tsar Alexander III, the construction of the railroad began in 1891 and proceeded simultaneously in several sections and across intermediate reaches by way of the Mid-Siberian Railway, the Transbaikal Railway, and other lines. Originally, in the east, the Russians secured permission to build a line directly across Manchuria, which was completed in 1901 and paved the way for the current Trans-Manchurian Route. After the Russo-Japanese War of 1904–5, however, Russia feared Japan's possible takeover of Manchuria and proceeded to build a longer and more difficult alternative route, the Amur Railway, which was completed in 1916. The Trans-Siberian Railroad thus had two completion dates: in 1904 all the sections from Moscow were linked and completed running through Manchuria; in 1916 there was finally a Trans-Siberian Railroad wholly within Russian territory.

What city does the mainline train stop at after its 5,726-mile (9,216-km) journey east from Moscow?

a) Khabarovsk
b) Lake Baikal
c) Irkutsk
d) Vladivostok

20. From which country would the Russians have had to secure permission to build a line directly across Manchuria?

a) Japan
b) China
c) Canada
d) The United States

21. Which route is longer? The Trans-Siberian Moscow–Vladivostok or the Trans-Manchurian, which runs from Moscow to Beijing and is serviced by a combination of trains?

22. The completion of the railroad opened up vast areas to exploitation, settlement and industrialisation and marked a turning point in the history of which part of Russia?

a) The Ural Mountains
b) Siberia
c) Moscow
d) Manchuria

23. Which is longest?

a) The Trans-Siberian route
b) The Great Wall of China
c) US Route 66
d) Hadrian's Wall

24. How cosmologically confident are you? Which of the following are true and which are false?

a) In around 150 CE, the Alexandrian astronomer and mathematician Ptolemy came up with a mathematical model of the universe in which he argued that Earth is a stationary sphere at the centre of a vastly larger celestial sphere that revolves at a perfectly uniform rate around the earth, carrying with it the stars, planets, sun and moon, thereby causing their daily risings and settings. Through the course of a year the sun slowly traces out a great circle, known as the ecliptic, against the rotation of the celestial sphere. (The moon and planets similarly travel backward – hence, the planets were also known as 'wandering stars' – against the 'fixed stars' found in the ecliptic.) The fundamental assumption of his 'geocentric cosmology' is that the apparently irregular movements of the heavenly bodies are in reality combinations of regular, uniform, circular motions.
b) German astronomer Johannes Kepler (1571–1630) came up with the three laws of planetary motion, which can be stated as follows: 1) all planets move about the sun in elliptical orbits with the sun at one focus; 2) the time necessary to traverse any arc of a planetary orbit is proportional to the area of the sector between the central body and that arc (the 'area law'); 3) the squares of the sidereal periods (of revolution) of the planets are directly proportional to the cubes of their mean distances from the sun; i.e. there is an exact relationship between the squares of the planets' periodic times and the cubes of the radii of their orbits (the 'harmonic law').

c) Kepler himself did not call these discoveries 'laws,' as would become customary after Isaac Newton derived them from a new and quite different set of general physical principles.
d) The prevailing cosmological view during the Middle Ages, and prior to Christopher Columbus, was that the earth was flat, not spherical.

25. Which seas are indicated on the map with the letters A to M?

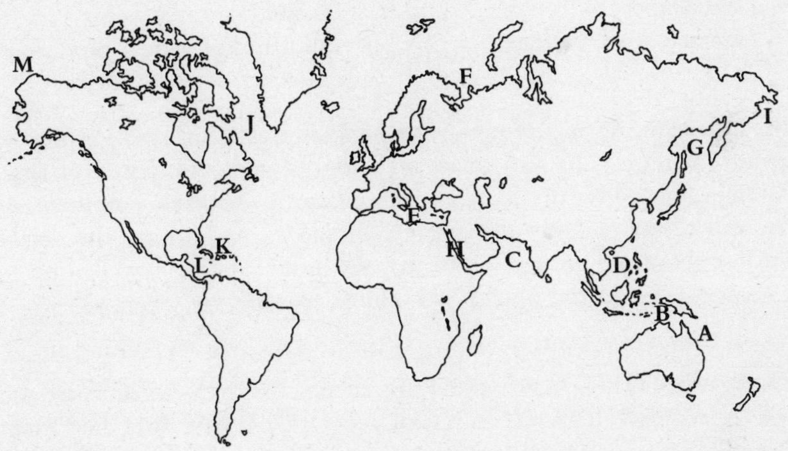

26. Which Hungarian towns amalgamated in 1873 to form what is now the nation's capital?

a) Buda, Pécs and Pest
b) Buda and Pest
c) Buda, Óbuda and Pest
d) Buda and Pécs

27. Population puzzle! Match the US Census Bureau's population figure for 2010 with the country of its inhabitants:

Brazil	1,330,141,295
Cape Verde	7,089,705
Hong Kong	1,354,051
Monaco	1,173,108,018
United Kingdom	62,348,447
China	57,637
Greenland	4,975,593
India	508,659
Swaziland	30,586
United Arab Emirates	201,103,330

28. Just before spring, the emperor penguin begins an epic journey of up to 75 miles (120 km) to its breeding grounds, composed of large colonies formed on the sea-ice surrounding the Antarctic continent. At the end of the summer the eggs hatch and by mid-winter the chicks are just about old enough to swim back home. Having travelled up to 75 miles, how do the plucky wee chicks manage the journey?

29. Agatha Christie novels aren't just crime classics of elegance, art and wit, they can also help you with your geography! Where does the Orient Express depart and terminate?

a) Paris and Istanbul
b) Venice and Istanbul
c) Paris and Constantinople
d) Geneva and Moscow

30. On its way to its destination, the legendary train passes through which of the following?

a) St Petersburg, the Ural Mountains and Xining
b) The Alps, Budapest and Bucharest
c) Amsterdam, Bratislava and Chişinău
d) The Pyrenees, Rome and Azerbaijan

31. The animals listed below are native to a specific continent, though some of them now live in a variety of continents. Return each animal to its original home (you'll notice that Antarctica is left off because, excepting a few mites and midges, most of the birds and fish live in and around the continent).

Anaconda
Aardvark
Babirusa
Blue jay
Cape buffalo
Cobra
Kangaroo mouse
Kodiak bear
Löwchen
Moa (extinct)
Musk turtle
Norway lemming
Orangutan
Oryctolagus cuniculus
Ostrich
Pyrenean ibex
Rhea
Sloth
Spectacled bear
Tasmanian devil
Wallaby
Warthog
Water buffalo
Wombat

North America	**Europe**	**Asia**
South America	**Africa**	**Australia**

32. Based on the example of the first analogy, solve the problem of the missing link in the second analogy in the examples below:

Eyjafjallajökull, Iceland: ____, Vesuvius (Answer: Mount Etna)

a) Native Americans, The United States of America: ____, Australia
b) Mount Everest, Nepal: K2, ____
c) Dead Sea, Israel and Jordan; ____, Kazakhstan and Uzbekistan
d) Nephology, study of clouds: Biogeography, ____
e) Lake Victoria, Africa: ____, North America
f) UNCED, Rio de Janeiro, 1992: UNFCCC, ____

33. What country is the easiest to defend in the game of Risk?

34. Test your knowledge of a miscellany of geographical terms by completing the crossword below.

ACROSS

4. A type of low cloud with a layer arranged in globular masses with joined edges (13)
7. An optical illusion in which images of distant objects are seen, caused by the refraction of light through layers of air of different density (6)
10. Instrument to measure the humidity of the atmosphere (10)
12. The scientific study of lakes and ponds with respect to their physical, chemical and biological properties (9)
13. The science of measuring the shape and size of the earth (7)
14. Periods of the year characterised by the inclination of the earth's axis to the plane of the ecliptic and the revolution of the earth about the sun (7)
16. Mid-latitude grasslands, consisting of level – generally treeless – plains of Eurasia (7)
18. An annoying and cold wind experienced on the shores of the north-west Mediterranean which, according to author Peter Mayle, 'can blow the ears off a donkey' (7)
19. Long, narrow inlet into the sea-coast (5)

DOWN

1. The subject which deals with the regional distribution of racial populations (11)
2. Depression in a range of mountains or hills (3)
3. An inland cliff or steep slope (10)
5. The degree of saltiness of bodies of water (8)
6. The largest known asteroid (5)
8. A vertical sheet of igneous rock formed when magma from the earth's interior has surfaced, cooled and solidified (4)
9. The time when the sun is vertically above the point which represents its farthest distance north or south of the equator (8)
11. A plant which requires an average amount of moisture (9)
13. Coarse-grained plutonic rock which contains quartz and feldspar (7)
15. A line on a map or chart joining places having equal atmospheric pressure (6)
17. Dwarf planet (5)

35. In which countries did these now defunct airports exist?

a) Renfrew Airport
b) Templehof Central Airport
c) Atarot Airport
d) W. H. Bramble Airport

36. Keep your seatbelt fastened and your tray table in the upright position for one more airport question. In which (abbreviated) time zones do the following airports operate?

CST, PET, CAT, CST, CET, ICT

a) George Bush International Airport
b) Guangzhou Baiyun International Airport
c) Jorge Chávez International Airport
d) Don Mueang International Airport
e) Esbjerg Airport
f) Sir Seretse Khama International Airport

37. What is the most ubiquitous place name in the United States?

a) Fairfield
b) Midway
c) Riverside
d) Springfield

38. Are these geographical places and terms really named after these particular people?

a) The Curzon line, marking the border between Poland and the Soviet Union and confirmed at the Yalta Conference of 1945, is named after the British politician George Nathanial 1st Marquis Curzon of Kedleston (1859–1925). As it was Lord Curzon who suggested that the Poles, who had invaded Russia in the Russo–Polish War (1919–20), should retreat to this line while awaiting a peace conference, the line was named after him.

b) The Richter scale, a scale for expressing the magnitude of earthquakes, is named after Gerhard Richter Senior, the father of the German visual artist Gerhard Richter.

c) The Mason-Dixon line was the name given to the boundary between the states of Maryland and Pennsylvania, set in 1763–7. Before the American Civil War the line came to be regarded as the demarcation line between the North and South, the free and the slave states. It was named after a poor slave called Mason Dixon.

d) The Linnaean system, in which all organisms have two names – the first which identifies the genus to which the organism belongs, the second its species (for instance members of the human race are *Homo sapiens*, *homo* being the genus and *sapiens* being the specific species) – was named after the Swedish botanist Carolus Linnaeus (1707–78). The Linnaean system, which he outlined in a number of books, marked the first significant attempt to bring all living beings together in a systematic classification.

39. We have a gaggle of geographical gee-gaws on the subject of agriculture for you here.

i. In which of these locations are you most likely to find hill sheep farming?

a) East Anglia
b) The M4 corridor
c) The Lake District
d) Greater London

ii. Which crop is often associated with terraced hillsides in South East Asia?

a) Rice
b) Corn
c) Sugar beet
d) Potatoes

iii. 'Ruminants' are:

a) Birds of prey
b) Mammals with cloven feet
c) Cud-chewing animals
d) Amphibians

iv. What does CAP stand for?

a) Common Agricultural Plan
b) Common Agricultural Policy
c) Common Arable Policy
d) Common Agricultural Police

40. In the following questions, a related pair of words or phrases is followed by four pairs of words or phrases. Select the pair that best expresses a relationship similar to that expressed in the original pair:

i. Tropical rainforest : biome

a) Boreal forest : precipitation
b) Savannah biome : tropical grassland
c) Coniferous trees : pinecones
d) Ecosystem : pond

ii. Glaciers : valleys

a) Freeze-thaw : rock fragments
b) Mount Everest : pyramidal peak
c) Rivers : tributaries
d) Glacier : downhill

iii. Inner core : concentric layer

a) Oceanic crust : water
b) Earth's crust : tectonic plates
c) Plate tectonics : earthquakes
d) Mantle : concentric layer

41. The notorious Nazi foreign minister Joachim von Ribbentrop worked for a bank in which Canadian city from 1910–1912?

a) Montreal
b) Ottawa
c) Toronto
d) Vancouver

42. The metre measurements below are in a muddle – can you sort them out?

1,637 metres is . . .	The mean elevation of the earth's land surface
980 metres is . . .	The depth of the world's deepest lake (Lake Baikal)
840 metres is . . .	The mean depth of the Pacific Ocean
1,343 metres is . . .	Where 52 per cent of the earth's surface is below
500 metres is . . .	The height of the world's highest waterfall, Angel Falls
4,280 metres is . . .	The height of Ben Nevis

43. The HMS *Beagle* was the naval vessel aboard which Charles Darwin served as naturalist on the voyage which gave him the essential materials for his theory of evolution by natural selection. From where did it launch?

a) Woolwich
b) Folkestone
c) Seaton
d) Dover

44. Below are the names of 18 important cultural and natural landmarks throughout the world. By unscrambling the names and copying the letters in the numbered cells to other cells with the same number, solve the seven-word mystery at the bottom of the puzzle that links all the clue words together.

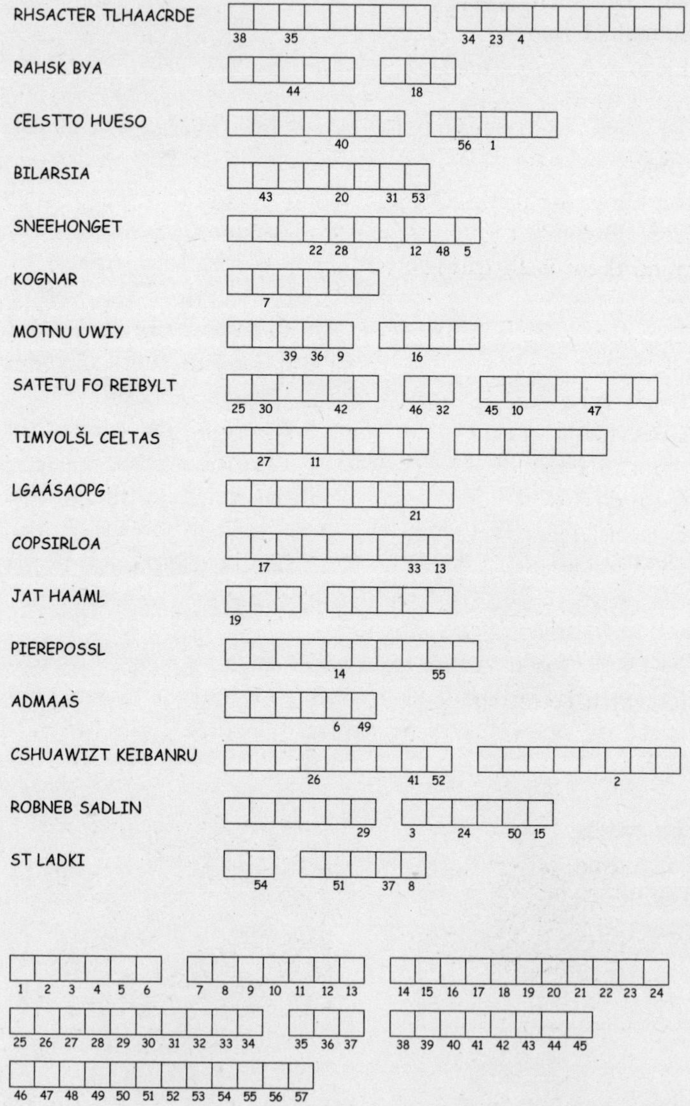

45. Lyme Regis, Dorset, was the site where which famous British fossil collector, dealer and palaeontologist, who became known around the world for a number of important finds she made in the Jurassic age marine fossil beds, lived and worked?

a) Jane Haldimand Marcet
b) Etheldred Benett
c) Eleanor Anne Ormerod
d) Mary Anning

46. You know the names of these countries (and you can certainly find them on a map), but can you guess their national adjectives? And avoid confusing them with national nouns?

Barbados
Benin
Burkina Faso
Comoros
Cook Islands
Côte d'Ivoire
Faroe Islands
Greenland
Isle of Man
Kiribati
Macau
Mauritania
Mayotte
Oman
Palau
Seychelles
Timor-Leste
Yemen

47. To which countries do these stylish flags belong?

a)

b)

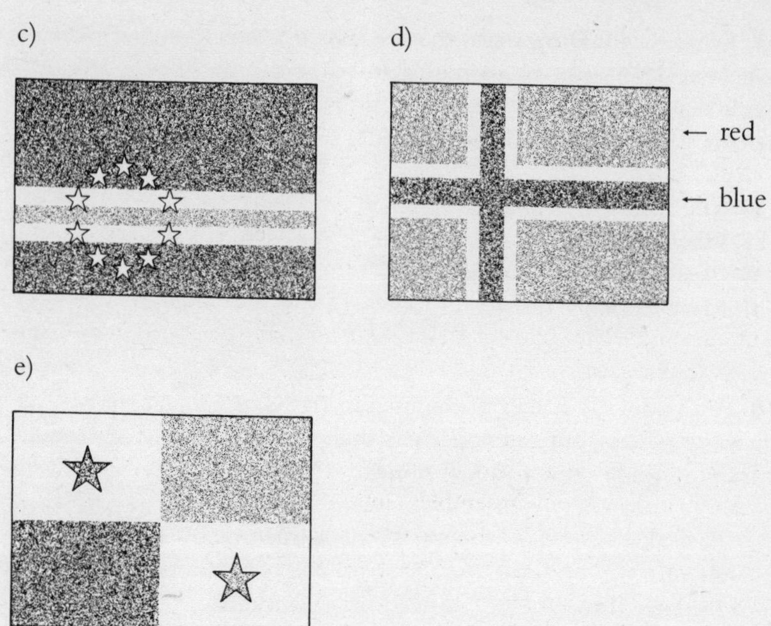

48. Back in the day, geography used to be about place names and maps. As a subject it has matured and expanded to incorporate wider social and geo-political topics, including development. Unfortunately the English language has not expanded at the same rate, leaving geographers to rely on a wide array of similar-sounding acronyms to communicate. Can you fill in the blanks with the acronyms below and decipher the code to discover what the acronyms actually stand for?

GNP, MEDCs, GDP, LEDCs, LDCs, WHO, UN, ILO, HDI, IMF, WEO

Countries exhibit different levels of development and studying development is about measuring how developed one country is compared to another, or to the same country in the past. The ____ measures the total economic output of a country while the ____ ____ is a weighted mix of indices that show life expectancy, adult literacy, and standard of living per capita.

The ____'s findings on how economically, socially, culturally or technologically advanced a country is are presented twice a year by the ____. ____ and their subset ____ focus on primary industries, such as farming, fishing and mining, and are countries with a low standard of living and a much lower ____. In the poorest rural areas, where the majority of people live at – or well below – subsistence level, relief is often supplemented by agencies such as ____ and the ____. ____ focus on secondary industries, such as manufacturing or service industries, like banking, and are countries that have a higher standard of living.

49. The aquatic food chain is a fascinating labyrinth of masticational complexity that barely resembles anything so simple as a chain (it's more like a circuitous, revolving-door maze . . .). Put the flora and fauna below in their place on the food chain, starting from the bottom.

Squid
Lancet fish
Copepods
Lantern fish
Large sharks
Marlin
Dinoflagellates

50. Have you been acing these geography questions? If so, perhaps you should consider a new career in something geography-related? Using the descriptions and the clue of every other letter, can you name the disciplines and sub-disciplines below?

P★l★o★r★p★y – the study of ancient handwriting
★i★e★a★o★y – the study of the physical, chemical and crystalline properties of minerals
A★c★a★o★o★a★y – the study of plant remains
★r★h★e★m★t★y – the study of the application of scientific methods to archaeology problems (i.e. radiocarbon dating techniques, remote sensing, and trace element analysis)

P*l*o*c*l*g* – the study of fossil data in the reconstruction of extinct ecosystems
*a*t*g*a*h* – the art and science of representing a geographical area
P*l*o*t*l*g* – the study of prehistoric life
*r*h*o*s*r*n*m* – the study of how we have historically related to the cosmos
P*i*o*o*y – the study of the history of written languages
*o*n*t*v* a*c*a*o*o*y – the study of the way past societies thought

GEOGRAPHY ANSWERS

1. Bouvet Island, in Bouvetøya Norwegian, in the South Atlantic Ocean. One of the world's most lonely islands, it lies about 1,500 miles (2,400 km) southwest of the Cape of Good Hope of southern Africa and about 1,000 miles (1,600 km) north of the mainland of Antarctica. Of volcanic origin, it is rocky and almost entirely ice-covered, with ice cliffs surrounding the coast, making landing extremely difficult. It has an area of 23 square miles (59 km^2), rises to 3,068 feet (935 metres), and is uninhabited. The perfect holiday destination for a bit of peace and quiet.

2. Croatia uses the kuna; Latvia uses the lats; Slovenia uses the euro; Armenia uses the dram; Georgia uses the lari; Laos uses the kip; Myanmar (Burma) uses the kyat; Thailand uses the baht; Ethiopia uses the birr; Mozambique uses the metical; São Tomé and Príncipe uses the dobra; Vanuatu uses the vatu; Haiti uses the gourde; Brazil uses the real; Peru uses the sol.

3. Seattle. Although its average climate is much milder, both in summer and winter, geographically it is located between the co-ordinates 47°37' North and 122°20' West while the Canadian city of Montreal is at 45°30' North and 73°35' West.

4. b) Longitude, of course, is the 'long' one: the angular distance of a place east or west of a standard meridian.

5. The **Earth** rotates on its polar axis once every 23.9345 **hours**. As an oblate sphere measuring a circumferential 360°, the Earth rotates through almost 15 angular **degrees** per hour. The Earth's lines of longitude (**meridians**) are great **circles** that meet at the north and south polar axis. They are referenced by an east or west displacement from the **prime meridian**. Accordingly, lines of longitude range from 0° E to 180° E and 0° W to 180° W. Degrees are further divided into arcminutes and **arcseconds**. The prime meridian runs through **Greenwich** and the line of longitude displaced 180° E and 180° W from the prime meridian is termed the international **dateline**. Standard **meridians** occur every 15° of longitudinal displacement from the **prime** meridian (e.g., 15° W, 30° W, 45° W, etc.) and establish the local **noon** for the time zone.

6. b) Berbers, who call themselves Amazigh (Imazighen), are any of the descendants of the pre-Arab inhabitants of North Africa. They live in scattered communities across Morocco, Algeria, Tunisia, Libya and Egypt and tend to be concentrated in the mountain and desert regions of those countries. Smaller numbers of Berbers live in the northern portions of Mauritania, Mali and Niger. They speak various languages belonging to the Afro-Asiatic language family and almost all Berbers are Muslims, but various pre-Islamic religious elements survive among them, chiefly the worship of local saints and the veneration of their tombs. Zulus live in KwaZulu-Natal province in South Africa, the Maori are native to New Zealand and the Kuba are a cluster of about sixteen Bantu-speaking groups settled in southeastern Congo (Kinshasa), living between the Kasai and Sankuru rivers east of their confluence.

7. She returns on 12 February at 16:50. Even though she lost two days flying to Sydney, on her return the 21-hour flight gets her into New York on the same day that she left (12 February) because the 16-hour time difference goes backwards.

8.

9. Afghanistan, Kazakhstan, Kyrgyzstan, Pakistan, Tajikistan, Turkmenistan and Uzbekistan. In some languages, 'Hindustan' is used as a synonym for India. As a generally accepted explanation, the suffix '*stan'* is an ancient word meaning 'country', 'nation', 'land', or 'place of' in several Middle, Near Eastern and Indo-European languages, including Persian. So the country name of Afghanistan would mean 'land of the Afghans', or 'place of the Afghans'. The political instability of many *-stans* has led to the use, since about 1960, of *-stan* (more recently still *-istan*) to form the names of fictional places which carry negative associations. The Gaza Strip area of Palestine controlled by Hamas was coined *Hamastan* in 2007; *Londonistan* is a disparaging term for the British capital that refers to the numbers of militant Islamists living there. Such invented names are often used humorously, as in *Blogistan*, a supposed country that is populated by online bloggers; *Nerdistan*, referring to concentrations of high-tech and science-based industries, such as Silicon Valley; and Robert

Frank's invention of *Richistan*, which became the title of his book in 2007, a state within a state in which only the seriously rich live.

10. Kazakhstan, Kyrgyzstan, Tajikistan, Turkmenistan and Uzbekistan.

11. Brunei, which joined the Commonwealth in 1984, Cameroon (1995), Rwanda (2009), Seychelles (1976) and Pakistan, which joined in 1947, left in 1972 and rejoined in 1989. Some of you may have also spotted Japan, Argentina and Poland, placed strategically in the word search to deliberately throw you off.

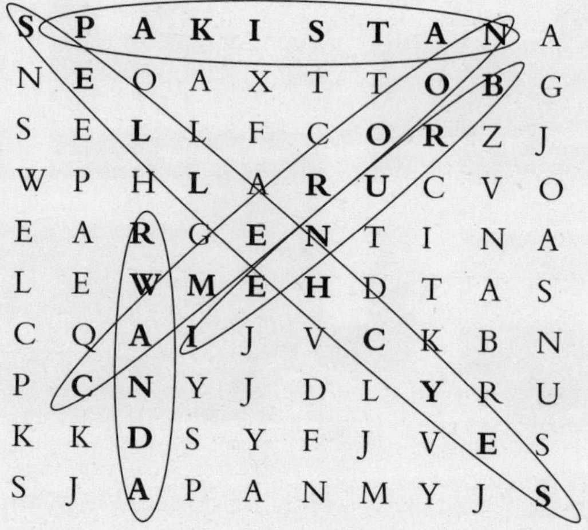

12.

a) Cumulus
b) Cumulonimbus
c) Stratus
d) Cirrus
e) Altostratus

13. c) The city of Reims is located in the Champagne-Ardenne *région* of northeastern France and is one of the main centres of champagne production. On the Vesle River, a tributary of the Aisne, and the Marne–Aisne canal, the city is situated in vine-growing country and is overlooked from the southwest by the Montagne de Reims. Take a tip from us that the best champagne comes from vineyards along the Marne River from Château-Thierry eastward to Épernay and on the plain from Épernay stretching north to Reims, which is dominated by the Montagne de Reims.

14. Philippines, Madagascar, Oaxaca, Bordeaux, Mississippi, Saskatchewan, Llangollen, Uppsala, Bologna, Azerbaijan, Riyadh, Bering Sea, Christchurch, Enniskillen, Minsk, Eritrea, Colombia, Xinjiang, Antwerp, Schleswig-Holstein.

15. c) The Juan de Fuca Strait, stretching approximately 80–100 miles (130–160 km) in length and 11–16 miles (18–27 km) in width, is the access route of the eastern North Pacific Ocean, between the Olympic Peninsula of Washington state, USA, and Vancouver Island, British Columbia, Canada. Part of the United States–Canadian international boundary lies mid-channel. The real name of Juan de Fuca (born 1536) was Ioánnis Foká.

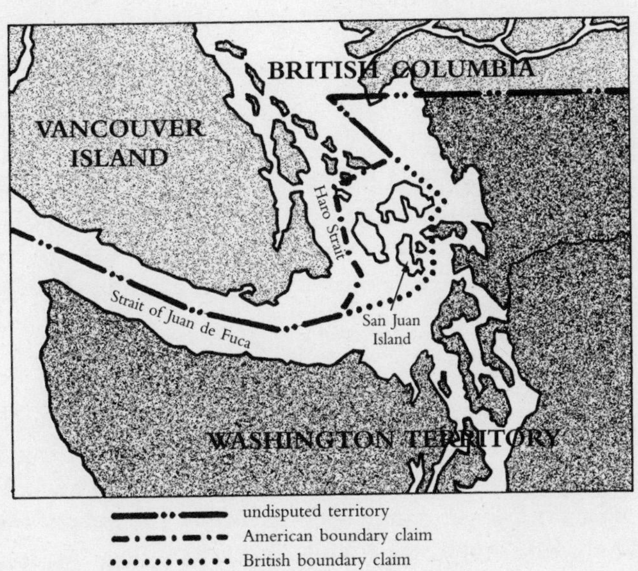

16. Alexander Nevsky (prince of Russia): Vladimir; Nelson Mandela (president of South Africa): Umtata; Catherine de' Medici (queen of France): Florence; Dorgon (prince of the Manchu people of Manchuria who played a major part in founding the Qing dynasty): Yenden; John F. Kennedy (president of the United States): Brookline; Julia Gillard (prime minister of Australia): Barry, Vale of Glamorgan; Adolf Hitler (leader of Germany): Braunau am Inn; Jânio da Silva Quadros (short-serving president of Brazil): Campo Grande; Benazir Bhutto (prime minister of Pakistan): Karachi; Mao Zedong (chairman of the People's Republic of China): Shaoshan; Léopold Senghor (first president of Senegal): Joal; Franklin D. Roosevelt (president of the United States): Hyde Park; Alexander the Great (king of Macedonia): Pella; Paul von Hindenburg (second president of the Weimar Republic): Posen; Sophie Friederike Auguste von Anhalt-Zerbst (more widely known as Catherine the Great, empress of Russia): Stettin; Andrew Bonar Law (prime minister of Britain): Kingston, New Brunswick; Che Guevara (Argentine-Cuban revolutionary): Rosario; Indira Gandhi (prime minister of India): Allahabad.

17. d) All the others are neighbourhoods in San Francisco, with Tenderloin being – from what we hear – one of the city's most exciting and diverse locales, with unpolished gems in the form of incredible cooking, great bars and live music.

18. Venus: 0; Mars: 2; Mercury: 0; Jupiter: more than 60, the four brightest of which are called the Galilean satellites and were the first objects in the solar system discovered by Galileo's telescope in 1610; Saturn: more than 60, of which Titan is the largest; Uranus: 27; Neptune: 13; Earth: 1 (obviously . . .) known as 'The Moon'; Pluto, the demoted 'dwarf planet': 3

19. d) Though the train passes through each of the three other possible answers. Today there are other routes serviced by the railway, but the 'Rossiva' Moscow–Vladivostok is the longest, direct-rail route. The full rail trip on the passenger train, which includes a compulsory overnight stay in lovely Khabarovsk, takes about eight days.

20. b) Throughout the early Chinese dynasties, China had only limited influence over the region of Manchuria, but in the late nineteenth-century

Manchuria was fully under Chinese control. While Canada and Russia both dominate the Arctic region and, as the two largest countries on earth, together account for three-quarters of the Arctic Ocean's coastline, any direct train line joining them would need the permission of either the US to cross through Alaska, or Santa Claus in the North Pole.

21. The Trans-Siberian Moscow to Vladistok, at 5,726 miles (9,216 km). The Trans-Manchurian is a mere 5,592 miles (9,001 km) long.

22. b) While Siberia has gained most of its notoriety as a place of exile for criminal and political prisoners, especially under Stalin, its mineral resources are plentiful; particularly notable are its deposits of coal, petroleum, natural gas, diamonds, iron ore and gold. With the completion of the railway, Siberia saw immigration and industry rise exponentially and even today about 30 per cent of Russian exports continue to travel on the line.

23. a) The Great Wall of China is approximately 4,500 miles (7,300 km) long. Although the length of Route 66 changed many times due to construction along the way, the historic length most often cited is 2,448 miles (3,939 km). Hadrian's Wall, built in 122 CE, ran from coast to coast across the width of northern Britain for 73 miles (118 km), from Wallsend (Segedunum) on the River Tyne in the east to Bowness on the Solway Firth in the west, and is the largest ancient monument in northern Europe.

24. a) True; b) True; c) True; d) False. The 'Myth of the Flat Earth' appears to have spread in the late nineteenth century and has become one of the most notorious pieces of dogma that contemporary historians have had to squash. By the Middle Ages, there was widespread belief (at least among the educated) that the earth was a globe. Columbus did face opposition from the Spanish Cardinals on his voyage, but not because they thought he'd drop off the edge of the world. Instead they believed he'd predicted too small a globe and would run out of supplies before he made it round to Asia, and they were right: the earth was a heck of a lot bigger than Columbus believed. People in Europe probably did believe that the earth was flat at one stage, but that was in the very early ancient period, possibly before the 4th century BCE. It was around this date that Greek thinkers began to not only realise the earth was a globe, but calculated – sometimes very closely – the precise dimensions of our planet.

25.
A: Coral Sea
B: Arafura Sea
C: Arabian Sea
D: South China Sea
E: Mediterranean Sea
F: Barents Sea
G: Sea of Okhotsk
H: Red Sea
I: Bering Sea
J: Labrador Sea
K: Sargasso Sea
L: Caribbean Sea
M: Beaufort Sea

26. c) Although the city's name Budapest suggests that the correct answer would be b), the village of Óbuda, which belonged to Pest *megye,* the autonomous county that was in the hands of the local Hungarian nobility, was also united into the single, municipal borough. Buda and Óbuda were located on the right bank of the Danube River while Pest was on the left.

27. Brazil, 201,103,330; Cape Verde, 508,659; Hong Kong, 7,089,705; Monaco, 30,586; United Kingdom, 62,348,447; China, 1,330,141,295; Greenland, 57,637; India, 1,173,108,018; Swaziland, 1,354,051; United Arab Emirates, 4,975,593.

28. This is easy as you guessed right off the bat that when we say 'Just before spring' we were referring (eurocentrically) to our own Northern Hemisphere seasons. But March is the start of autumn in the Southern

Hemisphere, so the sea waters the penguins live in become frozen for long distances, including the one to their breeding grounds. By 'mid-winter', i.e. high summer in Antarctica, temperatures rise and the ice melts, meaning the journey from the colonies on the sea ice to sea waters, where the penguins live, is considerably shorter.

29. a) Though if you were considering answer c) you would be partially correct because Istanbul was widely known as Constantinople between 326 CE and 1930 when it was officially renamed. (Another name for this many-monickered city that might be familiar to you is Byzantium, as this was what it was originally called at the time of its foundation in the seventh century BCE long before the Emperor Constantine came along.)

30. b)

31. **North America**: Kodiak bear, kangaroo mouse, blue jay and musk turtle; **Europe**: Norway lemming, Pyrenean ibex, Löwchen and *Oryctalagus cuniculus* (old world rabbit); **Asia**: Cobra, orangutan, babirusa and water buffalo; **South America**: Anaconda, rhea, sloth and spectacled bear; **Africa**: Aardvark, ostrich, warthog and Cape buffalo; **Australia**: Wallaby, Tasmanian devil, wombat and moa.

32.

a) Aborigines
b) Pakistan
c) Aral Sea
d) Study of distribution of species
e) Lake Superior
f) Cancun, 2010

33. Australia. Risk is a board game based on a political map of the Earth's territories and continents. The object of the game is for each player to gain as much control over as many territories as possible, with a view (of course) to gaining complete world domination by building up armies in specific territories and 'attacking' and 'capturing' other countries. Players control armies with results determined by dice rolls: the person who loses the dice roll loses the corresponding number of armies and players can keep 'attacking' this way until the loser's armies have been taken over and their country is wiped out. The reason Australia is so easy to defend? Well, as with the real Australia, there are very few neighbouring countries on the board from which you can attack it. On the flip side, though, different countries have different values and you get more credit for holding more difficult-to-defend countries, such as Italy, which can be attacked from – as with the real Italy – many different sides.

34.

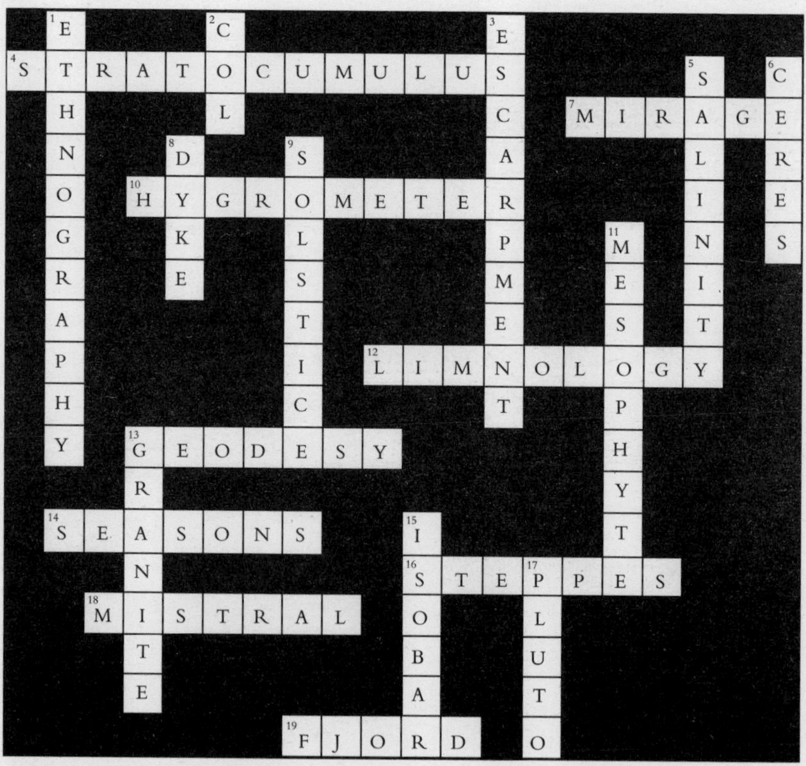

35.

a) Glasgow, Scotland. Before World War I, Renfrew was used as a practice ground for pilots and when war broke out, the military used it. In 1933 a scheduled air service bound for Campbeltown, then London, took off, but as air travel increased in the 1950s, the airport soon became too small to handle the traffic and closed in 1966.

b) Berlin, Germany. Barely 20 minutes from the Brandenburg Gate, Hitler's dream airport (and the airport in which US aircraft landed with essential food and coal when the Soviet Union sealed off West Berlin in 1948) was closed in 2008 because it could not be expanded to accommodate large aircraft.

c) Between Jerusalem and Ramallah and popularly known as the Jerusalem Airport, what was originally called Qalandia Airport was built by the British during the Mandate period and opened for business in 1936, but closed after the Second Intifada in 2001.

d) Named after Chief Minister William Henry Bramble, the airport was located near the now-abandoned capital of Plymouth on the island of Montserrat in the Caribbean but was destroyed in 1997 by the eruption of the Soufrière Hills Volcano.

36.

a) CST (Central Standard Time). George Bush International Airport is in Houston, Texas (time zone: UTC/GMT -6 hours.

b) CST (*China* Standard Time). Guangzhou Baiyun International Airport is in Guangzhou, China (UTC/GMT +8 hours).

c) PET (Peru Time). Jorge Chávez International Airport is in Cusco, Peru (time zone UTC/GMT -5 hours).

d) ICT (Indochina Time). Don Mueang International Airport is in Bangkok, Thailand (UTC/GMT +7 hours).

e) CET (Central European Time). Esbjerg Airport is in Esbjerg, Denmark (time zone UTC/GMT +1 hour).

f) CAT (Central Africa Time). Sir Seretse Khama International Airport is in Gaborone, Botswana (time zone UTC/GMT +2 hours).

37. c) According to the US Geologic Survey's Geographic Names Information Service, the place name of 'Riverside' can be found in all but four states (it does not exist in Hawaii, Alaska, Louisiana and

Oklahoma). The runner up was Centerville in 45 states, followed by Fairview (43 states), Franklin (42), Midway (40), Fairfield (39), Pleasant Valley (39), Troy (39), Liberty (38) and Union (38). Springfield – which is commonly thought of as the most prolific place name – isn't even in the top ten (only 35 states have a Springfield).

38. a) Yes. b) No. The Richter scale is named after the American seismologist Charles Richter (1900–85) who devised it in 1935 in association with the German Bruno Gutenberg. As far as we know, he bears absolutely no relation to the artist Gerhard Richter (whose father was called Horst Richter). c) No. The Mason-Dixon line was named after its English surveyors Charles Mason and Jeremiah Dixon. d) Yes.

39.

i. c)
ii. a)
iii. c)
iv. b)

40. i. b) A tropical rainforest *is* a biome (a large-scale ecosystem) in the same way that a savannah biome *is* a tropical grassland. A boreal forest *receives a lot of* precipitation; a coniferous tree *has* pinecones; an ecosystem *can be* a pond.

ii. a) Glaciers *produce* valleys just as freeze-thaw (the action of glacial meltwater on joints, cracks and hollows in rock) *produces* rock fragments. Mount Everest *is* a pyramidal peak (a peak formed when three or more corries and arêtes meet); rivers *have* tributaries (as the main glacier erodes deeper into the valley, a tributary is left higher up the steep sides of the glacier); a glacier *moves* downhill.

iii. d) The earth consists of four concentric layers: inner core, outer core, mantle and crust. The oceanic crust is one of two kinds of the earth's crust (the other is continental) and it *carries* water; the earth's crust is *made up of* tectonic plates; plate tectonics *cause* earthquakes (and volcanoes).

41. a) Ribbentrop was the son of an army officer in a middle-class family. After attending schools in Germany, Switzerland, France and England, he went to Montreal in 1910 and worked for the Molson's Bank, a prominent Canadian financial institution which was absorbed by the Bank of Montreal in the twenties. In 1912 he joined an engineering company and after working for the Trans-Continental Railway and as a journalist in New York City, Ribbentrop settled in Ottawa in 1913. When war broke out, he returned to Germany and settled in Berlin after World War I, becoming a successful liquor salesman. After meeting Adolf Hitler in 1932, he made the fateful decision to join the Nazi Party. Convicted at Nuremberg for his role in the Holocaust, Ribbentrop was executed on 16 October 1946.

42. 1,637 metres is the depth of Lake Baikal, in south-east Siberia; 980 metres is the height of Angel Falls, in Venezuela; 840 metres is the mean elevation of the earth's surface; 1,343 metres is the height of Ben Nevis, the Scottish Munro; 500 metres is where 52 per cent of the earth's land surface is below; 4,280 metres is the mean depth of the Pacific Ocean.

43. a) The HMS *Beagle* was launched on 11 May 1820, at Woolwich, the site of the Royal Navy's dockyards on the River Thames near London. The ship was designed as a flush-decked, 10-gun brig (a two-masted vessel intended for scouting, courier duty, and other light assignments). It carried eight 18-pounder carronades and two 6-pounder long guns; its length was 90 feet 4 inches (about 28 metres), its beam 24 feet 6 inches (about 8 metres). At the naval review for King George IV in 1820, it became the first ship to pass fully rigged under the old London Bridge.

44. Chartres Cathedral, Shark Bay, Stoclet House, Brasilia, Stonehenge, Angkor, Mount Wuyi, Statue of Liberty, Litomyšl Castle, Galápagos, Acropolis, Taj Mahal, Persepolis, Masada, Auschwitz Birkenau, Robben Island, St Kilda, Ironbridge Gorge. Unscrambled and re-worked, the various letters from these words spell: United Nations Educational, Scientific and Cultural Organization (UNESCO), the United Nations initiative which looks after the aforementioned heritage sites.

45. d) Mary Anning (1799–1847) was born in Lyme Regis. Her father was a cabinetmaker and occasional fossil collector and when he died he left his family in debt. To make ends meet the Anning family sold fossils from Lyme Regis and by the middle of the 1820s, Mary had established herself as the keen eye and accomplished anatomist of the family, and began taking charge of the family fossil business. Mary has been credited with the first discovery of ichthyosaur fossils. Although this is not entirely true, she did help to discover the first specimen of *Ichthyosaurus* to be known by the scientific community of London and several other fine ichthyosaur skeletons. But perhaps her most important find, from a scientific point of view, was her discovery of the first plesiosaur. The famous French anatomist, Georges Cuvier, doubted the validity of the specimen when he first examined a detailed drawing. Once Cuvier realised that this was a genuine find, the Annings became legitimate and respected fossilists in the eyes of the scientific community.

46. Barbados = Barbadian; Benin = Beninese; Burkina Faso = Burkinabe; Comoros = Comoran; Cook Islands = Cook Islander; Côte d'Ivoire = Ivoirian; Faroe Islands = Faroese; Greenland = Greenlandic; Isle of Man = Manx; Kiribati = I-Kiribati; Macau = Chinese; Mauritania = Mauritanian; Mayotte = Mahoran; Oman = Omani; Palau = Palauan; Seychelles = Seychellois; Timor-Leste = Timorese; Yemen = Yemeni.

47.

a) Albania. This flag is thought to have been designed by the fifteenth-century hero George Castriota Skanderberg, who led a successful uprising against the Turks that resulted in a short-lived independence for some Albanian regions (1443–1478). One possible explanation for the eagle symbol is the tradition that Albanians see themselves as descendants of the eagle and they refer to themselves as 'Shkypetars', which translates as 'sons of the eagle'.

b) American Samoa. The brown and white American bald eagle flying toward the hoist side is carrying two traditional Samoan symbols of authority, a war club known as a 'Fa'alaufa'I' (upper; left talon), and a coconut fiber fly whisk known as a 'Fue' (lower; right talon). The combination of symbols broadly mimics that seen on the U.S. Great Seal and reflects the relationship between the United States and American Samoa.

c) Cape Verde. The circle of stars represents the ten major islands united into a nation and the stripes symbolise the road to formation of the country through peace (white) and effort (red).
d) Norway. Red with a blue cross outlined in white that extends to the edges of the flag, the vertical part of the cross is shifted to the hoist side in the style of the Danish flag while the colours recall Norway's past political unions with Denmark and Sweden.
e) Panama. The blue and red colours of the Panamanian flag represent the main political parties (Conservatives and Liberals respectively) and the white denotes peace between them. The blue star stands for the civic virtues of purity and honesty, the red star signifies authority and law.

48. Countries exhibit different levels of development and studying development is about measuring how developed one country is compared to another, or to the same country in the past. The **GNP** measures the total economic output of a country while the **UN HDI** is a weighted mix of indices that show life expectancy, adult literacy, and standard of living per capita. The **IMF**'s findings on how economically, socially, culturally or technologically advanced a country is are presented twice a year by the **WEO**. **LEDCs** and their subset **LDCs** focus on primary industries, such as farming, fishing and mining, and are countries with a low standard of living and a much lower **GDP**. In the poorest rural areas, where the majority of people live at – or well below – subsistence level, relief is often supplemented by agencies such as **WHO** and the **ILO**. **MEDCs** focus on secondary industries, such as manufacturing or service industries, like banking, and are countries that have a higher standard of living.

IMF (International Monetary Fund); WEO (World Economic Outlook); LEDCs (Less Economically Developed Countries); LDCs (Least Economically Developed Countries); GDP (Gross Domestic Product); UN (United Nations); WHO (World Health Organization); ILO (International Labour Organization); MEDCs (More Economically Developed Countries); GNP (Gross National Product); HDI (Human Development Index)

49. Dinoflagellates, copepods, lantern fish, squid, lancet fish, marlin, large sharks. The food chain begins with phytoplankton, tiny little organisms like dinoflagellates and algae which usually have siliceous skeletons that exist through photosynthesis. Just above them are zooplanktons, the animal versions of the bottom feeders, made up of things like copepods, eggs, crustaceans and larvae. Above zooplankton are the first carnivores – the small predators or 'the filterers': the lantern fish, amphipods, ocean sunfish and herring. Then come the predators (squid or mackerel) followed by the top predators like marlins, sharks and some seabirds. Humans, obviously, are the absolute top predators, but only because we have weapons, not superior instinct or cunning.

50. The study of ancient handwriting: Paleography. The study of the physical, chemical and crystalline properties of minerals: Mineralogy. The study of plant remains: Archaeobotany. The study of the application of scientific methods to archaeology problems (i.e. radiocarbon dating techniques, remote sensing, and trace element analysis): Archaeometry. The study of fossil data in the reconstruction of extinct ecosystems: Paleoecology. The art and science of representing a geographical area: Cartography. The study of prehistoric life: Paleontology. The study of how we have historically related to the cosmos: Archeoastronomy. The study of the history of written languages: Philology. The study of the way past societies thought: Cognitive archaeology. Next time you meet an archeoastronomist at a party you'll know exactly how to engage him or her in small talk.

HISTORY

The great French leader Napoleon Bonaparte cannily said, 'History is the version of past events that people have decided to agree upon.' Up until recently people generally agreed that Napoleon was a short man, but it turns out that at 5′ 6½″ he was above average for his time. In fact there are many events that historians disagree about (although the consensus remains that, lanky or little, Napoleon was soundly whipped at Waterloo). The correct interpretation of history is supposed to mean that individuals and states learn from the past and don't make the same mistakes as their forefathers. However, as you will discover from the questions below, it seems that for a long time there have been plenty of bad historians out there in positions of power. In spite of this, a broad knowledge of the events of yesteryear is still a worthwhile attribute to cultivate. As well as the meat and potatoes of battles and kings, you'll find that this section of the quiz will challenge you on international happenings from South Africa to Russia, range back and forth in time from prehistory to the modern day and cover such varied beasts as dinosaurs and civil engineers.

1. The pugnacious-looking, yet plant-eating, Triceratops is a dinosaur from which of the following periods?

a) Jurassic
b) Cretaceous
c) Devonian
d) Cambrian

2. Using your common sense and the words in the box below, fill in the blanks in this précis of the Ancient Egyptian myth of Osiris and Isis.

ruler, earth, crocodiles, phallus, fish, Nile, underworld, casket, married, Seth, corpse, fourteen, spirit, peace, children, sky, scattered, thirteen, Isis

Seth, Nephthys, Isis and Osiris were all the ____ of Geb, the ____ god and Nut, the ____ goddess. Osiris and Isis were also ____, as were Seth and Nephthys, as was considered perfectly proper in Ancient Egyptian high society.

____ was extremely jealous of his brother, who became ruler of Egypt, bringing prosperity and ____ to the land and generally being a goody-two-shoes, so he tricked him into getting into a specially made cedarwood ____ which he then threw in the ____, killing him.

____ searched for the casket in order to give Osiris a proper burial but when she brought it back to Egypt Seth found it and chopped Osiris's ____ up into ____ pieces which he ____ in the Nile for the ____ to eat. Isis and Nephthys managed to collect together ____ of the pieces but Osiris's ____ had been eaten by a ____ so Isis had to make a new one for him. She then embalmed his body and his ____ was able to pass into the ____, where he became its ____.

Seth

3. When was the death penalty abolished in the UK?

a) 1808
b) 1908
c) 1949
d) 1998

4. Despite the fact that the laws of succession during the Tang dynasty in China precluded female rulers (in line with Confucius' rather hysterical view that 'when the hen crows, the state will fall'), who of the following rose from the position of an imperial concubine to become the first, and only, official ruling Empress of China?

a) Wu Zetian
b) Consort Xiao
c) Murasaki Shikibu
d) Empress Wang

5. God bless those Victorian do-gooders and their philanthropic plans. The nineteenth century saw a rise in social consciousness that led to reformers such as William Wilberforce opposing slavery, Joseph Livesey starting the Temperance Movement and Dr Thomas Barnardo campaigning for better treatment for children. Which area of society did Elizabeth Fry (1780–1845) turn her charitable attention to?

a) The police force
b) Prisons
c) The Catholic church
d) School dinners

6. The Christmas carol featuring the miraculously hot-footed 'Good King Wenceslas' is based on the life of a historical figure from which of the following countries?

a) Romania
b) Sweden
c) Scotland
d) Czech Republic

7. During the Boston Tea Party of 1773, some of the lively revolutionary fellows responsible for tossing the 342 chests of valuable tea from the British ships into the harbour were disguised as what?

a) French clowns
b) Policemen
c) Native Americans of the Mohawk tribe
d) Vicars and tarts

8. The celebrated Spanish Muslim philosopher and prominent polymath Abu al-Walid Muhammad ibn Ahmad ibn Rushd (plain old Ibn-Rushd to his friends) was famous in the twelfth century for his commentaries on the Greek philosopher Aristotle. These helped European scholars rediscover the work of the ancient Greeks, contributing to the glorious cultural flowering known as the Renaissance. However, due to the enthusiasm of the western scholars of the time for making exotic names more manageable he was more commonly known in Europe by which name?

a) Algazel
b) Averroes
c) Alkindus
d) Alkapone

9. Match up the following famous English kings with the impertinent nicknames they were given by their subjects:

Ethelred II	Lackland
William I	The Merrie Monarch
William II	The Bastard
John	The Unready
Charles II	The Be-shitten
James II	Rufus

10. Empress Catherine II of Russia has been ill-used by historians in the past, who invented scurrilous rumours about equine aspects to her love life. However, she fully deserved her title of 'Catherine the Great', as she made Russia into a key player in European politics and culture during her rule. When did she come to power?

a) 1682
b) 1696
c) 1725
d) 1762

11. Which country in the following list was the first to allow women to vote?

a) Great Britain
b) France
c) New Zealand
d) Norway

12. Find SIX of the names of months from the French Republican calendar, which was adopted by the French government after the Revolution of 1789, in the word search below:

B R I A N D G O F E
F N I V O S E A R T
J L B L U A R E U H
M I O R A N M U C E
J A N R U A I R T R
K T N A E M N S I I
O I E R O A A P D A
U E T I B E L I O L
T H E R M I D O R U
N M C E N T I M I E

13. When did the Korean War officially end?

a) 1950
b) 1953
c) 1975
d) never

14. The book-burning fifteenth-century firebrand Florentine priest Savonarola was a member of which religious order, distinguished by their black cloaks and white habits?

a) Dominican
b) Carmelite
c) Franciscan
d) Servite

15. We look back on the reign of Her Majesty Victoria, by the Grace of God, of the United Kingdom of Great Britain and Ireland Queen, Defender of the Faith, Empress of India (to give her her full title) as a time of gentlemen in pith helmets colonising distant lands, grubby chimney-sweep urchins and repressed women in big skirts sweeping through delightfully designed parks discussing the latest Dickens serial. However, this extraordinary age was also a time of great discovery and scientific progress. Which of the following were invented in the Victorian era?

Steel	Roads	Milk chocolate Easter eggs
Telephone switchboards	Electric tumble dryers	Advertising
Pedal bicycles	London Underground	Concrete
Lipstick	Submarines	Barometers
Synthetic heroin	Marmalade	Shoe polish
Refracting telescopes	Postage stamps	Radiography

16. Used by the British during the Second World War, the interestingly monickered Matilda, Cromwell and Challenger were all types of:

a) Uniform
b) Codeword cipher
c) Tank
d) Spaceship

17. In what year did Bangladesh become independent from Pakistan?

a) 1947
b) 1962
c) 1971
d) 1982

18. In honour of the plucky little upstarts who burn brightly and change the face of the world before the complacency of middle age sets in, please make yourself feel inferior by matching the following ages to the questions below:

14, 17, 21, 24, 25, 26, 26, 27, 28, 30, 33, 35, 41

a) How old was Queen Elizabeth I when she acceded to the throne?
b) How old was Joan of Arc when she took command of the French campaign against the English?
c) How old was the British Prime Minister William Pitt the Younger when he came to power?
d) How old was author Mary Shelley when her book *Frankenstein* was published?
e) How old was George Harrison when the Beatles split up?
f) How old was Carl Djerassi when he and his team invented norethindrone, leading to the development of the combined oral contraceptive pill?
g) How old was Orson Welles when he made *Citizen Kane*?
h) How old was Christopher Columbus when he landed in America?
i) How old was Martin Luther King when he won the Nobel Peace Prize?
j) How old was Paul Dirac when he published his paper explaining the concept of antimatter?
k) How old was Wolfgang Amadeus Mozart when he composed *The Marriage of Figaro*?
l) How old was Pablo Picasso when he painted *Portrait of Aunt Pepa*?
m) How old was Jesus said to be when he was crucified?

19. The technologically advanced and industrially significant machine invented by Lancastrian James Hargreaves in 1764 was called a:

a) Lazy Susan
b) Spinning Jenny
c) Catherine Wheel
d) Water Frame

20. Which of the following is NOT the codename for a beach used in the D-day landings in the Second World War?

a) Utah
b) Sword
c) Carolina
d) Omaha

21. The British Isles have always been proud of their marine prowess. Since the days of the Armada the navy has been a jewel in the crown of our defence forces. Put the following famous seafarers from history in order of rank from the highest to lowest:

James Cook
Horatio Nelson
Francis Drake
Fletcher Christian

22. The 1960 Sharpeville Massacre in South Africa began with a protest against which specific piece of apartheid legislation which was then in place in that country?

a) Prohibition of Mixed Marriages Act
b) Population Registration Act
c) Pass Laws
d) Reservation of Separate Amenities Act

23. Although in day-to-day life it's often harder to remember where you just left your keys than what your first kiss felt like, in world events most people feel more certain of their chronology when discussing recent historical happenings. Test your global knowledge of the more remote stretches of the past by identifying which came first out of the following?

a) The birth of Buddha
b) The construction of Stonehenge
c) The death of Attila the Hun
d) The foundation of the Roman Republic

24. We all know that Ming vases are very old and lovely and not cheap to replace, but what about artefacts from even further back in Chinese history? The Mings actually came on to the dynastic scene pretty late in the day, in the fourteenth century, and there were plenty of other ruling families preceding them. See if you can put the following Chinese dynasties in chronological order:

a) Tang
b) Han
c) Xia
d) Sui

25. Britain and the USA have always had a special relationship, even when that specialness was being expressed through brutal fighting in the War of Independence. But what do the British prime minister William Pitt the Elder and the American president John Adams particularly have in common?

26. Who were the Mensheviks?

27. These quotations are commonly attributed to which major historical character?

> 'Happiness is when what you think, what you do and what you say are in harmony.'
>
> 'I believe in equality for everyone, except reporters and photographers.'

'I cannot teach you violence, as I do not myself believe in it. I can only teach you not to bow your heads before anyone, even at the cost of your life.'

28. The far distant mists of time may seem just like an indistinguishable fog from our perspective in the dazzlingly fast-paced modern age. However, there is an awful lot of time to be filed in the pre-history drawer. To make this more manageable scientists have divided the time since the earth's creation into different units: eons of hundreds of millions of years divided into eras, in turn divided into periods. Put the following prehistoric periods in chronological order:

Ordovician
Jurassic
Carboniferous
Silurian
Paleogene

29. Who were the excellently named Lambert Simnel and Perkin Warbeck?

30. As you may have noticed from the news, the tiny island of Great Britain has messed around in the business of plenty of other nations in its time. Our current involvement in Iraq and Afghanistan is just the most recent activity of decades of dabbling in these areas for commercial and political gain. Using the words in the box below, fill in the blanks in this account of Afghanistan's recent history:

Taliban, 1979, Rawalpindi, Afghan, al-Qaeda, Saur, India, Soviet, 1747, Russia, Northern Alliance, Mohammad Daoud Khan, monarchy, 1973, 9/11, mujahideen, Ahmad Shah Durrani, 'Great Game'

Afghanistan was officially founded in ____ by the great military commander ____. In the nineteenth century Great Britain saw Afghanistan as a useful place of influence in the ____ to stem the spread of ____'s power, which threatened British ____. British forces invaded the country during the Anglo-Afghan Wars and the area remained subject to British meddling until the signing of the Treaty of ____ in 1919. Afghanistan was a ____ until the coup of ____ led by ____, who was later assassinated by the Communist People's Democratic Party of Afghanistan in the ____ Revolution of 1978. Opposition to this government led to ____ forces invading in ____ and fighting the ____ , backed by the US, until the Soviet withdrawal in 1989. The ensuing civil wars resulted in the foundation of the Islamic State of Afghanistan in 1992 which fell to the ____ in 1996. Resistance to the new regime took the form of the ____ which reclaimed most of the country in 2001 with US and UK support following the ____ attacks on the US by Taliban-backed ____. However, although a new ____ government was formed, this war still continues today.

31. The eighteenth and nineteenth centuries saw the face of Britain changed by the energies of the Industrial Revolution. No figure was more significant in the modernisation of our country than the great civil engineer and man voted second-best Briton of all time (after Churchill) in a BBC poll, Isambard Kingdom Brunel. Complete the following crossword based on his life and his wondrous works:

ACROSS

1. Brunel's first major design, a viaduct to carry trains across the Brent Valley (11)
5. ____ railway tunnel, between Bath and Chippenham on the Great Western Railway line, also a container (3)
7. 2 down and 10 across: structure across the River Tamar, opened the year Brunel died (5, 6, 6)
8. Famous Bristol bridge (7)
9. Brunel studied in this European capital during his youth (5)
10. See 7 across
13. Berkshire train station, also a pastime (7)
14. The name of the river tunnel Brunel first worked on with his father (6)
15. Brunel's second son, also a civil engineer (5)

DOWN

1. The Great ____ Railway (7)
2. See 7 across
3. This great British hero was half-____ (6)
4. The world's first iron-hulled, screw propeller-driven, steam-powered passenger liner, also the name of a country (5,7)
6. Famous London train station, also associated with bears (10)
9. Birthplace of Brunel (7)
11. Brunel's railway gauge, also a type of bean (5)
12. Brunel's wife's name (4)

32. Alexandre *père* and Alexandre *fils*, Pierre-Auguste and Jean, Kirk and Michael, Kingsley and Martin, Graham and Damon, Homer and Bart, but who was the famous son of Pepin the Short?

33. When we think of camouflage we generally think of squaddies smeared in mud with twigs in their hats lying in ditches, or the white ski-suits in the Alpine stand-offs of spy films. However, the art of disguising martial equipment has become ever more sophisticated. These days stealth bombers use their unique shape and radar-absorbent materials to render them all but invisible to tracking devices, but in earlier times the only thing available was good honest paint. What was the name of Norman Wilkinson's camouflage strategy used by the British navy during the First World War?

a) Clash
b) Dazzle
c) Chameleon
d) Divert

34. We all remember stubborn, scorned Catherine of Aragon and desirable but doomed Anne Boleyn, but what was the name of Henry VIII's fifth wife?

a) Anne of Cleves
b) Catherine Parr
c) Jane Seymour
d) Catherine Howard

35. Facts! Facts! Facts! There are different schools of thought about whether the study of history should involve rote learning or the development of transferable skills such as analysis and evaluation. Our view is a bit of solid knowledge never did anyone any harm. Use your erudition and your reasoning skills to fill in the following:

a) The *Golden Hind* is to Francis Drake as the *Santa Maria* is to ____.
b) 15th August is to India as 4th July is to ____.
c) Benito is to Italy as Francisco is to ____.
d) Chichen Itza is to the Maya as Tenochtitlan is to the ____.
e) Herbert Henry Asquith is to George V as Stanley Baldwin is to ____.
f) Luther is to Germany as Zwingli is to ____.
g) Michael Collins is to Fine Gael as Eamon de Valera is to ____.
h) Josephine is to Napoleon as Marie Antoinette is to ____.
i) The Kingdom of Kush is to Sudan as Mesopotamia is to ____.
j) Amerigo Vespucci is to America as Abel Tasman is to ____.

36. What are the Killing Fields?

37. Given the ingredients of a long, hot summer and a densely populated city built of wooden houses overhanging narrow streets, it's no surprise that when a spark escaped from a bakery in Pudding Lane in 1666, flaming devastation followed. Over 13,000 houses were destroyed and one sixth of the city's population was left homeless, but how many people were killed in the Great Fire of London, according to official records?

a) 4
b) 40
c) 400
d) 4000

38. Famed for eating off plates of solid gold and never wearing the same outfit twice, Suleiman the Magnificent was the most glorious and dashing leader of which Empire?

a) Roman
b) Byzantine
c) Ottoman
d) Mamluk

39. According to King George III, America was formally granted independence from the British Empire on 14 January 1784 as part of the Treaty of Paris, ending the hostilities of the American War of Independence. However, the US considered itself free from the date of the famous Declaration of Independence on 4 July 1776. How many states made up the United States of America when the Declaration of Independence was proclaimed?

a) 9
b) 13
c) 36
d) 50

40. Born the illegitimate son of a teenage Welsh girl, Sir Henry Morton Stanley went from a childhood in the workhouse to fighting on both sides in the American Civil War before becoming a famous journalist. He is most famous for having asked what question?

41. Which two heads of state were present at the Field of the Cloth of Gold?

a) Stalin and Roosevelt
b) Henry VIII and Francis I
c) Maximilian I and Ferdinand II
d) Napoleon and George III

42. As Mark Twain said, in his helpful essay, *How to Make History Dates Stick*, 'Dates are difficult things to acquire; and after they are acquired it is difficult to keep them in the head. But they are very valuable. They are like the cattle-pens of a ranch – they shut in the several brands of historical cattle, each within its own fence, and keep them from getting mixed together.' See if you can sort out the historical livestock below:

1988, 1517, 1718, 1337, 1865, 1815, 1955, 126, 1965,
1953, 1543, 1963, 1845, 1096, 1779

a) Religious reformer Martin Luther posts the *95 Theses* on the door of Castle Church in Wittenberg.
b) Civil Rights campaigner Rosa Parks refuses to give up her seat on a bus in Alabama for a white passenger.
c) The Emperor Hadrian rebuilds the Pantheon in Rome.
d) Rhodesian Prime Minister Ian Smith unilaterally declares independence from Britain in opposition to black majority rule.
e) President Abraham Lincoln is assassinated.
f) The Iranian leader the Ayatollah Khomeini pronounces a fatwa against the writer Salman Rushdie for his book *The Satanic Verses.*
g) The Beatles achieve their first Christmas number one with 'I Want to Hold Your Hand'.

h) Soviet Communist dictator Joseph Stalin dies.
i) Pope Urban II launches the first crusade.
j) The Hundred Years War between England and France begins.
k) Nicolaus Copernicus publishes his *On the Revolutions of the Celestial Spheres*.
l) The Battle of Waterloo sees Napoleon defeated by the Duke of Wellington.
m) New Orleans is founded.
n) The Great Famine begins in Ireland.
o) The explorer James Cook is killed in Hawaii.

43. The sinking of the *General Belgrano* took place during which conflict?

a) Crimean War
b) Second World War
c) Falklands War
d) First Gulf War

44. To many conspiracy theorists the history of the world is actually determined by shadowy forces acting behind what seem to be the obvious causes of events. For example it was reported that there were suspicions that the shark attacks in the Egyptian resort of Sharm el Sheikh in 2010 were planned by the Israeli secret services. How much or how little of the hearsay about the machinations of national intelligence agencies is true is impossible to establish so long as they are doing their sneaky business properly. Match up the following intelligence agencies with their countries:

Mossad	UK
FSB	Ireland
MI6	USA
CIA	Israel
G2	Russia
DGSE	Israel
Vevak	France

45. The British population has recently rediscovered the art of public protest. The million people who marched in London against the war in Iraq in 2003 failed to change the government's foreign policy but previous demonstrations have proved more effective. A series of riots across Britain broke out in March 1990. What were the rioters protesting against?

a) Student fees
b) Unemployment
c) Mine closures
d) Taxation

46. Between 1603 and 1868 Japan was ruled by the Tokogawa family in an era known as the Edo period because it saw the centre of political power shift from Kyoto to Edo (modern-day Tokyo). During this time Japan shut itself off from external foreign powers but enjoyed great domestic economic growth and cultural flowering while its society remained highly stratified and feudal. What was the name given to an unemployed warrior during this period?

a) Daimyo
b) Samurai
c) Ronin
d) Shogun

47. Who were the Huguenots and why might you find traces of them in Spitalfields in London?

48. Which side did Franco's Spain fight on in the Second World War?

a) Axis
b) Allies
c) Neither
d) Both

49. The Chilean leader Augusto Pinochet is said to have explained, 'I'm not a dictator. It's just that I have a grumpy face.' Name the countries 'looked after' by the following grumpy-faced politicians:

a) Idi Amin
b) Enver Hoxha
c) François 'Papa Doc' Duvalier
d) Jean-Bédel Bokassa
e) Nicolae Ceaucescu

50. We rely on historians, with their leather elbow patches and their ardent affection for archives and passion for primary sources, to log and interpret the world's events for us. Sometimes they do such a good job that they become part of history themselves. Which famous historical historian wrote *The Ecclesiastical History of the English People*?

a) Bede
b) Herodotus
c) Geoffrey of Monmouth
d) Edward Gibbon

HISTORY ANSWERS

1. b) During the Cretaceous period the Triceratops found itself a direct peer of the Tyrannosaurus Rex and Pteranodon but, despite what Hollywood might have you believe, not of other famous prehistoric beasts such as the Stegosaurus and Diplodocus (both from the Jurassic period) and the Mammoth and Sabre-toothed Tiger (both from the Quaternary Period).

2. Seth, Nephthys, Isis and Osiris were all the **children** of Geb, the **earth** god and Nut, the **sky** goddess. Osiris and Isis were also **married**, as were Seth and Nephthys, as was considered perfectly proper in Ancient Egyptian high society.

Seth was extremely jealous of his brother, who became ruler of Egypt, bringing prosperity and **peace** to the land and generally being a goody-two-shoes, so he tricked him into getting into a specially made cedarwood **casket** which he then threw in the **Nile**, killing him.

Isis searched for the casket in order to give Osiris a proper burial but when she brought it back to Egypt Seth found it and chopped Osiris's **corpse** up into **fourteen** pieces which he **scattered** in the Nile for the **crocodiles** to eat. Isis and Nephthys managed to collect together **thirteen** of the pieces but Osiris's **phallus** had been eaten by a **fish** so Isis had to make a new one for him. She then embalmed his body and his **spirit** was able to pass into the **underworld**, where he became its **ruler**.

3. d) The death penalty for murder was abolished in 1969 in Britain and 1973 in Northern Ireland. It remained officially available as a punishment for treason and piracy with violence until 1998. The last executions in Britain were of Peter Anthony Allen and Gwynne Owen Evans in 1964. The death penalty used to be applied for a range of 200 offences in the UK ranging from murder and treason to 'strong evidence of malice' in children aged seven to fourteen years of age.

4.
a) Beginning her court life as teenage concubine to Emperor Tang Taizong, Wu Zetian went on to become the next Emperor Gaozong's official consort, after shouldering aside the ill-fated Empress Wang. From this position she craftily governed behind the scenes until 690 when she made herself Sacred and Divine Empress Regnant until her deposition in 705. She is credited with an efficient and prosperous reign. However, she wasn't a great example of sisterhood, allegedly murdering her own baby daughter in order to accuse Empress Wang of the crime and replace her as Empress. She also eliminated other concubines whom she saw as a threat and established a secret police network to keep tabs on her enemies.

5. b) Elizabeth Fry was a devout Quaker who devoted her life to helping other people. When a friend told her about the terrible conditions he had witnessed at Newgate Prison she began to visit the female prisoners and provide clothes, schooling and supplies for the women to use for sewing. She reported on prison conditions to Parliament and campaigned against the death penalty. She was also the niece-in-law of the founder of J.S. Fry & Sons, originators of the moreish Fry's Turkish Delight.

6. d) Good King Wenceslas is Saint Wenceslas I (907–935) who was Duke of Bohemia, a region in what is now the Czech Republic. He is the patron saint of the country and there is a famous statue of him in Wenceslas Square in Prague.

7. c) The protestors were campaigning against the British government's tax on tea and, more generally, on British taxation being imposed on the American colonists without their having any representation in Parliament.

8. b) Averroes is a Latinisation of Ibn Rushd.

9. Ethelred II (ruled 978–1016): The Unready – So called because he was inclined to listen to bad counsel – 'unready' comes from '*un-raed*' meaning 'ill-advised' in Anglo-Saxon.

William I (ruled 1066–1087): The Bastard – So called because his parents weren't married. He probably preferred his other nickname, 'The Conqueror'.

William II (ruled 1087–1100): Rufus – So called because of his ruddy complexion ('rufus' comes from the Latin word for 'red').

John (ruled 1199–1216): Lackland – So called because as the youngest son of King Henry II he did not inherit land from his father and during his rule England lost territory to the French.

Charles II (ruled 1649–85): The Merrie Monarch – So called because of his jolly lifestyle, particularly seen in contrast to the dour old Puritan Commonwealth that came before his reign.

James II of England (ruled 1685–1688): The Be-shitten – So called in Ireland because of his abandonment of his Irish supporters after the Battle of the Boyne.

10. d) Catherine the Great was originally the consort of the unpopular Peter III of Russia but succeeded him in a coup in 1762, six months after he came to power. She ruled until her death in 1796, which, despite popular rumours, was not from an ill-fated sexual liaison with a horse.

11. c) New Zealand gave women the vote in 1893, a full twenty-five years before Britain made the move to allow women over thirty years of age, and therefore deemed grown-up enough not to be silly about it, to vote.

12. The word search contains Brumaire, Nivôse, Germinal, Floréal, Thermidor and Fructidor. The twelve months of the French Republican calendar were based on the weather and agricultural conditions around

Paris at the relevant time of year. The months ran from what we know as late September and were called Vendémiaire (grape harvest), Brumaire (fog), Frimaire (frost), Nivôse (snow), Pluviôse (rain), Ventôse (wind), Germinal (germination), Floréal (flower), Prairial (pasture), Messidor (harvest), Thermidor (heat) and Fructidor (fruit).

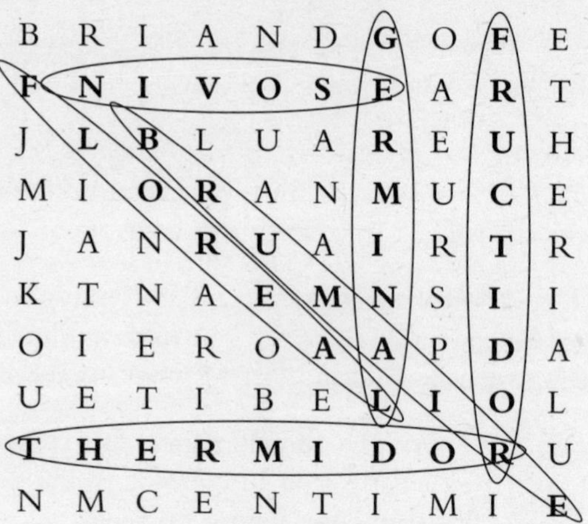

13. b) or d) After the Second World War the USSR and USA divided Korea into two separate areas of influence. The Korean War began in 1950 when Communist North Korea invaded South Korea in the hope of unifying the country and military action continued until the armistice of 1953. However, officially North and South Korea are still at war and at talks in 2009 North Korea declared that it no longer considered itself bound by the terms of the 1953 armistice.

14. a) Girolamo Savonarola (1452–1498) was a rather choleric Dominican friar who became the political leader of Florence for the four years before his death by burning for heresy in 1498. He came to popularity for his impassioned apocalyptic preaching against the lack of morality in the clergy (see the previous sentence for where that got him) and the loucheness of the Renaissance. He was responsible for the famous 1497 'Bonfire of the Vanities' in which books and works of art were piled up and set alight to represent a rejection of worldly luxuries. Legend has it that Botticelli was inspired to burn some of his own paintings in this conflagration.

15. Queen Victoria reigned from 1837 to 1901. The following were invented during this time: telephone switchboards; London Underground; pedal bicycles; milk chocolate Easter eggs; postage stamps; radiography; synthetic heroin.

16. c) They are all models of tank.

17. c) Bangladesh used to be part of India but became East Pakistan after Partition in 1947. It became independent after the Bangladesh Liberation War in 1971.

18.

a) Queen Elizabeth I was 25 when she acceded to the throne.
b) Joan of Arc was 17 when she took command of the French campaign against the English.
c) William Pitt the Younger was 24 when he came to power.
d) Mary Shelley was 21 when her book *Frankenstein* was published.
e) George Harrison was 27 when the Beatles split up.
f) Carl Djerassi was 28 when he and his team invented norethindrone.
g) Orson Welles was 26 when he made *Citizen Kane*.
h) Christopher Columbus was 41 when he landed in America.
i) Martin Luther King was 35 when he won the Nobel Peace Prize.
j) Paul Dirac was 26 when he published his paper coming up with the concept of antimatter.
k) Wolfgang Amadeus Mozart was 30 when he composed *The Marriage of Figaro*.
l) Pablo Picasso was 14 when he painted *Portrait of Aunt Pepa*.
m) Jesus was said to be 33 when he was crucified.

19. b) James Hargreaves (1720–1778) was born near the enchantingly named Oswaldtwistle in Lancashire. He is lauded as one of the heroes of the British Industrial Revolution for his invention of the Spinning

Jenny. His aim was to increase the supply of yarn for the textile industry in Blackburn. Previously yarn had been made on individual spinning wheels but Hargreaves' invention allowed several spindles to work at once creating much higher quantities of thread. However, his clever invention angered the mill workers of Blackburn who were scared it would lead to the loss of their jobs and Hargreaves had to move to Nottingham where his Jennies were embraced.

20. c) The codenames for the five beaches used in the Normandy landings on 6 June 1944 were Sword, Juno, Gold, Omaha, Utah.

21. Admiral Horatio Nelson (1758–1805)
Vice Admiral Francis Drake (1540–1596)
Captain James Cook (1728–1779)
Master's Mate Fletcher Christian (1764–1793)

22. c) In 1959 the pass laws, which meant that black citizens of South Africa could not travel outside their local areas without carrying pass books at all times, were extended to cover women as well as men. On 21 March 1960 black protestors against these laws congregated outside the police station in Sharpeville. Police opened fire killing sixty-nine people and shooting many others in the back as they fled. No police were ever convicted for this misconduct. The massacre stimulated the underground political struggle against apartheid within South Africa. Apartheid was abolished in 1994, forty-six years after being established.

23. b) The construction of Stonehenge is thought to have taken place around 3,000 BCE, Buddha was born in 563 BCE, the Roman Republic was founded not long after in 509 BCE and Attila the Hun died in 453 CE.

24. c); b); d); a). China is thought to have been ruled by various different dynastic families for around 4,000 years up until the end of the Qing dynasty in 1912, when the Chinese Revolution led by Sun Yat-sen led to the foundation of the Republic of China and the deposition of Emperor Pu Yi. At times, due to the vastness of China, various different areas were ruled by overlapping dynasties. The Xia dynasty (*c.*2100–*c.*1600 BCE) is thought to have been the earliest example of a ruling family controlling a large area of China although lack of documentary evidence leads some scholars to name the Shang dynasty (c.1600–c.1050 BCE) the first. The Han ruled from 206 BCE to 220 CE, the Sui from 581 to 618 and the Tang from 618 to 907.

25. Both of their sons, named after them, went on to hold the same public offices as them. William Pitt the Younger was British prime minister from 1783 to 1801 and 1804 to 1806 and John Quincy Adams was president of America from 1825 to 1829.

26. In 1903, at a meeting in Charlotte Street in London, the revolutionary Marxist Russian Social-Democratic Party, which opposed the rule of the Tsar, split into two factions: the Bolsheviks led by Lenin and the Mensheviks led by Julius Martov. Bolshevik comes from the Russian word meaning 'majority' and Menshevik from the word for 'minority'. Lenin believed that revolution could only be accomplished by a small party of professional revolutionaries, whereas Martov wanted a broader and more inclusive definition of party membership. The Mensheviks also came to believe in a more evolutionary, gradual path to revolution whereas the Bolsheviks were more radical. The party formally split in 1912 and both were instrumental in the 1917 Russian Revolution. However, once Bolshevik power was established the Mensheviks fell out of favour until they were suppressed in 1922.

27. These quotations are usually attributed to Mahatma Gandhi. Mohandas Karamchand Gandhi (1869–1948) is given the honorary title Mahatma, meaning 'great soul', for his work in achieving Indian independence from Britain. The last of the three quotations is the most significant as it refers to his famous pacifist campaign of civil disobedience. He was assassinated in January 1948 less than a year after independence.

28. Ordovician, Silurian, Carboniferous, Jurassic, Paleogene. The full list of periods in the correct order is:

Cambrian
Ordovician
Silurian
Devonian
Carboniferous
Permian
Triassic
Jurassic
Cretaceous
Paleogene
Neogene
Quaternary

Geological timescales are not divided into equal parts as their divisions are based on significant events deduced from fossils and other evidence: for example, the boundary between the Triassic and Permian periods is defined by what is known cheerfully as the 'mass extinction event' when a huge percentage of all kinds of life on earth disappeared. We live in the quaternary period, the most recent 2.6 million years of the earth's history (which in turn is broken down into the Pleistocene and Holocene epochs: the Holocene being the last 12,000 years).

29. They were both pretenders to the English throne. Bear with us, as the complex genealogy behind their claims needs some explanation.

The succession of the English monarchy had been fraught for several generations after the Wars of the Roses saw Edward of York depose the weak Lancastrian king Henry VI and become Edward IV. After his death, his twelve-year old son became Edward V but was usurped by his father's brother, Richard III, after just a couple of months. Richard III imprisoned both Edward V and his younger brother Richard (they seem to have had a limited imagination when it came to names in those days) in the Tower of London after declaring that Edward IV's marriage to their mother was invalid and hence also their claim to the throne. Richard's official line was that he was keeping them in the tower for their own protection, although in reality it was to prevent rebellions against his rule coalescing around them, and this 'protection' actually led to the disappearance of both princes: to this day no one knows exactly what became of them.

Richard III argued that he should accede to the throne, because the other obvious contender, the son of his older brother the Duke of Clarence, Edward Plantagenet, was barred from succession due to the said Duke's earlier treasonous plot against Edward IV (his brother, as you'll realise if you're keeping up with the family tree) which saw the Duke executed by being drowned in a butt of wine, if popular tales are to be believed.

In 1485 Richard III was deposed and killed in the Battle of Bosworth Field by Henry Tudor, who became Henry VII. Henry was a great-great-great grandson of Edward III and thus a claimant to the throne reaching back to the Lancastrians before those upstart Yorkists had shouldered their way into the monarchy (his claim was rendered somewhat tenuous by the fact that it came through his mother's side of the family and his great grandfather had actually been born out of wedlock, although his great-great grandparents had later married). Still with us?

In 1487 the tutor of ten-year-old Lambert Simnel attempted to usurp Henry VII by pretending that Simnel was Edward Plantagenet who was actually being held prisoner in the Tower at the time. He pretended that Edward had escaped from the Tower and managed to get various nobles on side to support his claim. After a battle with Henry VII's forces the conspiracy was undone and Henry mercifully gave Simnel a job in the royal kitchen.

Perkin Warbeck was not so lucky. In 1491 he emerged claiming to be Richard, the youngest of the Princes in the Tower. Various foreign and domestic enemies of Henry VII rallied around him but his forces were also beaten by the king's and, after escaping from custody once, Warbeck was imprisoned in the Tower in a cell next to the real Edward Plantaganet. In 1499 they were accused of plotting together and both executed, after Warbeck had written a confession admitting who he really was, conveniently ending the possibility of more shenanigans about their potential claims to the throne.

30. Afghanistan was officially founded in **1747** by the great military commander **Ahmad Shah Durrani**. In the nineteenth century Great Britain saw Afghanistan as a useful place of influence in the '**Great Game**' to stem the spread of **Russia**'s power, which threatened British **India**. British forces invaded the country during the Anglo-Afghan Wars and the area remained subject to British meddling until the signing of the Treaty of **Rawalpindi** in 1919. Afghanistan was a **monarchy** until the coup of **1973** led by **Mohammad Daoud Khan**, who was later assassinated by the Communist People's Democratic Party of Afghanistan in the **Saur** Revolution of 1978. Opposition to this government led to **Soviet** forces invading in **1979** and fighting the **mujahideen**, backed by the US, until the Soviet withdrawal in 1989. The ensuing civil wars resulted in the foundation of the Islamic State of Afghanistan in 1992 which fell to the **Taliban** in 1996. Resistance to the new regime took the form of the **Northern Alliance** which reclaimed most of the country in 2001 with US and UK support following the **9/11** attacks on the US by the Taliban-backed **al-Qaeda**. However, although a new **Afghan** government was formed, this war still continues today.

31.

	1 W	H	2 A	R	N	C	L	I	3 F	F	E		4 G		
	E		L						R				R		
	S		5 B	O	X				E				E		
	T		E			6 P			N				A		
	E		7 R	O	Y	A	L		8 C	L	I	F	T	O	N
	R		T			D			H				B		
	N					D					9 P	A	R	I	S
				10 B	R	I	D	G	E		O		I		
11 B		12 M				N					R		T		
13 R	E	A	D	I	N	G					T		A		
O		R				14 T	H	A	M	E	S		I		
A		Y				O					E		N		
D				15 H	E	N	R	Y			A				

32. Charlemagne (*c.*747–*c.*814 CE). Pepin the Short was King of the Franks. When he died Charlemagne took over the kingdom alongside his brother Carloman until Carloman's death. Charlemagne then became sole ruler and began to expand his territory in a series of successful military campaigns. In a canny career move he helped Pope Leo III subdue a rebellion and was crowned Holy Roman Emperor by the pontiff in return. Despite his father's epithet, Charlemagne was very tall for his time. Recent genetic studies have also shown that he is the ancestor of a large percentage of modern-day Europeans.

33. b) Norman Wilkinson was a marine painter who came up with the idea of daubing British navy warships with distorted geometric patterns in different colours in order to confuse enemy planes and submarines. This camouflage was not intended to hide the ships, as this was too difficult to achieve, but to confuse the eye as to their size, shape and heading, making it far harder to attack them successfully. The Vorticist artist Edward Wadsworth supervised the painting of many of the Dazzle ships.

34. d) Catherine Howard was one of the unlucky ones. Married to Henry in 1540, after catching his eye as a lady-in-waiting to his previous wife, Anne of Cleves (who got away with an annulment), Catherine was beheaded for treason in 1542. (A specially designed act of parliament was passed in the month before her execution making her sexual activity prior to her marriage treasonous.)

35.

a) Christopher Columbus. The *Golden Hind* was Francis Drake's most famous ship and the *Santa Maria* was Columbus's.
b) USA. These are the respective countries' Independence Days. The USA gained independence from the British Empire on 4 July 1776 and India on 15 August 1947.
c) Spain. Benito Mussolini was the fascist leader of Italy during the Second World War and Francisco Franco was his equivalent in Spain.
d) Aztecs. Chichen Itza is the famous ruin of a Mayan settlement

in the Yucatan in Mexico and Tenochtitlan is the ruin of an Aztec settlement in Mexico City.

e) George VI. Herbert Asquith was Prime Minister when George V ascended to the British throne and Stanley Baldwin was Prime Minister when his son George VI became king.

f) Switzerland. Luther was a German Protestant religious reformer and Zwingli was a Swiss reformer.

g) Fianna Fail. They are both considered the founders of their respective political parties.

h) Louis XVI. They are both these famous Frenchmen's wives.

i) Iraq. The majority of the ancient site of the kingdom of Kush falls inside the borders of modern-day Sudan, and the site of Mesopotamia falls mainly within the borders of modern-day Iraq.

j) Tasmania. America is thought to have derived its appellation from the Italian explorer Amerigo Vespucci's first name and Tasmania is named after the Dutch explorer Abel Tasman.

36. The Killing Fields are the areas of Cambodia where the Communist Khmer Rouge regime carried out mass murders and burials of the Cambodian population during their rule between 1975 and 1979. The Khmer Rouge is estimated to have killed over 1.7 million people, nearly a quarter of the national population, for being detrimental to the regime's aims of making Cambodia a classless, agrarian society. Many people were murdered on the grounds of their education, for having had contact with foreigners or for belonging to ethnic minorities.

37. The official record shows only four deaths in the fire but this is considered a hugely optimistic underestimate.

38. c) Suleiman the Magnificent was sultan of the Muslim Ottoman Empire from 1520 to 1566. The Ottoman Empire arose in the fourteenth century and at its peak included territories in North Africa, Turkey, Greece, Bulgaria, Romania, Hungary, Lebanon, Syria and Jordan. Suleiman's empire was extremely wealthy, sophisticated, cultured and well organised as well as commanding a formidable military force. After his death, the empire went into decline until it officially came to an end in 1922 due to internal change and the partition of its territories after its defeat in the First World War.

39. b) Thirteen states declared their independence from Britain in 1776. They were Delaware, Pennsylvania, New Jersey, Georgia, Connecticut, Massachusetts, Maryland, South Carolina, New Hampshire, Virginia, New York, North Carolina and Rhode Island. These were the states that went to war with Britain in the American War of Independence in protest against the fact that they were taxed by the British parliament without their interests being represented there.

40. 'Dr Livingstone, I presume?' Stanley was commissioned by the *New York Herald* to travel to Africa to look for the celebrated British explorer David Livingstone, who had gone missing on his search for the source of the Nile. Stanley found him in Ujiji near Lake Tanganyika in November 1871 and greeted him with these famous words. However, Stanley's more sinister and lasting legacy is his subsequent work in Africa helping King Leopold II of Belgium colonise the Congo, a process that involved great cruelty to the native population.

41. b) King Henry VIII of England and Francis I of France. This meeting in June 1520 between the two monarchs was held in order to forge an alliance between the two great European powers. It took place near Calais and both kings stayed in tents made of fabric woven with gold along with huge entourages in order to show off to each other about the sumptuous splendour of their respective courts.

42.

a) 1517
b) 1955
c) 126
d) 1965
e) 1865
f) 1988
g) 1963
h) 1953

i) 1096
j) 1337
k) 1543
l) 1815
m) 1718
n) 1845
o) 1779

43. c) The *General Belgrano* was an Argentinian warship that was torpedoed by a British submarine, killing over 300 sailors on 2 May 1982. The event remains controversial as the *Belgrano* was outside the exclusion zone that had been set by the British and was apparently sailing away rather than preparing to attack. Later commentators on both sides have noted that despite these factors the rules of engagement did not preclude action beyond the boundary if a hostile ship was deemed a threat to the naval forces within the zone.

44.

Mossad	Israel
FSB	Russia
MI6	UK
CIA	USA
G2	Ireland
DGSE	France
Vevak	Iran

45. d) March 1990 saw the Poll Tax riots in opposition to the new 'community charge' to pay for local services imposed by Margaret Thatcher's Conservative government. The protests are believed to have contributed to her downfall as she resigned later that same year. The poll tax was considered unfair as it was levied on individuals rather than properties. It was replaced by council tax three years later.

46. c) A ronin was a member of the samurai military class who had no noble master (daimyo) to serve. The samurai and ronin existed in Japan hundreds of years before the Edo period but the number of ronin increased at this time because the laws about how a samurai could act became more stringent, making it harder for a warrior who had lost his master in battle or through loss of favour to find a new one. Being a ronin was considered a shameful position and many samurai committed ritual suicide (seppuku) upon losing their employment. The most renowned ronin are the famous forty-seven whose master was forced to kill himself after losing his cool in an argument. His ronin bided their time, waiting two years in order to avenge his death and then committing seppuku all together.

47. The Huguenots were French Calvinist Protestants. After the Reformation began in the sixteenth century Protestantism spread throughout Europe. France, however, remained a Catholic country. Between 1562 and 1598 the French Wars of Religion saw conflict between French Catholics and Protestants up until King Henry IV came to power and signed the Edict of Nantes, granting freedom of religion to all French citizens. However in 1685 the mean old sun king, Louis XIV, revoked the Edict and the Huguenots began fleeing France for Protestant countries like Germany, the Netherlands, America and Britain. Many of those who came to Britain settled around Spitalfields in east London where they worked in the silk industry.

48. c) Spain was officially neutral during the Second World War, despite the help fascist leader General Franco had received from Nazi Germany during the Spanish Civil War. Spain did support the Axis powers economically and many Spaniards volunteered to fight with the Germans against Soviet Russia on the Eastern Front.

49.

a) Uganda. According to popular history, Amin gave himself the official title 'His Excellency President for Life, Field Marshal Al Hadji Doctor Idi Amin, VC, DSO, MC, Lord of All the Beasts of the Earth and Fishes of the Sea, and Conqueror of the British Empire in Africa in General and Uganda in Particular'.

b) Albania. The only western films allowed in Albania by Hoxha during his rule were those of Norman Wisdom.

c) Haiti. When Duvalier's former friend and leader of his dreaded Tonton Macoute, Barbot, became a rival and it was whispered that he could change into a black dog at will, Duvalier had his men shoot all the black dogs they could find.
d) The Central African Republic. Emperor Bokassa is said to have fed his enemies to the lions and crocodiles in his private zoo.
e) Romania. During Ceaucescu's reign newspapers were encouraged to mention his name forty times on every page.

50. a) The monk and exceptional Medieval scholar the Venerable Bede (673–735 CE) wrote *Ecclesiastica Gentis Anglorum* (*The Ecclesiastical History of the English People*) about the rise of Christianity in England. Written in Latin and completed in 731 CE, it is considered one of the most important resources for information about this period. Bede entered his monastery at the age of seven and described himself as 'Servant of Christ and Priest of the Monastery of Saints Peter and Paul which is at Wearmouth and Jarrow'. He was canonised in 1899 and you can celebrate St Bede's day on 25 May.

CLASSICS

Salve, lector! Welcome to the Classics conundrums section of our quiz. Despite the fact that chiton-wearing philosophers no longer stroll under porticos and legionaries no longer march in admirably straight lines across the map, the influence of the ancient cultures of the Mediterranean is still prominent in our world today. This is largely thanks to the intense crushes our more recent forebears had on those sophisticated Ancients' art, politics and philosophy. Here we will take our own mini Grand Tour of the major events and personalities of Greek and Roman history and examine the depth of your acquaintance with antiquity. Fittingly, some etymologists believe that the word 'quiz' comes from the Latin question '*qui es*?' meaning 'who are you?' We shall certainly be finding out if you can tell your Tully from your Tereus and your Hephaestion from your Hercules in the following *examen*.

1. However bohemian your neighbourhood you are unlikely to find children in your local nursery called Perdiccas, Antipater, Craterus, Antigonus and Ptolemy. However, these ancient names are surely worthy of revival and perhaps in years to come the ubiquitous 'Jack' and 'Mohammed' will be knocked off the top spot of most-popular names by one of them. The original holders of these names were all:

a) Fourth-century Greek dramatists
b) Generals of Alexander the Great
c) Roman centurions under the Emperor Hadrian
d) Followers of the philosopher Empedocles

2. CDXLVIII – CCCLXIX = ?

3. Perhaps you remember that the Roman Emperor Nero is supposed to have entertained himself on the lyre while Rome burned? That

Constantine aided the spread of Christianity? Or that Marcus Aurelius was a bit of a thinker? However, can you remember when these imperial highnesses were in charge? And who succeeded whom? Put the following Roman Emperors in chronological order:

Galba
Caligula
Nero
Constantine
Marcus Aurelius
Commodus
Domitian

4. The politically significant Peloponnesian War of 431–404 BCE was fought between:

a) Athens and Persia
b) Mycenae and Sparta
c) Athens and Sparta
d) Carthage and Rome

5. What do Beatrice Portinari, Lizzie Siddal, Yoko Ono, Edie Sedgwick and Isabella Blow have in common? They have all provided inspiration to the creative types they've been acquainted with. This has earned them the title of 'muse' after the ancient Greek goddesses who inspired imaginative endeavours. Match up the nine original Muses with their areas of patronage:

love poetry, mime, music, tragedy, comedy, epic poetry, astronomy, history, dance

a) Calliope
b) Cleio
c) Ourania
d) Thaleia
e) Melpomene

f) Polyhymnia
g) Erato
h) Euterpe
i) Terpsichore

6. Who of the following is NOT a famous Roman historian:

a) Herodotus
b) Tacitus
c) Livy
d) Plutarch

7. The ancient Greeks liked their heroes to take the business of heroism very seriously and none could be said to have worked harder for his renown than the lion-skin-wearing, club-wielding Heracles. Not a naturally lucky demigod, Heracles found himself beset by dangers from the moment of his conception, all of which he bravely battled off until, having survived attacks by men, monsters and the gods, he was finally finished off by a shirt. His exploits gained him everlasting glory and a place at the gods' table on Olympus. The Greeks had many different stories about his trials and triumphs and he later became a great favourite of the Romans as well, who called him Hercules. Can you name six of his twelve legendary labours?

8. 'Stichomythia' refers to:

a) A comic epic poem about a battle between frogs and mice
b) Fear of water
c) The wheels of a Spartan chariot
d) Dramatic dialogue where two characters speak alternate lines

9. When people bring to mind the greatest hits of ancient Greece they generally think of columns, democracy and philosophers. Not just concerned with questions of ethics and knowledge, Greek philosophers were also among the earliest scientists, investigating and analysing the physical world as well as the mental and moral. Find the names of FOURTEEN of them in the word search below.

H E R A C L I T U S P O
E M A N A X A G O R A S
S P Y T H A G O R A S E
P E Y C L E A N T H E S
R D I R O T H E D N M O
O O P A R I S T S T L E
T C L E A H O H I D E P
A L A C A X O A Y R R I
G E T O R A Z L E S E C
O S O C R A T E S N I U
R U C R E I T S N U S R
A C L E X A N E S O N U
S O C R E P L A S E S S

10. It's sometimes hard to imagine that the mythical-sounding kingdoms and territories in tales of the Greek and Latin empires and their enemies and allies correspond to real places. You probably guessed that Belgica matches today's Belgium and Britannia means Britain, but did you know that Lusitania refers to Portugal and ancient Phoenicia corresponds to parts of Lebanon and Syria? Or that the Medes came from what we would today call Iran? In which modern-day country would you find the following famous ancient cities:

Troy
Ephesus
Tyre
Mycenae
Carthage

Cumae
Babylon
Persepolis
Memphis
Massilia

11. The genius Roman poet Ovid's hexametric masterwork, *The Metamorphoses*, contains hundreds of stories from ancient myths, many of which are aetiological tales which explain the existence of certain plants and animals in the world. Match up the mortals with the flora and fauna they contributed to:

a) The daughters of Pierus	Hyancinths
b) Ajax	Swallows
c) Procne	Partridges
d) Galanthis	Magpies
e) Perdix	Weasels

12. What was so special about the fighting force called the Legio IX Hispana?

13. Everyone knows that prince Paris of Troy was one of those attractive young men who mean trouble. Responsible for the devastating Trojan War due to his weakness for the ladies, he is portrayed by Homer in the *Iliad* as a bit of a wuss as his only fighting ability is with a bow and arrow rather than in the more manly hand-to-hand combat. According to Greek legend, who killed Paris?

a) Achilles
b) Diomedes
c) Philoctetes
d) Menelaus

14. As in most ancient societies, Roman women were largely confined to the domestic sphere and didn't have an overt political role in life (although if you read Robert Graves' fantastic novel *I, Claudius* you will get a vivid sense of the ways in which wives and mothers could sneak into the corridors of power). Which of the following Roman matrons was influential in the founding of the Roman Republic?

a) Livia
b) Octavia
c) Lucretia
d) Agrippina

15. Homer's extraordinary epics the *Iliad* and *Odyssey* are dazzling examples of oral poetry and as such have many repeated formulas within them that helped the poets reciting the stories to remember the verses. The epithets of various characters are particularly famous. Complete the examples below:

a) ____-fingered dawn
b) ____-eyed Hera
c) ____-dark sea
d) ____-footed Achilles

16. It's time to turn our attention to the wonderful work of the greatest Latin poet of all time – Publius Vergilius Marro. His *Aeneid*, following the multifarious adventures of the Trojan prince Aeneas as he travels to Italy to found a settlement that would later become rather significant, essentially made Virgil the Poet Laureate of Imperial Rome. Using the names in the box, fill in Aeneas' family tree:

Silvius, Creusa, Priam, Venus, Ascanius, Lavinia, Hecuba, Anchises

17. *a, ab* – away; *absum, abesse, abfui* – to be absent; *ac, atque* – and; *accido, accidere, accidi* – to happen . . . There's no need to learn interminable lists of Latin vocab in order to understand many of the Romans' words. This is because many English words have been appropriated or developed from

Latin ones. Use your intellect (from the Latin *intellegere* – to understand) to match the following Latin words to the pictures they describe below:

bos, cattus, aquila, piscis, porcus

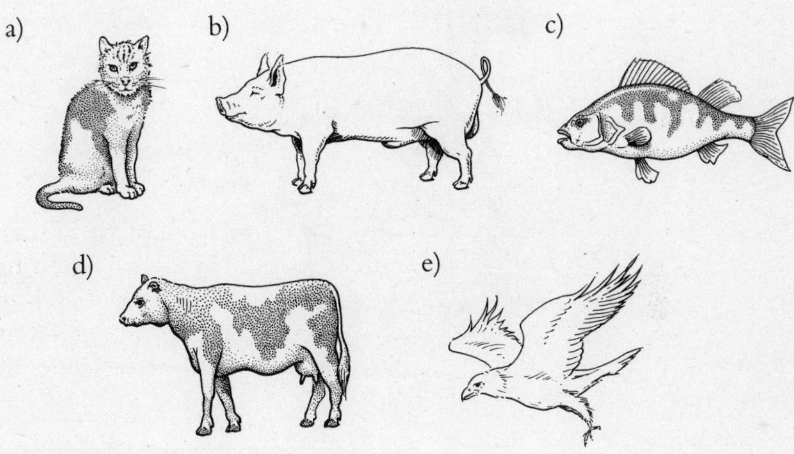

18. Full of violence, turmoil and excitement, the Greek myths deal with many taboos and dramatic crimes. Match up the transgressive act with the character responsible below:

a) Pasiphaë	Incest
b) Myrrha	Fratricide and infanticide
c) Clytemnestra	Bestiality
d) Medea	Mariticide

19. Which Greek philosopher said 'All is flux, nothing remains the same'?

a) Heraclitus
b) Socrates
c) Anaximander
d) Thales

20. The following picture refers to four works by which famous ancient Greek playwright?

a) Aeschylus
b) Euripides
c) Aristophanes
d) Sophocles

21. The ancient Greek philosophers were very fond of deductive logic so see if you can follow their example in answering the following brainteaser. If you know that the English word 'misogyny' developed from the ancient Greek language and means 'hatred of women' and that 'anthropology' means 'the study of humankind', what do you think the following Greek words mean?

a) μισέω (miseo)
b) ἄνθρωπος (anthropos)
c) γυνή (gynē)
d) λόγος (logos)

22. In 508 BCE the Athenian politician Cleisthenes suggested that every citizen had the right to vote on important matters, thus introducing democracy to the world. However, who among the following were not permitted to participate in the city-state's government?

a) Men without land
b) Women
c) Slaves
d) Foreigners

23. What object, important to ancient Athenians, is represented below:

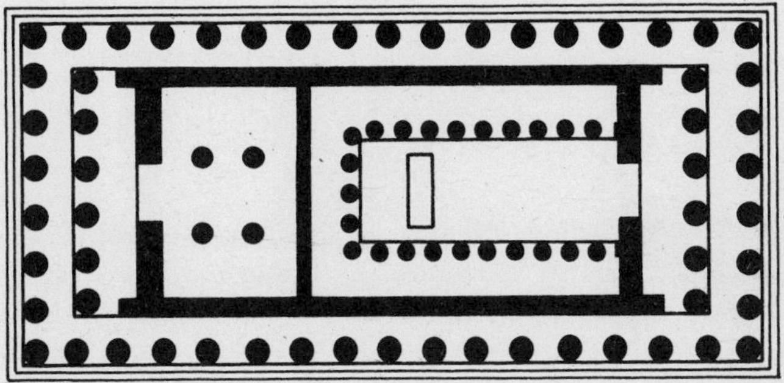

a) An ostrakon
b) The Parthenon
c) A domino
d) A unit of currency

24. All the attention on Latin literature tends to go on the glittery, glamorous Golden Age (first century BCE – mid-first century CE), when writers such as Virgil, Ovid, Catullus, Cicero, Horace and Livy were plying their trade. However all worthwhile artistic endeavour did not just suddenly stop at the end of this period. Fill in the names of the top Silver-Age (mid-first century CE – second century) writers below:

L_ C _ _

_A_I_ _S

J_ _ E _ _ _

_E_E_A

P_T_ _ _I_ _

_ _ _NY

MA_ _ _ _ _

_U_ _ON_ _ _

25. Born around 610 BCE on the island of Lesbos, this writer's work survives today only in fragments but is celebrated for its melodic qualities, directness and power. What is the name of this author?

26. Who was emperor of Rome at the time of the death of Jesus?

a) Augustus
b) Tiberius
c) Claudius
d) Constantine

27. Aristotle was a man destined to be significant in history: he studied with Plato, was tutor to Alexander the Great and wrote various texts which remain influential in the fields of philosophy, psychology and literature. Insert the correct terms from Aristotle's *Poetics* into the paragraph telling the sorry tale of King Oedipus below.

catharsis, peripeteia, anagnorisis, hamartia

In Sophocles' *Oedipus Tyrannos* the hero's …….. occurs when he kills King Laius of Thebes in a fit of road rage, little knowing that Laius is actually his real father. When the Thebans find themselves without a king, coincidentally at the same time as clever Oedipus turns up, he agrees to take the job. Things start to go downhill when a plague devastates the city and it is revealed that the unavenged death of King Laius is the cause. Diligent Oedipus then determines to discover the perpetrator. The ______ and ______ of the play happen at the same time when a helpful witness to Laius's murder reveals Oedipus to be the killer and also his true parentage. Poor Oedipus then realises that by marrying Laius' widow Jocasta, he has unwittingly married his own mother. ______ is achieved by Jocasta's suicide and Oedipus's decision to blind himself and leave Thebes. You'll be unsurprised to hear that this play is held up as a shining example of a tragedy.

28. For a decade from 43 BCE Rome was ruled by a trio of powerful men known as the Second Triumvirate. (The First Triumvirate was the name given to the unofficial dominance of the generals Julius Caesar, Crassus and Pompey from 59–53 BCE). Which of the members of the Second Triumvirate was the orator and intellectual Cicero's arch-enemy, denounced by him in several speeches known as the *Philippics* in 44–43 BCE? (Score a bonus point if you can explain why these speeches were so named.)

a) Octavian
b) Mark Antony
c) Lepidus
d) Philip

29. For what crimes was the prodigious pug-nosed philosopher Socrates condemned to death?

30. The following quotations are from which Golden Age Latin writer, celebrated for his turn of phrase and his outstanding odes?

Multa petentibus, desunt multa. Bene est cui Deus obtulit parca quod satis est manu.
(Those who seek for much will always be left in want of much. Happy is he to whom God has given, with sparing hand, as much as is enough.)

Carpe diem, quam minimum credula postero.
(Seize the day, trust little in tomorrow.)

Et semel emissum volat irrevocabile verbum.
(Once uttered a word flies abroad and cannot be recalled.)

Dulce et decorum est pro patria mori.
(It is sweet and fitting to die for one's homeland.)

31. Alexander the Great created an empire that stretched from Egypt to India. However, he still wasn't too big or too important to have a very special best friend. What was the name of Alexander's beloved companion?

a) Patroclus
b) Hephaistion
c) Antinous
d) Ganymede

32. The roar of the crowd, the smell of blood and sweat, the tension of whether the competitors will earn a thumbs up or a thumbs down: the Romans loved a good show. Although it was great fun watching Christians being crucified or criminals thrown to wild beasts, the top entertainment at the amphitheatres was gladiatorial combat. Match up the names and descriptions of the following types of Roman gladiator with the pictures below:

Thraex: The Thraex's armour was based on that of Rome's old enemy the Thracians. He had a slightly curved sword and a small rectangular shield.

Retiarius: Dressed like a fisherman, the retiarius had very little armour and fought with a weighted net and a trident and dagger.

Murmillo: Armed like a Roman legionary, the murmillo was named after a kind of fish, probably because of his fish-shaped helmet.

Secutor: The secutor had a rounded helmet with eye-holes, the better to protect him from the net and trident of the Retiarius who was his usual fighting opponent.

a)

b)

c)

d)

33. Do you know your alphas from your omegas? Mathematicians and engineers should find this question easy as they still use ancient Greek letters in their notation. What do you think the following Greek word means?

Αμνηοία

34. The Romans didn't spend all their time shouting at gladiators, writing poetry and worshipping capricious gods. Just like you and me they also had ordinary domestic lives, and although they had slaves to clean out the *impluvium* and work in the *culina*, their houses don't seem so very different to our own. Using the words below, label the following floor plan of a typical Roman townhouse:

Culina – kitchen
Vestibulum – porch
Ianua – door
Taberna – shop
Cubiculum – bedroom
Triclinium – dining room
Impluvium – rainwater pool
Atrium – hall
Hortus – garden
Tablinum – study

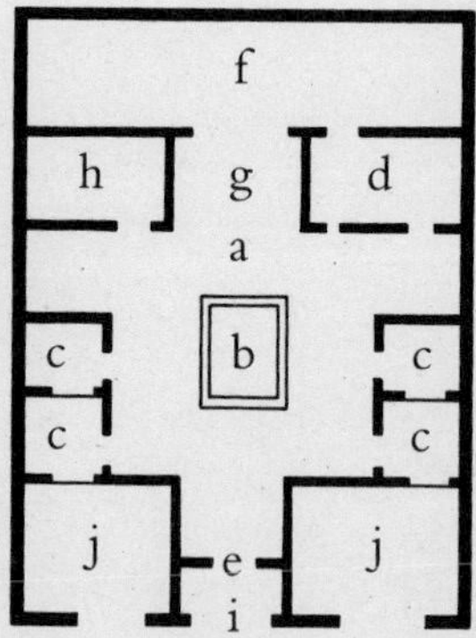

35. Which two famous Roman relatives were lovers of the Egyptian queen, Cleopatra VII?

36. The Greek gods and goddesses were very closely involved with the natural world. Aphrodite was born from sea foam, Hephaestus lived inside a volcano, Demeter controlled the ripening of the crops and

Hera loved to turn nymphs and mortal women who had slept with her husband into all kinds of animals and plants. Each of the Olympians also had various flora and fauna which were sacred to them. Match up the ancient gods and goddesses below with their associated animals:

Athene	Horse
Hera	Dove
Ares	Eagle
Poseidon	Peacock
Zeus	Owl
Aphrodite	Vulture

37. For the Romans, the best kind of life was one spent in service to the state and crowned with political glories. What was the name of the hierarchy of official posts taken by politically ambitious Romans?

38. Their reach was undeniably broad, as the ruins of their bathhouses and fancy underfloor heating across the globe attests, but which of the following were never provinces of the Roman Empire?

Egypt
England
Afghanistan
Spain
Luxembourg
Scotland
Greece
Malta
Syria
Norway
India

39. Probably the most notorious of all Latin despots, which is saying something, the Emperor Caligula ruled from 37–41 CE. Which of the following are NOT stories told about his infamous reign?

a) His name means 'Little Boots'.
b) His accession to power was greeted with great joy from the Roman populace.

c) He executed his adopted son.
d) He particularly liked to eat baby frogs cooked in honey.
e) He was a notorious spendthrift.
f) He liked to dress up as various Olympian gods.
g) He slept with his sisters.
h) He tried to make his favourite horse a consul.
i) He forced his troops to invade Mauretania naked.

40. Fifth-century Greece saw repeated bickering between the different *poleis* (city states) as well as significant conflicts with its main foreign rival, Persia, at battles such as Marathon and Thermopylae. Hollywood interpretations would have you believe that the Greek armies preferred to fight in breezy leather hot-pants but in fact they were rather better equipped. Which of the following is the correct word to describe the famously effective Greek foot soldiers?

a) Hippos
b) Hapax
c) Hydra
d) Hoplite

41. 'As with a tale, it is not how long life is, but how good it is, that matters.' For what reason did the Roman philosopher, politician and writer Lucius Annaeus Seneca commit suicide?

42. The great statesman Pericles (*c.*495–429 BCE) is famous for his role in Athens' rise in power in the late fifth century BCE, his military leadership, his cultural contributions to the city and his premature baldness (which is why he's always depicted with his helmet on). Which of the following surviving buildings on the Acropolis was NOT commissioned by Pericles?

a) The Parthenon
b) The Erechtheum
c) The Temple of Athena Nike
d) The Odeon of Herodes Atticus

43. Gaius Valerius Catullus (*c.*84–54 BCE) is rightly celebrated for the intense love poems he addressed to his girlfriend Lesbia. Lesbia is usually identified as the noblewoman Clodia Metelli who was by all accounts a bit of a goer – certainly her affair with Catullus doesn't end well and Cicero was fairly scathing about her morals too. What is Catullus asking Lesbia for in the following lines from his famous '*Carmen V*'? (N.B. '*Carmen*' just means 'song' or 'poem' so no clues there.)

Da mi basia mille, deinde centum,
Dein mille altera, dein secunda centum,
Deinde usque altera mille, deinde centum.

VOCABULARY
Dare – to give
Basiare – to kiss
Dein/Deinde – then
Alter – another

44. 'I am Spartacus!' Who can forget Kurt Douglas's bronzed chin-cleft and gladiatorial pants in the 1960 Stanley Kubrick swords-and-sandals movie about the Third Servile War. Spartacus's famous revolt took place in which of the following years?

a) 73 BCE
b) 45 BCE
c) 14 CE
d) 27 CE

45. After the years of power-hungry nobles competing for influence, the architects of Athenian democracy in the fifth century were keen to defuse potential future conflicts. For this purpose they invented the procedure of ostracism, whereby male Athenian citizens could vote to kick another citizen out of the city and exile them for ten years. What was the crucial ingredient of this process?

a) Abacuses
b) Papyrus
c) Broken pottery
d) Horses

46. What does the word '*libertus*' in Latin mean?

a) Libertine
b) Ex-slave
c) Victim of libel
d) Homeowner

47. Ancient Greek philosophers such as Thales, Pythagoras and Anaxagoras were scientifically interested in the celestial bodies they saw glimmering in the night sky above them. They made various discoveries about the movements of stars and the composition of the sun and moon. However, the Greeks also saw a connection between the arrangement of groups of stars and mythological stories. What is the name of the constellation below and why is it so called?

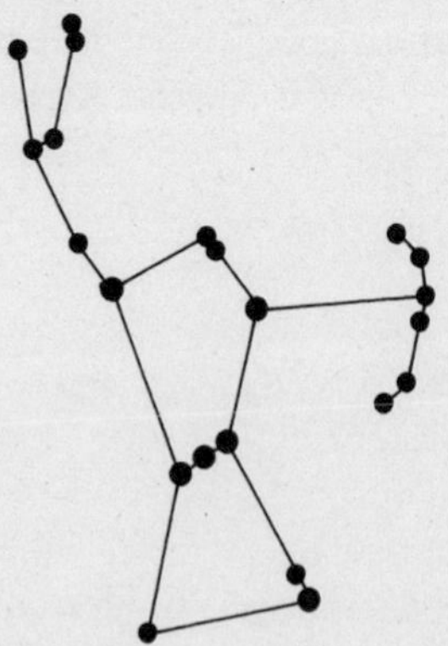

48. Latin may be what non-believers heartlessly call a 'dead language' but individual phrases still cling on to enrich our communication in English. What are the Latin phrases that match the following definitions?

a) Beneath one's dignity
b) The things that need to be done
c) From the library of
d) Dry land

49. The famous Gaulish chieftain Vercingetorix was beaten by which Roman general after he attempted to resist the conquest of his territories?

a) Belisarius
b) Pompey
c) Agrippa
d) Julius Caesar

50. If you were a young girl in ancient Rome what would be the most politically powerful job you could hope to obtain?

CLASSICS ANSWERS

1. b) You may have heard that Alexander was a pretty good soldier and his troops were fairly efficient at conquering everything they put their mind to. After 'the Great's death in 323 BCE the question of who should succeed him posed a problem. Alexander's baby son and brother officially became kings of the empire but Perdiccas acted as regent. He also organised a settlement at Babylon where the other generals were given satraps (the Persian term for provinces) to rule over. There is some confusion over who took over which area but it is generally held that Antipater and Craterus ruled Greece and Macedon, Antigonus ruled Lycia, Pamphylia and Phrygia and Ptolemy took Egypt, beginning the Ptolemaic dynasty which ended with famous ophiophilist Cleopatra. Other generals took over territories such as Persia, Thrace, Syria, Mesopotamia, Parthia and Punjab.

2. CDXLVIII – CCCLXIX = LXXIX. This is the Roman numeral for 79. The sum in full is 448-369 = 79.

3.

Caligula (ruled 37–41 CE)
Nero (54–68)
Galba (68–69)
Domitian (81–96)
Marcus Aurelius (161–180)
Commodus (180–192)
Constantine (306–337)

4. c) The Peloponnesian War was fought between Athens and Sparta and its allies. Sparta emerged triumphant and its victory saw the end of democratic Athens' dominance of Greece.

5. The Muses were the divine daughters of Zeus and Mnemosyne, the goddess of memory. They were responsible for inspiring creative work in the arts and sciences.

a) Calliope inspires epic poetry
b) Cleio inspires history
c) Ourania inspires astronomy
d) Thaleia inspires comedy
e) Melpomene inspires tragedy
f) Polyhymnia inspires mime
g) Erato inspires love poetry
h) Euterpe inspires music
i) Terpsichore inspires dance

6. a) Herodotus was a fifth-century BCE Greek historian. Cicero calls him the father of history, because he wrote the first extended historical narrative that we know of, called, fittingly enough, *The Histories*. He was born in Halicarnassus but spent a great deal of time travelling around the Hellenic world collecting information for his writing. Plutarch (*c*.46–120 CE) was also Greek by birth, but became a Roman citizen.

7. Any six from the list below.

The greatest of Greek heroes was originally called Alcides and was the product of one of Zeus's many affairs with mortal women. Because of this, Zeus's wife, Hera, took against Heracles and devoted herself to making his life hell, from sending two snakes to try to murder him in his cradle as a baby to driving him mad so that he killed his own children. In order to expiate this terrible crime, Heracles was told by the oracle at Delphi that he must spend twelve years serving the king of Tiryns, Eurystheus. Eurystheus originally set Heracles ten tasks but meanly decided that he had cheated by having some help on two of them so set him two more, taking the full total to twelve.

Heracles' to-do list looked like this:

1. Slay Nemean Lion
2. Slay Hydra of Lerna
3. Capture Hind of Ceryneia
4. Capture Boar of Erymanthus
5. Clean Augean Stables in one day
6. Shoo away Birds at Lake Stymphalia
7. Capture Cretan Bull
8. Steal Diomedes' Horses
9. Bring back Hippolyta's Girdle
10. Steal Geryon's cattle
11. Bring back Apples of the Hesperides
12. Capture Cerberus

None of these tasks was particularly straightforward: the lion had famously weapon-proof fur so Heracles had to strangle it with his bare hands; the hydra was a many-headed monster who produced two new heads for every one that was cut off until Heracles had the bright idea of cauterising the stumps; the hind could run faster than an arrow and was sacred to the goddess Artemis, who wasn't keen on handing it over until Heracles negotiated with her; the boar was astonishingly fierce and had to be driven into thick snow to hobble it enough to allow Heracles to catch it; Augeas had thousands of livestock and Heracles had to divert two rivers through the stables to rinse away all their muck; the flock of birds at Stymphalia was huge and dangerous and he had to use a rattle given to him by Athena to frighten them out of the trees; the bull (the father of the minotaur) was as rambunctious as the boar before Heracles wrestled it into submission; Diomedes' four horses were man-eaters who managed to kill one of Heracles' pals before he subdued them; Hippolyta was the queen of the Amazons and although she was friendly Hera caused a misunderstanding that led to him killing her; Geryon was the giant grandson of Medusa and although Heracles defeated him fairly easily his cattle kept escaping on the journey back to Eurystheus; the apples belonged to Zeus and Heracles had to beat up and trick several people to find out where they were and get his hands on them; and, finally, Cerberus was the many-headed dog who guarded the entrance to the underworld and no easy puppy to control. However, Heracles managed all these labours, and was released from his bondage in time to join Jason's Argonauts for some more adventures. He remained unstoppable until a laundry error occurred when his wife Deianeira mistakenly gave him a poisoned shirt, thinking it had been impregnated with love potion rather than toxic centaur's blood.

8. d) Stichomythia is an effect used in many ancient Greek plays, and in later playwrights' work as well as in modern plays and films. It is a particularly effective method of adding pace and tension when characters are disagreeing with one another: Euripides' *Medea* has some wonderful, and surprisingly contemporary-sounding, examples in his dramatisation of the bitter and spiteful marital ding-dongs between Jason and Medea.

9. Anaxagoras, Aristotle, Cleanthes, Crates, Empedocles, Epicurus, Heraclitus, Plato, Protagoras, Pyrrho, Pythagoras, Socrates, Thales, Zeno.

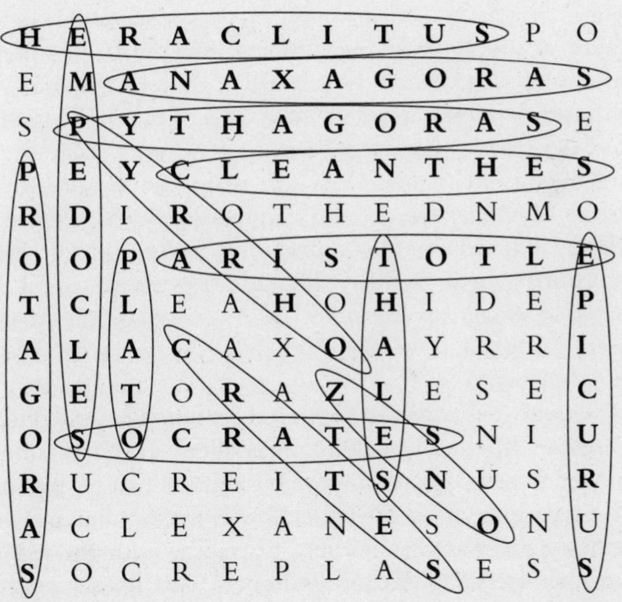

10.

Troy (now called Hisarlik) – Turkey
Ephesus (near modern-day Selçuk) – Turkey
Tyre – Lebanon
Mycenae – Greece
Carthage – Tunisia
Cumae – Italy
Babylon (near modern-day Al Hillah) – Iraq
Persepolis (now Takht-e Jamshid) – Iran
Memphis (near modern-day Helwan) – Egypt
Massilia (now Marseilles) – France

11. a) Magpies; b) Hyacinths; c) Swallows; d) Weasels; e) Partridges

The nine daughters of Pierus in Emathia were such bad losers after taking part in a singing competition with the Muses that the goddesses transformed them into magpies: '. . . and since that time their ancient eloquence, their screaming notes, their tiresome zeal of speech have all remained.'

After losing a competition for Achilles' armour to resourceful old Odysseus, the great warrior Ajax somewhat overreacted and fell on his sword. Where his blood splashed on to the ground hyacinth flowers grew. The plant's leaves from this point on have been marked with 'AI', the first letters of his name. Ovid also refers to another aetiological myth for the hyacinth flower – this involves Apollo accidentally killing a mortal boy he was fond of, called Hyacinthus, during a game of discus (ancient Frisbee). In this version, the letters 'AI' on the leaves of the flower that sprang up from the youth's blood are said to represent Apollo's cries of grief.

Poor old Procne was married to the charming Thracian king Tereus who decided to rape her sister Philomela, then cut out her tongue and imprison her. When Procne discovered this she killed her own son, Itys, and served him up to his father Tereus for his dinner. Because of her infanticide she was changed into a swallow with the red 'mark of murder' on her breast. Tereus and Philomela were transformed into the hoopoe and the nightingale.

Galanthis was the maid of Hercules' mother Alcmena (we are calling him Hercules rather than Heracles here because Ovid is a Roman. You'll also notice that Hera is referred to as Juno in Roman myth). Under orders from the Hercules-hating Juno, the goddess of childbirth, Lucina, delayed Alcmena's efforts to give birth to him. Galanthis tricked Lucina into allowing Hercules to be born and then, rather foolishly, laughed at the goddess for her mistake. For this impertinence she was transformed into a weasel. A nice ending to the story is that Alcmena still let her live in her house, perhaps as a wily pet.

Perdix was the nephew and pupil of the great inventor Daedalus who began to outstrip his teacher in ingenuity, inspiring his jealous relative to throw him to his death from Minerva's temple. Minerva however transformed him into a partridge. His fate explains why the partridge doesn't like to fly very high these days. Partridges still carry the official genus name Perdix.

12. Legio IX means 'the ninth legion' and the 'Hispana' was added to their name in honour of their part in the conquest of the final northern parts of Hispania (Spain) to fall to the relentless Romans in 19 BCE. This legion is famous for having been involved in many high-profile Roman campaigns, including the invasion of Britain, and for having disappeared from Roman army records suddenly in 108 CE, after building a fortress near Eboracum (York). The author Rosemary Sutcliffe wrote a popular book on this subject called *The Eagle of the Ninth* in 1954 where she imagined the legion being annihilated by northern tribes. Recent scholarship has in fact turned up various later references to the legion elsewhere in the Roman Empire although it is still thought that it was wiped out at some point before the reign of Marcus Aurelius as it is absent from a list of all the active legions that was made during his rule.

13. c) Achilles was in fact killed by one of Paris's arrows, rather than the other way around, when he was hit on the only vulnerable place on his body, his heel. Diomedes and Menelaus both fought Paris during the war but he escaped from them. He was not so lucky with Philoctetes, who fatally shot him with Heracles' bow and arrows (which he was given by the great hero for helping him commit suicide to escape the pains of his poisoned shirt). The rest of the Greeks had actually abandoned Philoctetes on the island of Lemnos during the journey to Troy as he had received a snakebite which made his foot unbearably stinky. However, when a prophecy revealed that Troy could only be defeated if Heracles' weapons were present, they rushed back to collect him.

14. c) Lucretia was a Roman noblewoman who was raped by Sextus Tarquinius, the son of the last king of Rome, Lucius Tarquinius Superbus. After telling her family of the assault Lucretia, unable to live with the stain on her virtue, stabbed herself with a dagger. This incident led to the nobles driving the royal family out of Rome and founding the republic which endured from 509 BCE to 44 BCE when Julius Caesar was made dictator-for-life, taking on king-like powers.

15.
a) Rosy-fingered dawn
b) Ox-eyed Hera
c) Wine-dark sea
d) Swift-footed Achilles

16. In the *Aeneid*, Virgil makes Ascanius an ancestor of Julius Caesar, thereby linking the new Emperor Augustus (Caesar's great-nephew and adopted son) with the foundation of Rome and with the age of mythological heroes (as well as giving him a touch of deity by making him a descendant of the goddess Venus).

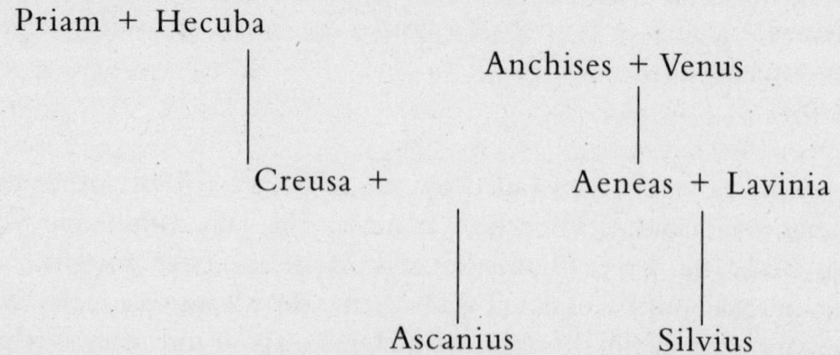

17. a) Cattus; b) Porcus; c) Piscis; d) Bos; e) Aquila

18. a) Pasiphaë was a daughter of the sun god Helios who was married to King Minos of Crete. She committed bestiality (and, concomitantly, adultery) by having relations with a bull, leading to the birth of the Minotaur.

b) Myrrha tricked her father into sleeping with her and so was guilty of incest. When her father discovered this he tried to kill her but the gods transformed her into the myrrh bush (the sap from this bush is said to be her tears). Adonis, of Aphrodite (Venus in Latin) and Adonis fame, was born from this union.

c) Clytemnestra murdered her husband Agamemnon so is guilty of mariticide. She killed Agamemnon in the bath when he returned from the Trojan War to avenge the fact that he had sacrificed their daughter Iphigenia to the gods in order to get a fair wind to sail to Troy. She was also miffed that he had brought back Cassandra, a Trojan princess, as his concubine so she killed her too. This murder was just part of a cycle of incredibly destructive behaviour that haunted the House of Atreus, Agamemnon's family, right back to his ancestor Tantalus (who was himself a proponent of infanticide) and only ending with his son Orestes.

d) The maestra of mythical murderers, Medea was a princess of Colchis who fell in love with the Greek hero Jason. She helped him steal the golden fleece from her father Aeetes and when they were making their escape by ship she came up with a horrific plan to slow Aeetes' pursuit: she dismembered her little brother Apsyrtus and threw his limbs into the sea, forcing her father to stop to collect his body parts in order to bury them properly. Despite this devotion, Jason later tired of Medea's charms and she murdered their two sons in order to get back at him for going off with another princess. She also murdered the princess and her father. Medea was a relative of Pasiphaë, so their clan could be said to give the House of Atreus a run for their money in the families-from-hell stakes.

19. a) Heraclitus was an influential Presocratic philosopher from Ephesus who was born around 540 BCE. He believed that the universe was constantly changing and that it was controlled by a rational force which he called the 'Logos'. His work does not survive directly and was considered by later commentators to be famously difficult to interpret, earning him the catchy nickname 'the Obscure one'. However, the references to his thought that have been preserved through the centuries went on to influence philosophers such as Hegel and Heidegger.

20. c) *The Frogs*, *The Clouds*, *The Wasps* and *The Birds* are all plays by the fifth-century BCE comic playwright Aristophanes.

21.
a) μισέω means 'I hate'.
b) ἄνθρωπος means 'man' or 'human'.
c) γυνή means 'woman'.
d) λόγος means 'study', 'word' or 'story'.

22. b), c) and d).

23. b) This is a floorplan of the iconic Athenian temple, the Parthenon. This magnificent building was constructed by the architects Ictinus and Callicrates between 447 and 432 BCE on the site of a previous shrine that had been destroyed in the wars with Persia. The temple was dedicated to the patron goddess of Athens, justice, war and wisdom, Athene. (Its name comes from the word '*parthenos*' meaning 'virgin', as Athene was celebrated as an unmarried and chaste deity.) It housed a huge chryselephantine depiction of the goddess by the famous sculptor Phidias and, despite our conception of Greek architecture and sculpture as icy-white and minimalist, it was decorated in brightly coloured paint.

24.

Lucan
Tacitus
Juvenal
Seneca
Petronius
Pliny
Martial
Suetonius

25. Sappho (*c*.610–570 BCE) is considered one of the best ancient Greek lyric poets and her poems were widely read by her contemporaries and many later generations. Unfortunately for us not much of her work survives today. Even though he wasn't a big fan of poets in general, banning them from the ideal state he depicts in his *Republic*, Plato referred to Sappho as 'the tenth Muse'.

26. b) Tiberius was emperor from 14–37 CE. Jesus' home region of Galilee was under Roman rule via the client-kingdom of Herod Antipas during his lifetime and the province of Judea, where Jesus was killed just outside Jerusalem, was brought under direct Roman rule when Jesus was six years old. This is why the Roman Prefect Pontius Pilate had to approve Jesus' crucifixion.

27. Aristotle's *Poetics* outlines his ideal ingredients for a successful tragedy. These include 'hamartia' referring to the hero's tragic mistake or flaw, 'peripeteia' referring to the necessary reversal of fortunes in the hero's life, 'anagnorisis' referring to the revelation of a key element of the plot that the hero has been ignorant of and 'catharsis' referring to the purgation of emotions of either the hero or the audience.

In Sophocles' *Oedipus Tyrannos* the hero's **hamartia** occurs when he kills King Laius of Thebes in a fit of road rage, little knowing that Laius is actually his real father. When the Thebans find themselves without a king, coincidentally at the same time as clever Oedipus turns up, he agrees to take the job. Things start to go downhill when a plague devastates the city and it is revealed that the unavenged death of King Laius is the cause. Diligent Oedipus then determines to discover the perpetrator. The **peripeteia** and **anagnorisis** of the play happen at the same time when a helpful witness to Laius's murder reveals Oedipus to be the killer and also his true parentage. Poor Oedipus then realises that by marrying Laius's widow Jocasta, he has unwittingly married his own mother. **Catharsis** is achieved by Jocasta's suicide and Oedipus's decision to blind himself and leave Thebes. You'll be unsurprised to hear that this play is held up as a shining example of a tragedy.

28. b) Cicero hated Mark Antony: he thought he should have been assassinated alongside his friend Julius Caesar and considered him extremely dangerous to the principles of the Roman Republic. Alas for poor Tully (as he was called in later times, from his first names Marcus Tullius) Mark Antony came out on top when he came to power in the Second Triumvirate alongside Octavian (later the Emperor Augustus) and Lepidus. Cicero was proscribed in 43 BCE as an enemy of the state, leading to his murder. His speeches against Mr Cleopatra were named after the Greek Demosthenes' prescient speeches warning the Athenians about the ambition of Philip II of Macedon in the fourth century BCE.

29. What we know of Socrates' fall from grace comes from the work of his top student, Plato. In 399 BCE Socrates was put on trial for introducing new gods to Athens and corrupting the youth. During the proceedings he made his famous pronouncement that 'an unexamined life is not worth living'. He was found guilty and sentenced to death. Despite his friends' efforts to convince him to escape, he carried out his own sentence by drinking hemlock. In the *Apology*, Plato has Socrates blaming Aristophanes' play, *The Clouds*, for contributing towards his bad reputation.

30. These quotations are from the work of Quintus Horatius Flaccus (65–8 BCE), more often known to us as Horace. Despite fighting on the side of Brutus after the assassination of Julius Caesar, Horace was luckier than Cicero in the aftermath of the conflict, losing only his property and keeping his life. He was later favoured by the Emperor Augustus and today is considered the leading lyric poet of his time.

31. b) Hephaistion was Alexander's closest confidant from his childhood up until Hephaistion's death in 324 BCE which left the great leader distraught. On a similar theme, Patroclus was Achilles' beloved in Homer's great epic the *Iliad*, Antinous was the Roman Emperor Hadrian's companion and Ganymede was a young boy abducted by Zeus in Greek myth (our word 'catamite' developed from the name 'Ganymede').

32.

a) Murmillo
b) Retiarius
c) Secutor
d) Thraex

There were many types of Roman gladiator, with different specialised fighting styles and armours. These are four of the most recognisable. Gladiatorial contests are thought to have developed in Italy as part of the rites surrounding funerals. In imperial Rome the Emperor was responsible for putting on often lavish and elaborate gladiatorial displays in the amphitheatres. In 107 CE, to celebrate his victory over the Dacians (a people from around the region of modern-day Romania), the Emperor Trajan not only built the impressive column still visible in Rome today but also put on repeated gladiatorial games that were said to involve 10,000 gladiators and 11,000 animals over the course of about four months. Gladiators were usually slaves and convicts who had been condemned for crimes such as treason, murder and tax evasion, although there were also a few citizens who volunteered to fight. They were pitted against each other or wild beasts and if they fought well they were sometimes spared by the will of the audience, even if they had been defeated. It is thought, however, that the majority only lasted for ten competitions at most.

33. This word transliterates as 'amnesia' and, as you might expect, means 'forgetfulness'.

34.

a) *Atrium*. The atrium was the main room of the house. It had an opening in the roof to let in light. Luckily Rome was generally a warm and sunny place or this could be considered a grave design flaw.
b) *Impluvium*. The impluvium caught rainwater that came in through the opening in the roof of the atrium.
c) *Cubiculum*. The cubicula were rooms used as bedrooms and for other general purposes.
d) *Culina*.
e) *Ianua*.
f) *Hortus*.
g) *Tablinum*. The tablinum was where the paterfamilias (father of the household) would receive visits from his clients.
h) *Triclinium*. The triclinium was the dining room where the household ate lying on couches.
i) *Vestibulum*.
j) *Taberna*. The rooms at the front of town houses were often rented out as shops.

35. Julius Caesar and Mark Antony. Mark Antony's mother was a distant cousin of Caesar's. Both of them are thought to have had children with Cleopatra. Her son Caesarion was said to be Julius Caesar's child and she had three children with Mark Antony. Caesar's grand-nephew and adopted son, Octavian (who went on to become the Emperor Augustus), wasn't keen on a rival son of Caesar's hanging about and had Caesarion killed after Mark Antony and Cleopatra's suicides following their defeat at the Battle of Actium in 31 BCE.

36.

Athene	Owl
Hera	Peacock
Ares	Vulture
Poseidon	Horse
Zeus	Eagle
Aphrodite	Dove

You might be interested to know that, along with the oak tree, celery was one of Zeus's sacred plants. Think about that next time you're letting it wilt in the bottom of the fridge: what's good enough for the king of the gods should be good enough for you.

37. The sequence of public offices followed by Roman politicians was called the *cursus honorum* (course of honours). The first step was Quaestor, followed by Praetor, followed by Consul. There were only two Consuls each year and they were the most powerful men in the Roman Republic until the emperors came along. They left these offices in place as a sop to the sentimental affection for those old Republican days, but in practice they held absolute power.

38. Afghanistan, Scotland, Norway and India were never part of the Roman Empire. The Romans did make some incursions into Scotland but they never fully conquered those courageous Caledonians. Interestingly, several decades before the Romans started running riot over the world map, the Macedonian ruler Alexander the Great had invaded both India and Afghanistan.

39. d) and i) The emperor we know as Caligula was actually named Gaius. 'Caligula', meaning 'little boots', was a nickname from when he was a sweet-faced young boy in miniature army boots visiting his popular father Germanicus on his military campaigns. His father's heroic status meant that Caligula was initially received as emperor with great enthusiasm by the Roman citizenry. They soon changed their minds and, rather than retiring gracefully in his old age, Caligula was stabbed to death in a widely supported conspiracy at the age of twenty-eight. All the other answers are eccentricities and crimes attributed to him by writers such as Suetonius, Tacitus and Cassius Dio.

40. d) The hoplites were heavily armed infantrymen who fought for the various city-states. They wore distinctive helmets, breastplates and bronze greaves and also carried swords or spears and large bronze shields which were an essential factor in their nifty formation fighting method.

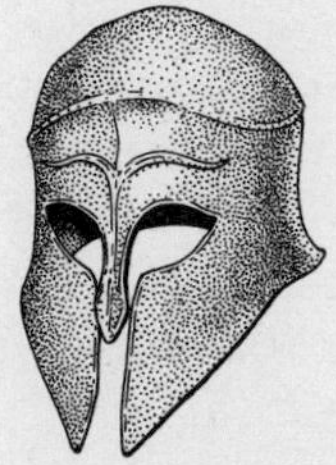

41. Seneca committed suicide on the orders of his former pupil, the Emperor Nero. Nero had been told that Seneca was involved in a conspiracy to replace him with the orator and statesman Gaius Calpurnius Piso. He sent a messenger to his old teacher to inform him that his death was required. According to Tacitus' account, Seneca received this news calmly. However, he had a rough ride quitting this mortal coil: he cut his own wrists and when that didn't work took poison, but was finally only successful after suffocating himself in a bath.

42. d) The Odeon of Herodes Atticus was commissioned in 161 CE by, you guessed it, Herodes Atticus. All the other monuments were planned during the golden days of Pericles' influence in Athens. Pericles is also famous for his exhilarating speech at the funeral of the Athenian soldiers killed in the first year of the Peloponnesian War. This oration was recorded by the historian Thucydides in his *History of the Peloponnesian War*. It was so inspiring that Pericles' words on the subject of freedom were printed on the sides of London buses during the First World War.

43. Catullus is asking Lesbia for 3,300 kisses in this poem. The lines quoted read: 'Give me a thousand kisses, then a hundred, then another thousand, then a second hundred, then yet another thousand, then a hundred'. You should have been able to work out '*centum*' meaning 'one hundred' from our English word 'century', '*secunda*' meaning 'a second' from our word 'second' and '*mille*' meaning 'a thousand' from our word 'millennium'. However, if you translated this last one as a 'million' by mistake don't chastise yourself too heavily; the gist of the poem remains the same.

44. a) Spartacus was a Thracian slave (a member of a Balkan tribe which had fought against the Romans in the second century BCE) who became a gladiator. After escaping from his gladiatorial school in 73 BCE with a group of fellow fighters he defeated the Roman forces sent against them and recruited thousands of slaves to their cause. Finally in 71 BCE his army was brutally destroyed by the Roman generals Crassus and Pompey.

45. c) Citizens would vote for whom they would like to see exiled by scratching their name on to a spare broken piece of pottery called an '*ostrakon*'. As with our ballot papers, these were deposited in containers and counted by officials. The citizen with the most votes was exiled. In theory you could vote to exile anyone you liked, that bloke who looked at your wife funny in the agora or pushed past you at the gymnasium, but in practice it was men of power and influence who were ostracised.

46. b) '*Libertus*' was the word used to describe a slave who had been freed by his or her master in the ceremony called manumission. Slaves could buy their freedom or earn it through dedicated service. Once free, they could live a similar life to ordinary Roman citizens although they were not allowed to hold public offices. Despite this prohibition several *liberti* went on to hold important roles as advisors to emperors, such as Narcissus who worked for the Emperor Claudius, and Epaphroditus who was secretary to the Emperor Nero.

47. This is the constellation of Orion which is named after an ancient Greek mythological hunter. There are various versions of the story of how he came to shine down upon us from the night sky: one of the most popular is that he was such an enthusiastic hunter that he boasted of his intention to hunt down all the animals on earth. The Earth goddess Gaia was not best pleased by this and sent a giant scorpion to kill him for his effrontery. After a plea by Artemis, the goddess of hunting, Zeus took him up and placed him in the heavens, but the scorpion (the constellation Scorpio) was also given this honour.

48.

a) *Infra dig*
b) *Agenda*
c) *Ex libris*
d) *Terra firma*

49. d) Vercingetorix was beaten by Julius Caesar at the Battle of Alesia in 52 BCE, as is recorded in Caesar's *Gallic Wars*. He surrendered and was taken back to Rome as a prisoner where he was displayed in Caesar's triumphal procession and then executed. Rome went on to conquer all of Gaul (unless the stories of one tiny indomitable village in Armorica are to be believed).

50. Virgo Vestalis Maxima, or Chief Vestal Virgin, was the most powerful job available to women in Rome. The Vestal Virgins were priestesses of the temple of Vesta, the goddess of the hearth. They were enrolled as little girls and sworn to keep an oath of chastity for thirty years, with the threat of being buried alive should they behave inappropriately. They kept the sacred fire in Vesta's temple burning, which was thought to safeguard the city. Rhea Silvia, descendant of Aeneas and mother of the founders of Rome, the touchy twins Romulus and Remus, was made a vestal virgin by her uncle when he usurped her father as king of Alba Longa. The nasty uncle's plan was to prevent Rhea from providing any heirs to the throne by employing her in this chaste occupation. However, Rhea got around this problem by claiming to be impregnated by the god Mars.

BREAK TIME

As the great sage George Bernard Shaw once said, 'We don't stop playing because we grow old, we grow old because we stop playing', and there's nothing we would like to see more than the font of eternal youth to be forever supped at. So it's time to down tools, stop looking at the clock, get silly and have a little fun – here's where we'll rib-tickle you with some rather resplendent riddles, test your lateral thinking with some vicious verbal reasoning, and let you in on some of the sacred secrets of crafty card conjurors. Enjoy!

Galvanise your grey matter with these brain teasers and riddles:

1. Two dusty and well-read books, Volumes One and Two, stand side by side in order from left to right on a bookshelf. Not including bindings, each book is one inch thick; the bindings are each an eighth of an inch thick. Starting from page one, Volume One, a hungry and destructive bookworm chomps her way to the last page of Volume Two. How many inches did she consume?

2. A circular pool, twenty-five feet in diameter, has a remarkable and possibly magical lily in its centre. This lily grows by doubling its area each day. At the end of thirty days, the lily exactly covers the pool. In how many days does this lily cover half the pool's area?

3. A salty seadog, looking up from his tot of rum, noted a rope ladder dangling from a ship in a harbour with its lowest six rungs underwater. Also, he saw that each rung was four inches wide and that the rungs were ten inches apart. If the tide rose at the rate of five inches per hour, how many rungs would be submerged in three hours?

4. Roger Bottomley-Smythe bumped into a friend at the races wearing a lieutenant's uniform. They shook hands and greeted each other warmly as they had not seen one another in ten years. With his friend was an adorable little girl. 'I've been married since you saw me the last time to someone you don't know,' said the lieutenant. 'This girl is my daughter.' Richard asked the child's name, and she replied that it was the same as her mother's. 'So your name is Margaret!' How did he know her name?

5. What four weights would you use for a balance scale to weigh any number of pounds from one to forty inclusive? You can place the weights on both sides of the scale at the same time.

6. Three railway men named Smith, Robinson and Jones, and three businessmen, similarly named, live in London. The businessman Robinson and the brakeman live in Notting Hill, the businessman Jones and the fireman live in Stratford, while the businessman Smith and the engineer live halfway between the two. The brakeman's namesake earns £3,500 a month; the engineer earns one-third of the businessman nearest him. The railway man Smith beats the fireman at billiards. Name the engineer.

7. Three men – Alexander, Balthazar and Caleb – are tested for quick thinking. On the forehead of each a cross is marked which, they are told, may be either blue or white. They are then taken to an empty room. None of the three knows the colour of his own cross or is allowed to speak to the others, but each one is told he may leave the room if he either sees two white crosses or determines the colour of his own cross. Alexander is a sharp fellow. He notes that both Balthazar and Caleb have blue crosses, and after a few seconds of quick thinking, he leaves the room having determined the colour of his own cross. What was the process by which he determined the answer? And what was the colour of his cross?

8. A farmer is in happy possession of a fox, a goose and some corn. Unhappily, he must cross a river, and due to the size of the boat, he can only transport one at a time. If he leaves the goose with the corn to take the fox over, the goose will eat the corn. If he leaves the fox alone with the goose, the fox will devour it. How will he get each safely across?

9. Invented by Lewis Carroll, the notoriously playful author of *Alice in Wonderland*, a Doublet is a word transformation puzzle. Using two words of similar length, the objective is to transform the first word into the second word by forming successive words of the same length by substituting one letter at a time. For instance, changing HEAD to TAIL in only six steps can be done as follows:

HEAD
HEAL
TEAL
TELL
TALL
TAIL

Can you turn WORK into PLAY in just six steps, using 'P' as the first letter substitute, 'E' as the third letter substitute, and 'L' as the fifth letter substitute?

10. Ted and June were long-distance lovers living in different cities (Ted in Chicago and June in New York). Ted was eager to get married soon but June wanted to wait a while to be sure that Ted was Mr Right. Knowing full well that Chicago and New York have a time difference of one hour (and assuming this would make a speedy marriage impossible), after much pestering June promised Ted that if he proposed when Chicago and New York were on the same time, she would agree to get married right away. In November of that year, they were married. How did this happen?

11. Perhaps only a rabid mathematician would feel thoroughly at home with the difficulties of the man who had ten young trees to plant and an *idée fixe* as to how they ought to be planted. But here we go.

Pernickety Peter wanted his saplings arranged in five rows, with four trees in each row, and he could afford only ten trees. Can you work out how it can be done?

12. Two competitive cyclists start at the same instant from opposite ends of a twenty-mile road and ride towards each other at a constant speed of ten miles per hour until their front wheels meet. At the instant they start, a fly leaves the front wheel of one of them and flies straight towards the other at a constant speed of fifteen miles per hour until he touches the other wheel; he at once flies back until he touches the first wheel, and so on, his journeys naturally getting shorter and shorter as the cyclists approach each other, until he is crushed between the wheels. How far did the fly fly?

13. The combined ages of Mary and Ann equal forty-four years. Mary is twice as old as Ann was when Mary was half as old as Ann will be when Ann is three times as old as Mary was when Mary was three times as old as Ann. How old is Ann?

Wily words and problematic punctuation:

14. Punctuate to make sense of the following sentence: 'Williams where Johnson had had had had had had had had had had been approved of by the critics.'

15. Complete the following sentence using either *complements* or *compliments*:

> 'Dan thinks Rachel looks absolutely ravishing in her yellow dress, which her green scarf really ____, and he wasn't afraid to pay her a few ____.'

16. Complete the following two sentences using either *which* or *that*:

Just William is the first in the series of William Brown books and is also the one ____ I like best. The books, ____ are written by Richmal Crompton, have been made into numerous television series, films and radio adaptations.

17. Complete the following pedagogical tidbit using the grammatical terms below:

clauses, independent, phrase, semicolon, comma, semicolon, ideas

A ____ normally joins two independent ____ or complete ____, not an ____ clause and a dependent clause or ____. In other words, a ____ is not just a lengthened or strengthened ____.

18. Which is the odd word/phrase out in the following set of sequences, and why?

a) Hexagon, hexadecimal, hexahedron, polygon
b) Pendant, didactic, sanctimonious, clamorous
c) Self-rule, free reign, autonomy, sovereignty

19. What is the longest word in the English language with the least number of vowels?

20. What are oft considered to be the longest words in the English language in which no letter appears more than once? (Hint: there are three, beginning with D, M and U respectively.)

21. Concerning the above question, we say 'oft considered' because despite our ability to define each fifteen-letter word – in which no letter occurs more than once – only the one beginning with D can be found in the dictionary. And while many people, we are sure, often use the other two in their everyday speech, their non-dictionary status means they are what kind of words?

a) Neologisms
b) Homonyms
c) Hapax legomenons
d) None of the above

22. Which of the following words/phrases is an example of a palindrome?

a) Ex grata
b) Reminder
c) Coffee
d) Redivider

23. Devilishly demanding definitions:

What are the meanings of the following words?

a) Jumentous (*a.*)

– To be in the process of becoming youthful
– Pertaining to the smell of horse urine
– Imitative in colour, or shape
– Many-coloured (literally, like a rainbow)

b) Maculation (*n.*)

– Thriving in rubbish or waste
– The systematic classification of all organisms
– An intense dislike of undressing in front of another person
– The condition of being covered in spots (like a leopard or a Dalmatian)

c) Zarf (*n.*)

– A type of turmeric root that has the medicinal function of strengthening the activity of the stomach
– A filigree metal holder for a hot coffee cup
– The knob on a toadstool cap, a shield, or a seashell
– A sudden uneasiness, generally about some action or proposed action of one's own

d) Shandygaff (*n.*)

– An old-fashioned term for 'monster'
– A doctrine or principle once held essential by a particular group or party, but which now seems dated
– The full (and proper!) name for what most people call a shandy (beer and ginger beer)
– A person who shares the opinions of the character Tristram Shandy in the novel of that name by Laurence Sterne

Complex clans: some kinship puzzles

24. In-laws are the source of much trouble, not only from a domestic standpoint. Here is a snatch of conversation two women were overheard having in a café, which goes to prove the aforementioned statement. 'That man's mother was my mother's mother-in-law, but he had a terrible argument with my father, and they still don't speak.' The question for us is, what was the relation of the gentleman in question to the speaker?

25. Another combination of in-law-ship is involved in the following horrible-sounding snippet of conversation overheard on a bus as one man speaks to another: 'It's really quite simple, my dear chap. You happen to be my father's brother-in-law, my brother's father-in-law, and my father-in-law's brother.' Can you list the appropriate marriages (within the legal limitations, of course) that would have had to have brought about this astonishing triple relationship?

26. A man – Andrew – had two friends, a brother and a sister whose names were Stuart and Hannah Smith. One day, while Andrew was at lunch with Stuart and Hannah, a handsome young man appeared at their table whom Stuart introduced to Andrew as his nephew. Andrew then naturally referred to Hannah as the young man's aunt, but the youth corrected him, saying that while he was the nephew of Stuart Smith, he was not the nephew of Hannah Smith. How come?

27. At a certain family party there were present: one grandfather, one grandmother, two fathers, two mothers, four children, three grandchildren, one brother, two sisters, two sons, two daughters, one father-in-law, one mother-in-law, and one daughter-in-law. The party was held in a small flat with room for only seven people around the table, and yet all were served at once without the slightest inconvenience. Perhaps you can explain this without recourse to relativity? Or the fourth dimension?

28. And now for the modern family. Verity's mother Patsy has two sisters, Jenny and Barbara. Barbara has three children: Nancy, Ben and Stephen, and Jenny has two daughters, Maggie and Pru. Maggie and Pru's father has two other daughters from his second marriage, Evelyn and Andrea, and Maggie has two children of her own, Estelle and Jack. This makes Andrea Jenny's:

a) Stepdaughter
b) Stepdaughter once removed
c) There is no relation between Andrea and Jenny
d) Half-cousin

29. Estelle and Jack, however, are Patsy and Barbara's:

a) Third cousins
b) Second cousins, once removed
c) Step-niece and nephew
d) Great-niece and great-nephew

30. Andrea and Evelyn are Estelle and Jack's:

a) Grandparents
b) Cousins
c) Step-aunts
d) Half-aunts

31. If Estelle has a daughter, that daughter will be Verity's:

a) First cousin once removed
b) Second cousin once removed
c) Third cousin twice removed
d) Second cousin

32. Nancy, Ben and Stephen would be Estelle's daughter's:

a) Second cousins once removed
b) Third cousins
c) Step-aunts and uncles
d) Half-aunts and uncles

33. If Jenny got married again to a man with two sons, those sons would be Pru's:

a) Half-brothers
b) Half-nephews
c) Half-cousins
d) Step-brothers

34. Finally, the wife of Maggie and Pru's father would be Stephen's:

a) Step-niece
b) No relation
c) Great-aunt
d) Half-aunt

Verbal reasoning – it's time for some lateral thinking

35. Match the relationship to the words below to create the appropriate analogies:

Relationship:	Words:
Type of	Abhorrence : Dislike
Degree of	Philanthropist : Benevolence
Used to	Conceited : Self-awareness
Characterised by	Anger : Emotion
Lacking in	Ultimatum : Coerce

36. In the following questions, a related pair of words or phrases is followed by four pairs of words or phrases. Select the pair that best expresses a relationship similar to that expressed in the original pair:

i. Rain : Puddle

a) Lake : Flood
b) Heat : Evaporation
c) Jealousy : Trust
d) Education : Ignorance

ii. Sonnet : Stanza

a) Computer : Machine
b) Room : House
c) Dog : Paw
d) Colour : Pigment

iii. Drawl : Speak

a) Cultivate : Grow
b) Dawdle : Walk
c) Pare : Cut
d) Spurt : Expel

37. Though many of the answers could be correct, which is the *most correct* word with which to complete the two incomplete sentences?

i. Libraries, because they contain a great number of books, maps and private papers about the development of different cultures, are good places for students of ____.

a) Religion
b) English literature
c) Biography
d) History

ii. Because Laura had always been a staunch defender of women's rights, her audience was confounded by her ____ stance during the debate.

a) Wavering
b) Credulous
c) Absolute
d) Passionate

38. Find FIVE antonyms for **maladroit** in the wordsearch below:

R R A Z I N I H T S F J J Y I
Z Y F J H V S J Y M I Z L L B
Q I W S C I T S E Y F L K D T
O C P Z G R T U W K X W L R S
T K V G F E N D U R I N G A K
B N U X M T Q P F I O Z O W I
M L E A S U O R E T X E D O L
S A T I C K Q X B P G Y O C F
L I L Q C Z T B S T P E D A U
C H O A T I C O I C L J I D L
L K F O I L F E N K P I N H W
K C L V U S E F X U Q R Y G W
J Z F M X K E N E B J J U U S
F E S D F F T W G Q Y E U B Y
N Y V O S T S P U D B Q Z A G

Riddles:

39. Solve each of these anagrams to give the names of classic card games:

DAD LIMO
PASSED
RECHUE
RUNG MIMY
TEA PIC EN
HWITS
RAT SHE
SERIAL ITO
A FLAME HIP YIPS

40. Which word in group B fits in group A? And why?

A.
solve
unpressed
tent
cod
act
poll
claim
pose
it

B.
pillow
dark
sad
create
cite
pail
posture
pen
den

41. Can you uncover what each group of three has in common?

a) Greenhouse, car, doll's house
b) Onion, snake, elephant
c) Sewer, mine, valley
d) Wolf, kite, comet
e) Pluto, Sirius, Laika

42. It's sometime between 1972 and 1981 and you have fifty-five coins totaling £10. There are more 5ps than pennies, more 10ps than 5ps, and more crowns than 10ps. How many of each coin do you have?

43. What expression is represented below?

Chloe
Tennis
Tennis
Tennis
Tennis
Tennis

Optical illusions

44. The 'Blivet' below is an impossible object. Why?

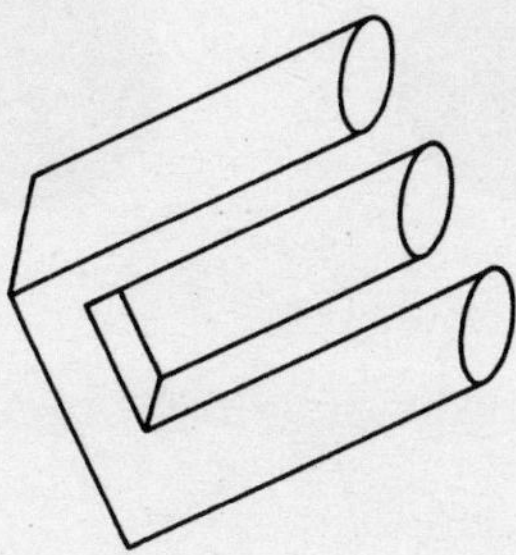

45. Which of the two central circles is smaller?

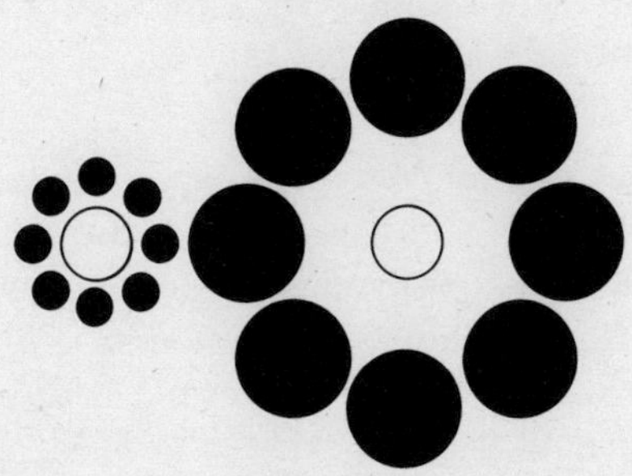

46. There are three images in this picture. What are they?

47. Eponyms. Are these expressions really named after these particular people?

a) 'Christopher Columbus!', used to show great surprise ('Christopher Columbus! What the heck are you doing with that can of petrol in one hand and a cigarette in the other!') and named after Christopher Columbus Langdell, the American educator and dean of the Harvard Law School who originated the case method of teaching law.

b) 'Buckley's Chance' is an Australian expression meaning 'a very remote chance' ('you haven't got a Buckley's Chance of persuading that banker that smaller bonuses should be paid'). Two chances, Buckley's and none, amounts – in reality – to virtually no chance at all. The expression is thought to have been named after William Buckley who lived, against all odds, with Aborigines for thirty years.

c) 'John Hancock', an expression used to denote the issuing of one's signature, was named after Jean Anock, the brother of the French educator Louis Braille with whom he developed a system of printing and writing that is extensively used by the blind.

d) 'Keeping Up With the Joneses' refers to the drive to maintain the same living and material standards as one's neighbours and comes from the American comic strip of the same title by Arthur R. Momand which began running in the New York *Globe* in 1913.

48. Cryptograms. For centuries, military strategists encoded secret documents by simply changing letters to other letters in the alphabet or giving them a numeric value so that they appeared illegible to anyone who didn't know their ciphers. In keeping with usual 'enemy' practices, we have given you three cryptograms which, once decoded, will reveal the names of some classic card games. Unlike usual 'enemy' practice, we have generously provided one clue to the ciphers, which is a lot more than the codebreakers at Bletchley Park ever got . . . (Rules to the tricks can be found with the answers . . .)

a) 1 15 12   13 8 19 26 12   10 22 2 21 1

(clue: the substitute for the letter T is the number 1)

b) 16 4 1   14 1 17 10 5 11 10

(clue: the substitute for the letter R is the number 14)

c) Now, let's try one with substitute letters. If A is Z, what does this spell?

SGD SNO BGZMFD

49. Fallen phrases.

Below are three grids and a series of letters which appear to have fallen out of the grid and got jumbled up on the journey down. Can you place them back into their original squares to spell out the opening lines of theme songs to some classic British TV shows? (In case you are wondering what 'skill' is required to solve these particular brainteasers, we'll be straight with you and say right up front that putting the letters in the right boxes involves nothing more than mere guesswork, though as we've provided the punctuation within the lyrics, you can use that as a handy clue. And once you get the first word, you should be able to get the others if you spent more time watching telly than you did doing your homework . . .)

a)

O E R
R G L O N R
G F U O N T
A N D L O U A D Y
P E F R I M E S H E
S T A T O O D E R Y R

b)

T T
A E N T H R N
Y O O M E O O Y K I H E N I G
W H I F D Y H I O L D I H R N N
W E U R R R O U T U E D I K U K

c)

By decoding the ciphers in the cryptograms below – and taking advantage of the generous clue letters we have also supplied – can you determine what classic card tricks are encrypted? (Rules to the tricks can be found with the answers . . .)

a)

A	B	C	D	E	F	G	H	I	J	K	L	M	N	O	P	Q	R	S	T	U	V	W	X	Y	Z
5											17							2	14						

T _ _   _ A L S _   _ _ _ _ T
14 3 18   12 5 17 2 18   6 19 10 9 14

b)

A	B	C	D	E	F	G	H	I	J	K	L	M	N	O	P	Q	R	S	T	U	V	W	X	Y	Z
																	D			A					

_ _ _   R _ U _ _ _ _
J X F   D F A I Z E I

c)

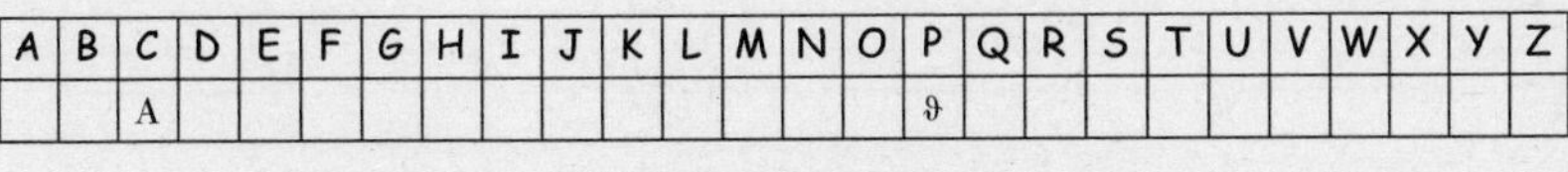

A	B	C	D	E	F	G	H	I	J	K	L	M	N	O	P	Q	R	S	T	U	V	W	X	Y	Z
		A													ϑ										

_ _ _   _ _ P   C _ _ _ _ _
ς N Θ   ς Ω ϑ   A N K T M Θ

50. Mazes. Can you find your way out of these labyrinths?

a)

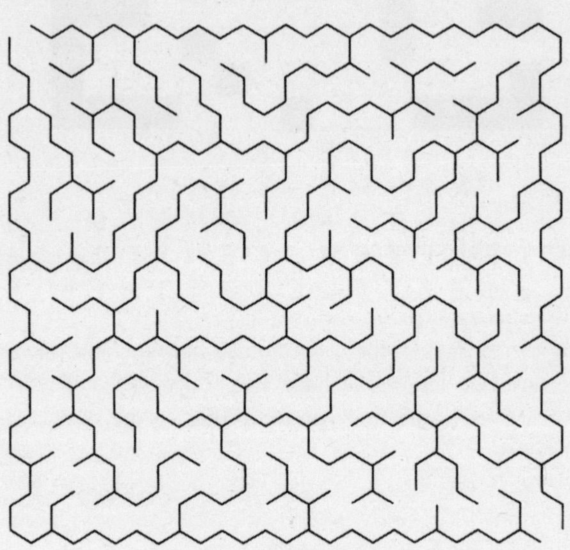

b)

BREAK TIME ANSWERS

Brain teasers and riddles:

1. The bookworm consumed only a quarter of an inch. When two volumes are in order from left to right on a bookshelf, the first page of Volume One and the last page of Volume Two are separated only by two covers.

2. Twenty-nine days.

3. Six rungs would still be submerged. The ship with the ladder rises with the tide, of course!

4. The friend that Roger Bottomley-Smythe happened to meet was a lady lieutenant. Please don't tell us you *still* don't get it? . . .

5. 1, 3, 9, 27 pounds.

6. Smith. The businessman living nearest to the engineer is named Smith, and the engineer's monthly income is exactly a third of his. Therefore, this businessman cannot be the brakeman's namesake as the latter earns £3,500 which is not divisible by three. Hence, the brakeman's name is not Smith. Neither is the fireman's name Smith since the railway man Smith beats him at billiards and so must be a person with a different name. This leaves the engineer to whom the name Smith may be correctly applied, thus answering the question.

7. Alexander's cross was blue. He figured it out this way: 'If I were white, Balthazar would decide he is blue, for otherwise Caleb would see two whites, and would leave the room. Likewise, Caleb would know that he is blue or else Balthazar would have gone out. Since both of them stay in the room, I must be blue also.'

8. There are two ways to get all across in one piece. The farmer can take the goose, return and fetch the fox and take the goose back. Leaving the goose, he can then take the corn, leave the corn with the fox and return for the goose. *Or*, for variety, he can transport the goose, return and fetch the corn, at which time he then takes the goose back, leaves the goose at the starting point and takes the fox over, after which he returns to collect the goose.

9.

WORK
PORK
PORT
PERT
PEAT
PLAT
PLAY

10. Ted proposed on the last Sunday of October when, at 2 a.m., the clocks in New York were set back one hour to Standard Eastern Time. In Chicago, however, it was still Daylight Time, which ends an hour later, so for this one hour both New York and Chicago were on the same time, which is when crafty Ted proposed . . .

11. The amateur solver can only juggle and juggle, like some demented circus act until she strikes on the following arrangement (a five-pointed star with a tree at each angle will do it just as well . . .).

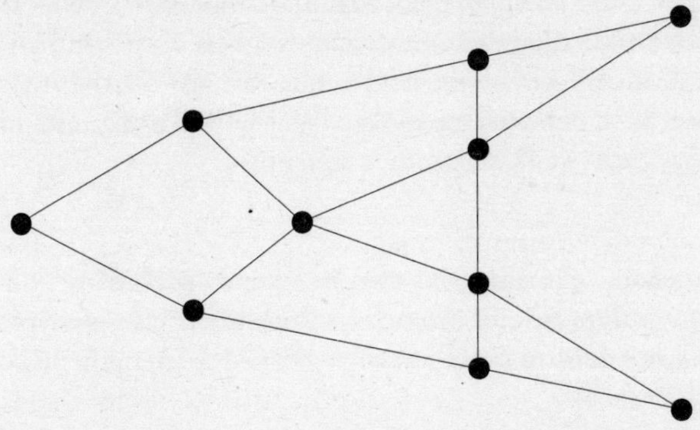

12. It is easy to see that the cyclists ride for exactly one hour. The fly was flying between them at a constant speed of fifteen miles per hour, then, for one hour. Consequently he flew just fifteen miles.

13. Ann is 16½ ; Mary is 27½.

Words and punctuation:

14. The situation depicted is probably some bitter and pedantic literary controversy over a point in translation from the Sanskrit, recording that: 'Williams, where Johnson had had 'had had' had had 'had': 'had had' had been approved of by the critics.'

15. Complements/compliments. Rachel's green scarf *complements* her yellow dress (as it adds to it in a way that enhances or improves the whole ensemble), prompting Dan to give her a number of *compliments* (praise) on her style.

16. That, which. Many writers ignore the 'that/which' rule and many editors no longer go on a 'which' hunt when checking copy nowadays. Yet the distinction is not only correct English usage, but will add clarity and rigour to your prose. While the pronoun 'that' is used in *restrictive* clauses ('apples are the only fruit that I do not buy'), 'which' should only really be used in *non-restrictive* clauses ('You'll not find any apples, which I hate, in my kitchen'). And while we are on the 'that/which' topic, 'whose' is a personal pronoun *that* should not stand in for 'of which'. 'Who', not 'that', refers to a person . . .

17. A **semicolon** normally joins two independent **clauses** or complete **ideas**, not an **independent** clause and dependent clause or **phrase**. In other words, a **semicolon** is not just a lengthened or strengthened **comma**.

18.

a) Hexadecimal which, according to the OED, is an adjective 'relating to or using a system of numerical notation that has 16 rather than 10 as its base'. Hexagon, hexagram and hexahedron can be seen as 'equal words' since they are all – to put it rather unpoetically – shapes. Plane figures composed of straight lines and angles (hexagon); with at least three straight sides and angles, and typically five or more (polygon); a solid figure with six plane faces (hexahedron). Aren't you glad you asked?

b) Pendant, which is a piece of jewellery that hangs from a necklace chain and is not to be confused, of course, with pedant, which is synonymous with the three other words, all of which refer to characteristics associated with a self-righteous, know-it-all, bossy sort of person.

c) Free reign. But why, you ask? Surely all four phrases and words refer to 'freedom'? Well, had the phrase 'free rein' (which derives from the literal meaning of allowing a horse to move freely without being controlled by reins) been in the sequence, there would be no odd-one-out answer. As it stands, however, 'free reign' does not exist as a phrase in the English language. Reign, of course, is a monarchical term meaning head of state; head of a team; to currently hold a particular title; to prevail over something; the period of rule of a monarch; the period during which someone or something is predominant or pre-eminent. Yet we would still be required to describe the *reign* of Henry

VIII as one in which a king *reigned* strongly over the religious institutions of England, yet did not have complete *free rein* to simply divorce his first wife, Catherine of Aragon, though his wish was granted later on during his *reign*.

19. Strength.

20. *Dermatoglyphics* (which, according to our dictionaries, is the scientific study of fingerprints or skin markings and patterns on fingers, hands and feet), *misconjugatedly* (an adverb which describes the act of an erroneous conjugation: '"He stealed my jumper!" cried the boy, misconjugatedly . . .') and *uncopyrightable* (the inability to copyright something).

21. d) None of the above. Our own definition would be, however, 'made up, silly, unofficial, probably non-existent words'.

22. d) As you know from *Homework for Grown-ups: Everything You Learned at School and Promptly Forgot*, a palindrome is 'a word, phrase or sentence which reads the same forwards or backwards. "Deed", "madam", and "I prefer pi" are all palindromes'.

23.

a) Jumentous: Pertaining to the smell of horse urine.
b) Maculation: The condition of being covered in spots (like a leopard or a Dalmatian).
c) Zarf: A filigree metal holder for a hot coffee cup.
d) Shandygaff: The full (and proper!) name for what most people call a shandy (beer and ginger beer).

Kinship puzzles:

24. The gentleman spoken of by the ladies in the café was the speaker's uncle.

25. To explain the brother-in-law and father-in-law tangle, we had best resort to a family tree. Here it is. Let us call the families involved Smith and Jones, just to be original.

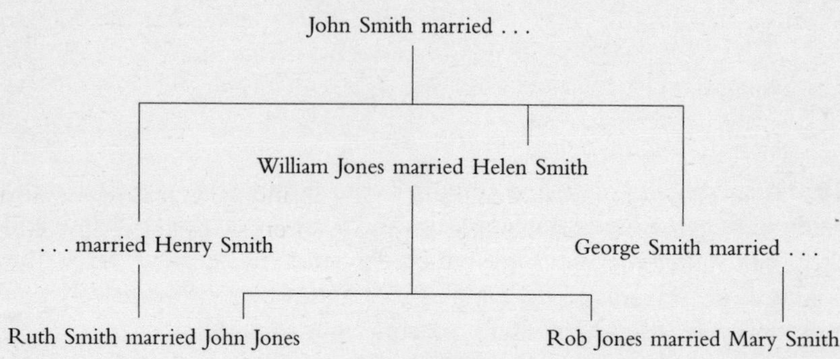

The legal limitations, by the way, might be summarised to read: a man may not marry his aunt or his niece or the daughter of his deceased wife's sister (though he may, as stated above, marry said sister). Nor may he marry his mother, his grandmother, or his great-grandmother. This last bit may sound preposterous, we know, but solvers of puzzles partake of the quality which the Scots impute to kings: they are '*kittle cattle to shoe behind*' . . .

26. Obviously you've got this one figured out already, as it's super simple. The young man is Hannah Smith's *son*.

27. The family gathering consisted of seven people: two little girls and a boy, their mother and father, and their paternal grandparents. This accounts for everyone in their various familial roles.

28. c) As Andrea is the child of Jenny's ex-husband – not Jenny's present husband – there is no relation.

29. d) As Estelle and Jack are the children of Patsy's and Barbara's niece.

30. d) As Andrea and Evelyn are Maggie's half-sisters.

31. b) As Maggie is Verity's first cousin, Maggie's daughter Estelle is Verity's first cousin once removed, as 'removal' indicates the number of generations that separate two cousins from one another, so Estelle's daughter would be Verity's second cousin once removed.

32. a) As Nancy, Ben and Stephen are Verity's and Maggie's first cousins, they have the same relationship to any children that Estelle may have as Verity does.

33. d) As Pru is Jenny's daughter, Jenny's stepchildren would be both Maggie and Pru's step-siblings.

34. b) Stephen's cousin's stepmother opens up a line of familial relations that is completely 'unrelated' to Stephen's family, though if there were a terminology for that line we suppose the wife of Maggie and Pru's father would be Stephen's step-aunt, which more technically refers to the sister of one's own stepmother.

Verbal reasoning

35. Anger is a **type of** emotion; abhorrence is a **degree** of dislike; an ultimatum is **used to** coerce; a philanthropist is **characterised by** benevolence; someone who is conceited is **lacking** in self-awareness.

36.

i. b) Just as rain can *cause* a puddle, so too can heat *cause* evaporation. A lake, on the other hand, will not cause a flood (unless it rains and the lake becomes overflooded, but in that case it is the rain that is the cause); jealousy certainly does not cause trust, and we generally like to believe that education *combats* ignorance . . .

ii. c) In the same way that a stanza is a *part of* a sonnet, a paw is a *part of* a dog (usually). A computer is a *type of* machine, a house is *characterised by* – among other things – rooms, and colour is *made of* pigment. But you knew all this already.

iii. b) Does drawl mean to speak slowly? Yes! Does cultivate mean to grow slowly? No . . . Does pare mean to cut slowly? Erm, nope. Does spurt mean to expel slowly? Not quite. Does dawdle mean to walk slowly? We thinketh yes.

37.

i. d) Libraries are good for the study of all sorts of subjects, but as the statement specifically states that libraries contain books about the development of cultures, the best answer can't simply be based on our idea of libraries. Instead we must conclude that a library with many texts on the evolution of a culture is best for a student of history, as history is the subject which most charts the developments of culture. Since culture expands to include religion, but history is the study of both, religion is not the best answer. And since biography is the history of a person, not a culture, it isn't so great either. We assume libraries are best for students of literature because we think they read the most number of books.

ii. a) The clue, of course, is that the audience was 'confounded' by her position during the debate, which means her position must have been one that was seemingly in opposition to her usual one as a 'staunch defender' of women's rights.

38. Since antonyms are opposite words, those of you who spotted **clumsy**, **malaise**, **cowardly**, **sluggish** and **enduring** but did not circle them win gold stars! The five antonyms of **maladroit** (which means inefficient or clumsy) are: **dexterous**, **skilful**, **adept**, **systematic** and **efficient**, words we would, of course, use to describe our quiz-takers . . .

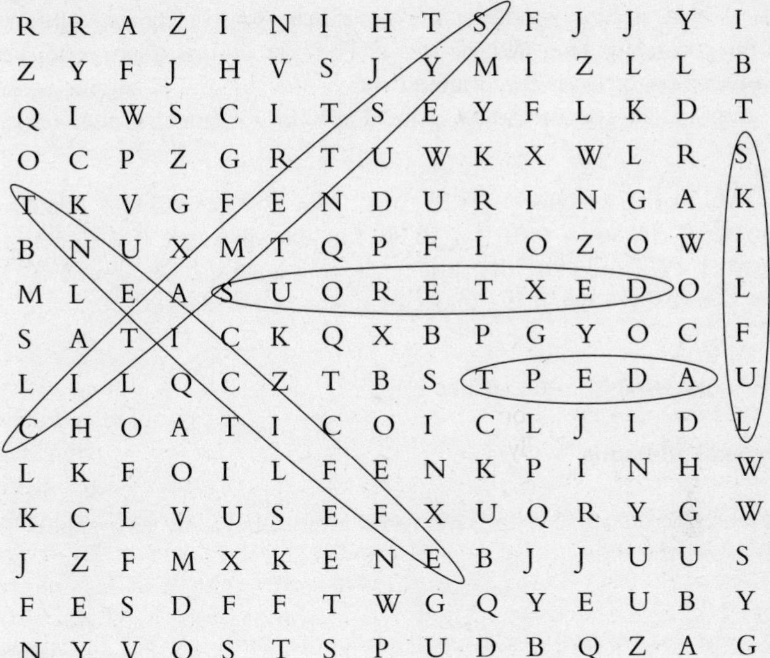

Riddles:

39. Old maid, spades, euchre, gin rummy, patience, whist, hearts, solitaire, happy families.

40. cite. All the words in group A, and 'cite' from group B, form another word if you add 'ex' to them:

solve (exsolve)
unpressed (unexpressed)
tent (extent)
cod (codex)
act (exact)
poll (pollex)
claim (exclaim)
pose (expose)
it (exit)
cite (excite)

41. a) They all have windows; b) They all have skin; c) They are all holes in the ground; d) They all have tails; e) They are all dogs (Pluto is Mickey Mouse's dog, Sirius is the brightest star in the sky and is known as 'the dog star', Laika was the Soviet space dog who was launched into orbit).

42. Thirty-five crowns = £8.75; nine 10ps = 90p; six 5ps = 30p; five pennies = 5p. So in total = £10.00. But why, pray tell, is it sometime between 1972 and 1981? Because (excepting some special, commemorative coins) that's when the 25p crown was in circulation.

43. Chloe is at 'the top of her game'.

Optical illusions

44. This blivet appears to have three prongs, but only two appear to rise from the base.

45. The two central circles are exactly the same size but the circles around them make them appear to be different sizes.

46. You should see two faces and also a vase. Which do you think best describes the image?

47.

a) False, but you knew that already . . . 'Christopher Columbus!' comes from the Italian navigator and explorer in honour of his rather unexpected arrival on San Salvador island in 1492, and is now also a euphemism for other more expletive phrases which also denote surprise.

b) True.

c) False. As far as we know there is no such Jean Anock because we made him up. The expression's proper namesake was John Hancock (1737–93), the Boston merchant and revolutionary patriot who was the first to sign the American Declaration of Independence and also the chap who signed his signature most prominently, 'so that no Britisher would have to use his spectacles to read it'.

d) True. And the comic itself was based on Momand's own attempts to keep up with his neighbours.

48. a) **The False Count**. In this cipher, the alphabet begins with T so its substitute is the number 1, meaning the rest of the cipher can be decoded with this key:

A	B	C	D	E	F	G	H	I	J	K	L	M	N	O	P	Q	R	S	T	U	V	W	X	Y	Z
8	9	10	11	12	13	14	15	16	17	18	19	20	21	22	23	24	25	26	1	2	3	4	5	6	7

Counting forwards from T as 1, H would be number 15 and E number 12. From then on, F=13, A=8, L=19, S=26. E=12, C=10, O=22, U=2, N=21, and T=1.

Do you know this trick? It involves a very deceptive sleight in which the conjurer leads his audience to suppose that he has many more cards in his hands than he really has. For example, let us suppose that the performer holds only six cards, while from the nature of his trick the audience believe he has eight. He holds the pack in his left hand, backs up, and keeps the front cards pointing in a slanting direction towards the stage. The first card is pushed by the thumb of the left hand into the right hand, the thumb of that hand drawing it away, and the hand itself moving away a trifle towards the right. Then the hands come together again and the next card is pushed off in the same way, falling on number one. Now the third card ought to follow, but at the very moment that the right hand is about to draw it away it is quickly drawn back by the left thumb on top of the cards in the left hand. The hands separate again, as in the case of the first two cards, as shown in the figure below.

Bear in mind that the performer counts 'one, two, three,' etc. whether or not a card leaves the left hand. So, when he counts 'three' this time, he has only two cards in his right hand. Then he continues 'four,' really counting a card into his hand; 'five' (drawing back the card), 'six, seven, eight'. Apparently he has eight cards in his right hand, when in fact he has only six. As there is always a sound when a card is drawn away, the performer is careful to imitate it when a false count is made by sliding his right thumb downward along the card just at the moment the left thumb draws it back.

b) **The Reunion.** If R is 14, then T=16, H=4, E=1, U=17, N=10, I=5, O=11, N=10.

The performer forces the Queen of Hearts on a lady in the audience. When it is returned the pack is shuffled and a rubber band is put around it lengthwise. It is then momentarily placed aside while the performer explains the situation. 'I noticed,' he says 'that in replacing the Queen of Hearts, which was drawn, the lady took no pains to put her side by side with the King. That is wrong. They should be together, and we must try to remedy the wrong.' He turns now to get the pack, but instead of taking the one just used he substitutes for it a prepared pack. From this the King and Queen of Hearts have been removed, after which a fine, small rubber band is placed, lengthwise, about the pack. The pack is then stood on one end on a table, opened in the middle, bookwise, and laid flat as shown in the figure below. The King and Queen are now laid, faces down, over the rubber band, and the part with the faces upward is folded over. Two or three cards are placed top and bottom of the pack and another rubber band is put around it, lengthwise, to keep the cards in place. Turning to his audience with this pack, he says, 'Let us hope that their exalted highnesses have met. Will your Majesties kindly make your appearance?' Removing the outside rubber band, but holding the pack tightly pressed together, the performer slightly relaxes his hold, when the two cards will rise slowly from the pack. 'Ah, that is well,' exclaims the conjurer. 'And now for a trip in an aeroplane,' saying which he relaxes the pressure entirely so that the two cards will go soaring into the air.

c) **The Top Change**. If A is Z, then each letter in the alphabet is substituted with the one that precedes it, so the cipher is:

ABCDEFGHIJKLMNOPQRSTUVWXYZ

ZABCDEFGHIJKLMNOPQRSTUVWXY

When the top card is to be changed the pack is held in the left hand, the thumb resting across the back and the fingers at the bottom. The card that is to be changed for the top card of the pack is held between the tips of the right-hand thumb and the forefinger, the thumb on top of the card and the forefinger below it. The hands are brought together for just a moment, and the left thumb pushes the top card of the pack an inch or so to the right. At the same time the card held in the right hand is laid on the top of the pack and slid back by the left thumb. At that moment the first and middle fingers of the right hand clip and carry off the original top card of the pack, as shown in the figure below. Care must be taken to bring the forefinger, which, with the thumb, is on top of the card to the bottom, thus replacing the second finger, so that the card will be between the thumb and forefinger. The slight noise which is unavoidable, must be reduced to a minimum, and as soon as the change is made the left hand is drawn away, but not too quickly, while the right hand is held motionless. The body must not be turned sideways to the left at the critical moment, nor should the hands be brought together suddenly and then separated in a jerky fashion, as if something were snatched away. The necessary moves ought to be made in a natural, careless way in the course of the remarks that accompany the trick. While it may seem that these moves will be apparent to every one, they are, in fact, almost imperceptible.

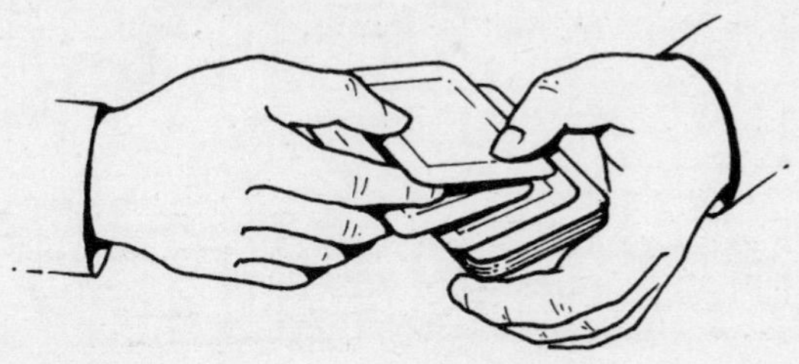

49. a). 'Ground floor: Perfumery, Stationery and Leather Goods' from *Are You Being Served?* (1972–85).

b) 'Who do you think you are kidding, Mr Hitler, if you think we're on the run?' from *Dad's Army* (1968–77).

c) 'Stick a pony in me pocket, I'll fetch the suitcase from the van' from *Only Fools and Horses* (1981–2003).

50. a)

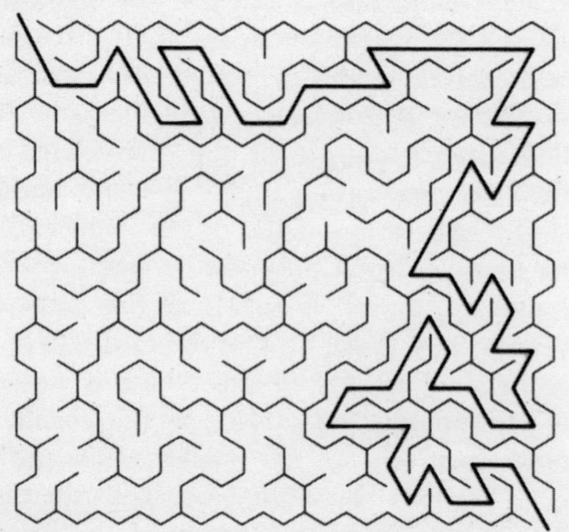

b)

SCIENCE

We are all scientists. On some small level at least we all believe certain facts about the world around us. Most of us are in agreement that the earth is a planet orbiting the sun, and that our hearts pump blood around our bodies, that babies do not arrive because of the assistance of long-legged wading birds, and that if you jump off the top of a tall building you will fall rapidly through the air until you meet the pavement below. These seemingly obvious truths were not always held to be self-evident and it is thanks to the enquiring minds of men and women stretching back to the dawn of civilisation that we have this measure of understanding about our universe. Science is brilliant because it has something for everyone: whether you are interested in the minutiae of an ant's daily existence or the magical hold the giant nuclear-powered star we call the sun has over our lives, the delights of Physics, Chemistry and Biology are open for your delectation. Below we will check that you were concentrating in class and not just trying to melt your eraser in the Bunsen burners and shove copper sulphate down the back of your lab partner's uniform.

1. Who did our greatest living boffin, Stephen Hawking, describe as 'responsible for the birth of modern science'?

a) Claudius Ptolemaeus
b) Nicolaus Copernicus
c) Galileo Galilei
d) René Descartes

2. Which double Nobel-Prize-winning scientist, who was also the parent of another Nobel-winner, named one of the elements they discovered after their country of birth?

a) Sir Humphrey Davy
b) Albert Ghiorso
c) Daniel Rutherford
d) Marie Curie

3. If you have children you may not remember what energy feels like, but can you remember all the different forms? Which of these are NOT types of energy?

a) Kinetic
b) Nervite
c) Radiant
d) Dormant
e) Magnetic
f) Vibrant

4. Albert Einstein's elegant equation $E=mc^2$ is as familiar as *A Brief History of Time* and about as readily understood, although you're less likely to find it hanging about on bookshelves attempting to make the owners look clever. What do these legendary letters stand for?

a) E: Energy, m: Mass, c: Speed of light
b) E: Energy, m: Magnitude, c: Speed of sound
c) E: Electricity, m: Mass, c: Acceleration
d) E: Energy, m: Magic, c: Crystals

5. You're not getting off that lightly. What does $E=mc^2$ mean? Rote learning won't help you here, so spark up your synapses and concentrate hard.

a) Mass and energy can travel at an equivalent speed when acceleration is directly proportional to the mass.
b) Mass and energy are interchangeable; they can be converted into each other.
c) Mass travelling at the square of the speed of light will have a greater magnitude than mass travelling at the square of the speed of sound.
d) Light can be converted into mass when it contains the correct amount of energy.

6. Some astronomical identification for you stargazers here. In Greek mythology the hero Perseus slew Medusa, the mother of the useful flying horse Pegasus, and then kept himself busy by rescuing Andromeda, daughter of Cassiopeia and Cepheus, from the sea monster Cetus. Can you match these classical characters to their constellations?

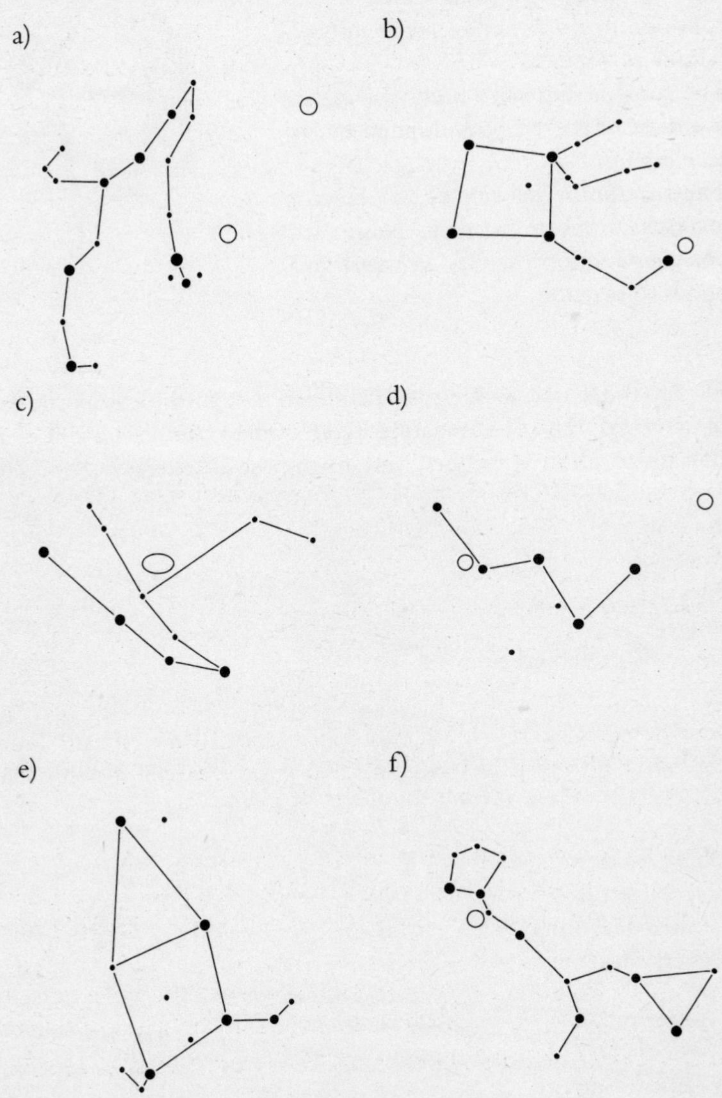

7. It is often forgotten that the famous catflap inventor and keen alchemist, Sir Isaac Newton, also came up with three influential laws of motion. Which of the four laws below is the fake?

a) If a body is at rest or moving at a constant speed in a straight line, it will continue to do so unless acted upon by a force.
b) The force acting on a body is equal to the mass of the body multiplied by its acceleration.
c) The maximum velocity of an object is inversely proportional to its mass.
d) For every action there is an equal and opposite reaction.

8. You may think that locking your toddlers out in the garden to run wild is a useful way of dissipating their endless *joie de vivre* but, in scientific terms, what is the best way to dispose of energy?

a) Burn it
b) Freeze it
c) Bury it
d) Split it
e) None of the above

9. Which modest master of physics said: 'If I have seen further than others it is by standing on the shoulders of giants.'

a) Albert Einstein
b) Isaac Newton
c) Stephen Hawking
d) Robert Hooke

10. We are all grateful to lightning for making golf more exciting to watch. But which three of these are NOT types of lightning?

a) Cloud-to-ground
b) Cloud-to-cloud
c) Surface-to-air
d) Bead
e) Whip
f) Dry
g) Wet
h) Ribbon
i) Staccato

11. You are travelling in a car at 60 mph. A fly buzzing along towards you minding its own business at 5 mph hits your windscreen leaving a grisly viscous smear. According to Newton's third law of motion, which of the two forces is greatest?

a) The force on the fly.
b) The force on the windscreen.
c) The forces are the same.
d) The forces cancel each other out.

12. Quick thinking required here. What is the speed of light?

a) 300,000,000 km per second
b) 300,000 km per second
c) 3,000 km per second
d) About 70 mph, officer

13. If you were a serious, white-coated researcher, noting down measurements of frequency in hertz, which of the following would you be studying?

Longitudinal waves
Mexican waves
Transverse waves
Marcel waves

14. There are three types of radioactive emission, but which is the scary Geiger counter-rattling, time-for-an-uncomfortable-shower one?

Alpha
Beta
Charlie
Gamma

15. We're sure you remember the nifty model of the coloured balls revolving around each other from the Science lab at school. We all learned the composition of atoms as one of the first lessons of Physics but can you remember the key facts about this most essential ingredient of everything? Which of these can't be found in an atom?

a) Positron
b) Electron
c) Neutron
d) Quark

16. The most well-known face – and crazy hairstyle – of Physics is undoubtedly Nobel Prize-winner and all-round scientific superstar Albert Einstein. Fill in the blanks with the words in the box below to complete this quote from the great man:

truth, possessions, ideals, beauty, courage, kindness, luxury, trite

'The ______ which have lighted my way, and time after time have given me new ______ to face life cheerfully, have been ______, ______, and ______. The ______ subjects of human efforts, ______, outward success, ______ have always seemed to me contemptible.'

17. It's time to undertake your own Battle of the Planets: rearrange the various heavenly bodies of the solar system in order of the size of their diameters, with the smallest first.

Sun
Mercury
Venus
Earth
Mars
Jupiter
Saturn
Uranus
Neptune

18. Poor dear, angry, neglected seventeenth-century scientist Robert Hooke never felt he got his due for his discoveries and investigations. Let us honour him by asking – what is Hooke's Law?

a) A law of gravity
b) A law of motion
c) A law of thermodynamics
d) A law of elasticity

19. It is a wonderful aspect of scientific endeavour that individuals, poring over their microscopes, fixing their eyes on the heavens, or scratching out their arcane mathematical equations, can arrive at conclusions that totally change our concept of the world in which we live. Match the following game-changing theories to their creators:

Heliocentrism	Isaac Newton
Special Theory of Relativity	Charles Darwin
Natural Selection	Nicolaus Copernicus
Theory of Gravity	Albert Einstein

20. Larking about with the Vandegraff generator and rubbing balloons on your head in Science lessons at school made for good fun and bad hair, but what, on an atomic level, was actually happening to make your hair stick to the balloon?

a) The balloon removed some of the electrons from your hair.
b) The balloon deposited protons in your hair.
c) The neutrons in both the hair and the balloon were charged.
d) The protons are forced out of both the hair and the balloon.

21. What is the Theory of Everything?

a) An attempt to reconcile the theory of gravity with accepted subatomic processes to generate an equation describing the earth's orbit.
b) An attempt to reconcile the differing causal theories of climate change to generate a model of future weather patterns.
c) An attempt to reconcile quantum mechanics and general relativity to generate a complete picture of the universe.
d) An attempt to reconcile religious theory with scientific theory to generate a complete picture of the human condition.

22. Erwin Schrödinger is hailed as one of the fathers of quantum mechanics for his centrally important wave theory. However, he is more widely known to the common man for his 1935 feline thought experiment. Is the cat in Schrödinger's box dead or alive?

a) Dead
b) Alive
c) Dead and alive
d) Come again?

23. Hello Dolly! Why did a white, woolly quadruped become the talk of the town in scientific circles and beyond in the mid-1990s?

a) Dolly was the first sheep on Mars.
b) Dolly was the first cloned sheep.
c) Dolly was the first mammal cloned from adult cells.
d) Dolly was the first sheep to have her genome sequenced.

24. Look at the Periodic Table below. Rearrange the individual letters from the element symbols for Curium, Cobalt, Lithium, Tantalum, Palladium, Europium and Nitrogen to give you a word which you may or may not feel applies to this question.

THE PERIODIC TABLE

1 H 1.0079																	2 He 4.0026
3 Li 6.941	4 Be 9.0122											5 B 10.811	6 C 12.011	7 N 14.007	8 O 15.999	9 F 18.998	10 Ne 20.180
11 Na 22.990	12 Mg 24.305											13 Al 26.982	14 Si 28.086	15 P 30.974	16 S 32.065	17 Cl 35.453	18 Ar 39.948
19 K 39.098	20 Ca 40.078	21 Sc 44.956	22 Ti 47.867	23 V 50.942	24 Cr 51.996	25 Mn 54.938	26 Fe 55.845	27 Co 58.933	28 Ni 58.693	29 Cu 63.546	30 Zn 65.38	31 Ga 69.723	32 Ge 72.64	33 As 74.922	34 Se 78.96	35 Br 79.904	36 Kr 83.798
37 Rb 85.468	38 Sr 87.62	39 Y 88.906	40 Zr 91.224	41 Nb 92.906	42 Mo 95.96	43 Tc -	44 Ru 101.07	45 Rh 102.91	46 Pd 106.42	47 Ag 107.87	48 Cd 112.41	49 In 114.82	50 Sn 118.71	51 Sb 121.76	52 Te 127.60	53 I 126.90	54 Xe 131.29
55 Cs 132.91	56 Ba 137.33	57–71	72 Hf 178.49	73 Ta 180.95	74 W 183.84	75 Re 186.21	76 Os 190.23	77 Ir 192.22	78 Pt 195.08	79 Au 196.97	80 Hg 200.59	81 Tl 204.38	82 Pb 207.2	83 Bi 208.98	84 Po -	85 At -	86 Rn -
87 Fr -	88 Ra -	89–103	104 Rf -	105 Db -	106 Sg -	107 Bh -	108 Hs -	109 Mt -	110 Ds -	111 Rg -							
			57 La 138.91	58 Ce 140.12	59 Pr 140.91	60 Nd 144.24	61 Pm -	62 Sm 150.36	63 Eu 151.96	64 Gd 157.25	65 Tb 158.93	66 Dy 162.50	67 Ho 164.93	68 Er 167.26	69 Tm 168.93	70 Yb 173.05	71 Lu 174.97
			89 Ac -	90 Th 232.04	91 Pa 231.04	92 U 238.03	93 Np -	94 Pu -	95 Am -	96 Cm -	97 Bk -	98 Cf -	99 Es -	100 Fm -	101 Md -	102 No -	103 Lr -

25. We generally think of acids as corrosive substances you can use to get rid of the evidence that you've murdered your wife. It is true that acids are often caustic, but their opposites, alkalis, can also have this property. The official definition of an acid is a substance with a high concentration of hydrogen ions that scores less than seven on the acidity-measuring pH scale. Alkalis are substances that react with acids to neutralise them and have a pH of more than seven. Which of the liquids below are acidic and which are alkaline?

a) Milk
b) Pure water
c) Oven cleaner
d) Tomato juice
e) Bleach

26. If you are of a certain age you will recall that Tony Hart's little Plasticine pal Morph could change from a solid little brown man into a puddle of liquid clay at will. Morph lived by his own rules, but the rest of creation observes certain principles when solids, gases or liquids change state. What is the name of the process that refers to the change from a solid to a gas, missing out the liquid phase?

a) Sublimation
b) Subjugation
c) Subversion
d) Ridiculation

27. Now for the practical. Let's see if you can make a human being. And no cheating like Dr Frankenstein: you must start from scratch. You will need just six elements to create 99% of the human body. But which six?

a) Osmium
b) Oxygen
c) Mercury
d) Carbon
e) Tin
f) Hydrogen
g) Nitrogen
h) Barium
i) Iridium
j) Calcium
k) Phosphorus
l) Radon

28. What is this sign trying to tell you?

a) Complex one-way system up ahead
b) Biohazard
c) Explosive
d) Radioactive

29. When different elements collide and combine, chemical reactions result. Diana Ross's love of Chemistry led her to sing a passionate song about chain reactions, a special brand of chemical event where the results of a reaction keep it going. Match the following chemical reactions to their characteristics.

Endothermic reaction	Involves the gain of electrons
Neutralisation	Involves the loss of electrons
Oxidation	Is accompanied by a drop in temperature
Reduction	Produces a salt

30. The eagle-eyed among you will have noticed in the illustration on page 221 that each element in the periodic table has its very own unique atomic number. This tells you the number of protons in the nucleus of an atom of that element. Not terribly handy information to have on hand in everyday life we grant you, but very important in your quest to understand the chemical make-up of the world around you. Match up the following atomic numbers and their elements:

1	Iodine
53	Gold
79	Hydrogen
111	Roentgenium

31. A closer look at the natural world often reveals beautifully intricate, interdependent systems, whirring like the many cogs inside a daedal clock mechanism. When you next walk past a humble tree, think about all of the creatures and plants that rely upon it and the ways in which they contribute to its existence and it contributes to theirs. Check your orientation in this microuniverse by using the words in the box below to fill in the blanks in the passage underneath.

population, ecosystem, niche, habitat, community

A tropical rainforest is an ____, in which a mahogany tree is a ____. On the tree is a ____ of insects, one of which is an ant ____. The ____ of the ant is to be the primary consumer of the leaves.

32. What can be pinnate, palmate, linear or lanceolate?

a) Solids
b) Blood cells
c) Atoms
d) Leaves

33. What crucial, life-giving process does this equation describe?

$6CO_2 + 6H_2O \longrightarrow$ (in the presence of light energy) $\longrightarrow$
$C_6H_{12}O_6 + 6O_2$

34. And this one?

$C_6H_{12}O_6 + 6O_2 \longrightarrow$ (in the presence of enzymes) $\longrightarrow$
$6CO_2 + 6H_2O +$ energy

35. Let's play Biological Guess Who now. I've got anthers, pistils and style. What am I?

a) Cowboy
b) Leaf
c) Flower
d) Tree

36. We would never suggest that you are anything but special and unique. But humour us for a moment and categorise yourself according to influential eighteenth-century Swedish biologist Carolus Linnaeus's rules of classification:

Kingdom: ____
Phylum: ____
Class: ____
Order: ____
Family: ____
Genus: ____
Species: ____

37. Barring any major surgery, how many major organs should you have? Can you name them?

a) 8
b) 16
c) 24
d) 32

38. Why are leaves green?

a) Because chlorophyll is green and is the most abundant pigment within a leaf cell, masking the yellow/orange/brown carotenoid and the red/purple anthocyanin pigments.
b) Because chlorophyll is blue and carotenoids are yellow/orange/brown and together they produce the green.
c) Because green is the only colour reflected by the leaf.
d) Because they are jealous of the showy flowers.

39. Another bloody word search. Can you prove you're not a clot by finding EIGHT of the constituent parts of blood floating around in the gobbledegook below?

Q	U	E	R	Y	T	H	R	O	C	Y	T	E	S	P
U	P	Y	I	K	H	G	Y	I	A	Y	R	C	V	O
A	D	L	E	U	C	O	C	Y	T	E	S	O	G	T
S	P	K	A	S	A	D	O	L	S	F	P	R	W	H
S	H	L	F	S	X	H	J	L	K	I	Z	P	D	B
A	A	S	X	C	M	J	V	Y	B	N	M	U	Q	W
B	G	D	G	C	K	A	U	M	O	P	Z	S	R	E
M	O	N	F	A	P	N	P	P	I	U	W	C	T	Y
R	C	G	N	X	Y	T	J	H	L	G	F	L	U	U
C	Y	T	Z	A	Q	I	H	O	Y	T	J	E	I	P
R	T	H	R	O	M	B	O	C	Y	T	E	S	N	P
D	E	S	R	V	Z	O	S	Y	F	T	P	C	T	O
R	S	Y	A	W	R	D	Y	T	J	H	I	D	E	I
X	R	C	U	G	K	I	D	E	R	H	L	C	R	U
Y	E	P	H	G	L	E	Y	S	D	N	G	D	W	T
S	N	T	E	G	N	S	G	H	E	W	J	E	Q	G

40. You are standing in your local bookshop. There is only one copy of the *Homework for Grown-ups Quiz Book* left. If you do not secure it for your Aunt Maude there will be hell to pay. Another browser has spotted the book and is advancing even as you reach toward the shelf. Before your fingers brush the book's elegant cover you find you have been rugby-tackled to the ground. Your opponent kneels over you brandishing the coveted volume and looks a lot like he's going to thwack you with it. Your endocrine system kicks into action offering you two response options. But which options are they?

a) Freeze or flee
b) Fight or flight
c) Slap or tickle
d) Bolt or bawl

41. Remember the boy at school who ate an eyeball during dissection class? Not that we wish to regurgitate such unpleasant memories, but which two of the following would have been swilling around his stomach?

a) Aqueous humour
b) Sensov Humour
c) Vitreous Humour
d) Gelatinous Humour
e) Humerus

42. Ah, your glorious grey matter. Freak yourself out by thinking about your brain right now; yes, your unique, exceptional personality is contained in one of those wrinkly, jelly-like loaves, just like everyone else's. Match up the different parts of your brain with the processes they control below.

Cerebrum	Digestion, blood pressure, breathing
Brainstem	Growth, water balance
Cerebellum	Senses, speech, thought, memory
Hypothalamus	Muscular activity
Pituitary Gland	Body temperature, sleep, hunger, thirst

43. What colour is deoxygenated blood?

a) Red
b) Green
c) Blue
d) Yellow

44. Who said, 'I think it's far more important than walking on the moon; not much has happened since walking on the moon,' and what was he talking about?

a) Albert Einstein on splitting the atom
b) Craig Venter on decoding the human genome
c) Stephen Hawking on the creation of the Large Hadron Collider at CERN
d) Crick and Watson on the double helix structure of DNA

45. As you settle down to Chateaubriand with Béarnaise sauce, Pommes Pont-Neuf and French beans, your digestive system creaks into action. Where would you find your much-abused duodenum, jejunum and ileum?

a) Stomach
b) Small intestine
c) Large intestine
d) Pancreas

46. Nociception, or the perception of pain, is an unpleasant but very important factor in human survival. When you accidentally slam your fingers in the car door, you are probably aware that it is your nerves that kindly transfer the sensation from your poor, injured hand to your brain where it can register pain, distress and wrath at the stupid motor vehicle for being so badly designed as to allow this travesty. The human nervous system is divided into two parts: the central nervous system (CNS) and the peripheral nervous system (PNS). The PNS in turn can be broken down into three parts. Which three?

a) The reactive nervous system
b) The somatic nervous system
c) The sensory nervous system
d) The autonomic nervous system
e) The supersonic nervous system

47. Where would you find the corpora cavernosa? We don't suggest you look for them now unless you are with people who know you intimately and will respect you in the morning.

a) The penis
b) The testicles
c) The buttocks
d) The urethra

48. Laid end to end, your ____ would stretch to the moon and back about 130,000 times. What on earth (and beyond) is it?

a) Large and small intestines
b) Veins
c) DNA
d) Ignorance

49. Headache destroyer, blood thinner and all-round wonder-drug, aspirin, was developed from a natural source – what was it?

a) Coal dust
b) Chytridiomycota fungi
c) Willow bark
d) Shark fins

50. If a tree falls in a forest and there is no one around to hear it, does it make a sound?

a) Yes, of course it bloody well does, it still smashes into other trees and creates sound wave vibrations.

b) No, a sound is a vibration transmitted by the ear to our brains and recognised there as such; if there are no ears to hear, there will be no sound.

SCIENCE ANSWERS

1. c) Hawking doffed his scientific cap to the Renaissance genius, Galileo Galilei, because he identified Galileo as the first philosopher-scientist-mathematician to believe that man was capable of understanding how the world works, and because he had the audacity to come into conflict with the all-powerful, and less than forward-thinking, Catholic Church in the course of his studies. Galileo was condemned by the Inquisition for his support of Copernicus's theory that the earth rotates round the sun, rather than vice versa.

2. d) Scientific heroine Marie Sklowdowska Curie (1867–1934) discovered the elements polonium and radium with her husband Pierre in 1898. She won the Nobel Prize in Chemistry in 1911 for this breakthrough (her first Nobel was in Physics in 1903 for her research into radioactivity). She named polonium after the Latin word for Poland, 'Polonia'. Her daughter Irène Joliot-Curie won the Nobel Prize in Chemistry with her husband in 1935 for their discovery of artificial radioactivity. We bet the conversation round that family dinner table was pretty impressive.

3. b), d) and f). Kinetic energy is the energy of movement, radiant energy is a posh way of saying 'light' and magnetic energy is . . . wait for it . . . the energy held in magnets.

4. a) Nowadays it is conventional Physics shorthand to use the letter 'c' to stand for 'the speed of light'. It is thought that this either comes from the Latin word '*celeritas*' meaning 'speed' or, simply, 'constant'. In the nineteenth century the capital letter 'V' was more often used for this purpose.

5. b) Mass and energy can be converted into each other and are essentially expressions of the same thing. You can find out the amount of energy that could be released from a piece of matter by multiplying its mass by the speed of light squared. As the speed of light squared is such a large number even a tiny amount of mass can be converted into a huge amount of energy, a discovery that sadly led to the Manhattan Project and the creation of the atomic bomb.

6.

a) Perseus
b) Pegasus
c) Andromeda
d) Cassiopeia
e) Cepheus
f) Cetus

7. c)
a) is the first law, the law of inertia, which rules that an object in motion will stay in motion until it is acted upon by an outside force; b) is the second law which says that a force acting on an object is equal to its mass multiplied by its acceleration – or, more snappily, F=ma; d) is the third law which dictates that every action has an equal and opposite reaction, probably the most familiar of the three.

8. e) Energy cannot be destroyed or created, only converted. This a marvellous, magical scientific fact that means that everything that has ever existed has been made up of the same stuff, endlessly being recycled through the universe.

9. b) Isaac Newton wrote this line in a letter to his colleague and rival Robert Hooke: 'What Descartes did was a good step. You have added much several ways, and especially in taking the colours of thin plates into philosophical consideration. If I have seen a little further it is by standing on the shoulders of giants.' Dubbed 'England's Leonardo', Robert Hooke was a multitalented scientist as well as being an architect, the inventor of Hooke's Law and the sash window and the man responsible for the use of the word 'cell' in Biology. Men of genius in those days certainly kept themselves busy. He also claimed to have told Newton his ideas about gravity which Sir Isaac then developed into his famous theory. Hooke was miffed not to receive more credit for this.

10. c), e) and g). Lightning occurs when storm clouds are charged by the movement and collision of water droplets and ice. The upper part of the cloud becomes positive and the lower part negative. As opposites attract, this causes a positive charge to build up on the ground beneath the cloud. The charge concentrates around any vertical structures such as trees, lampposts or golfers, which then take the full force of the lightning.

11. c) The forces are the same but because the poor fly's mass is so much smaller it comes off rather worse than the car.

12. b) We think you'll agree that light is a pretty zippy customer. A light year is how far light would travel in one year: 9.46 trillion km. To put that in perspective, the Milky Way is 100,000 light years in diameter.

13. a) Sound waves are measured in hertz and they are longitudinal waves, meaning that the vibrations of the wave move in the same direction as its forward movement. Light and water waves are transverse waves, where the vibrations of the wave move at right angles to its forward movement. Mexican waves are co-ordinated celebratory actions by crowds of people at sporting occasions where individuals stand up and raise their arms in turn around the arena. Marcel waves are a wavy style of hairdo popular in the 1920s and 30s.

14. d) Gamma is a very short electromagnetic wave which can pass through metals and human tissue. Exposure to unhealthy doses can cause cancer and, in the case of Dr Bruce Banner, turn a person a putrid shade of green and make them cross. Gamma waves' destructive powers are used in sterilising processes and also to treat certain cancerous tumours as its penetrative properties can be harnessed and used in spookily futuristic-sounding gamma-knife surgery. Alpha and Beta particles can be contained by physical barriers. Charlie is a harmless chap and doesn't have much to do with any of this, so best leave him out of it.

15. a) Little wee quarks are components of protons and neutrons which can be found in the nuclei of atoms with electrons whizzing in orbit around them. A positron is actually an antimatter version of an electron.

16. 'The **ideals** which have lighted my way, and time after time have given me new **courage** to face life cheerfully, have been **kindness**, **beauty** and **truth.** The **trite** subjects of human efforts, **possessions**, outward success, **luxury** have always seemed to me contemptible.'

17.

Mercury	4,878 km
Mars	6,795 km
Venus	12,104 km
Earth	12,756 km
Neptune	50,538 km
Uranus	51,119 km
Saturn	120,537 km
Jupiter	142,985 km
Sun	1,392,000 km

18. d) Hooke's is a law of elasticity that says that the tension of a spring is proportional to the weight hanging from it.

19.

Heliocentrism	Nicolaus Copernicus
Special Theory of Relativity	Albert Einstein
Natural Selection	Charles Darwin
Theory of Gravity	Isaac Newton

20. a) Inside an atom you will find protons and neutrons cuddling up together in the nucleus with electrons floating around outside. Protons are positively charged, electrons are negatively charged and neutrons are not charged. Rubbing the balloon on your hair removes some of the negatively charged electrons from your hair and gives the balloon a negative charge. As electrons have been removed from your hair it becomes positively charged. Now your hair and the balloon are of opposite charge and as such are attracted to each other.

21. c) We hope you were able to reconcile your brain with the correct answer to generate smugness.

22. c) No need to call the RSPCA; Schrödinger's famous brain-cramping thought experiment was formulated to demonstrate the limitations of quantum mechanics in relation to classical physics. In quantum mechanics particles such as atoms can be in two or more different states at the same time. In classical physics, however, objects made of a larger number of atoms, such as a cat, cannot.

The scenario is as follows: a cat is locked in a box with a radioactive isotope that has a 50/50 chance of decaying. If it does decay the cat will be killed. If it does not decay then Tiddles will merely be irritated at being shut in a box. When the box is closed it is not possible to know what has happened to the isotope or whether the cat is dead or alive. Schrödinger postulated that because we can't observe what has happened then the isotope can be in both a decayed and non-decayed state at the same time and therefore the cat can be both dead and alive at the same time; something that clearly doesn't happen in classical physics. Clear? Try a cool compress and a little lie-down.

23. c) Dolly was the first mammal to be cloned using adult rather than embryonic cells. She was born on 5 July 1996 at the Roslin Institute in Scotland. A year earlier two other ewes called Megan and Morag had been cloned from embryonic cells. Dolly was cloned using DNA from a six-year-old sheep and many believe this is the reason she died relatively young in 2003. However, she has left her hoof print in the history of genetic research for ever.

24. Cm, Co, Li, Ta, Pd, Eu, N. UNCOMPLICATED

25.

a) Milk – Acidic: pH of 6
b) Pure water – Neutral: pH7
c) Oven cleaner – Alkaline: pH13
d) Tomato juice – Acidic: pH4
e) Bleach – Alkaline: pH12

26. a) Sublimation. Dry ice is solid carbon dioxide that sublimes directly into gaseous carbon dioxide. Mothballs also sublime, their gases fill every crease and seam, leaving the pesky garment-munchers no place to hide.

27. b), d), f), g), j) and k). Oxygen, carbon, hydrogen, nitrogen, calcium and phosphorus are the dominant elements in our bodies. We also contain small amounts of other elements such as aluminium, arsenic, boron, bromine, cadmium, chlorine, chromium, cobalt, copper, fluorine, germanium, iodine, iron, magnesium, manganese, molybdenum, nickel, potassium, selenium, silicon, sodium, sulphur, tin, titanium, tungsten, vanadium and zinc.

28. b) If you saw this sign on a container you would be unwise to unscrew the top, slosh the contents into a highball glass, top it up with tonic and a slice of lemon and slug it back. This sign means biohazard. Logically enough, a biohazard is a biological substance that is hazardous to humans. It can signal viruses or bacteria from the severity of chickenpox to Ebola and, depending on the level of hazard, can be an indication that you should think about wearing some disposable gloves or wrap yourself up in a full Hazmat suit.

29.

An endothermic reaction is accompanied by a drop in temperature.
Neutralisation produces a salt.
Oxidation involves the loss of electrons.
Reduction involves the gain of electrons.

30.

1	Hydrogen
53	Iodine
79	Gold
111	Roentgenium

31. A tropical rainforest is an **ecosystem**, in which a mahogany tree is a **habitat.** On the tree is a **community** of insects, one of which is an ant **population**. The **niche** of the ant is to be the primary consumer of the leaves.

32. d) These are common leaf shapes, along with trifoliate, cordate and acicular. The word 'pinnate' comes from the Latin word for 'feather' as these leaves are shaped like feathers. Palmate leaves have four or more lobes or leaflets making them shaped something like the palm of a hand, albeit one that has been in a bit of an accident. The word 'linear' comes from the Latin for 'line' and as you might expect these leaves are long, narrow and straight. You'll readily recognise a lanceolate leaf when you come across one as it will look like the head of a lance. The word 'trifoliate' comes from the Latin for 'three' and 'leaves' and these have three leaflets, like a clover. Cordate leaves are romantically shaped and their label comes from the Latin word for 'heart'. 'Acicular' comes from the Latin for 'needle' so I think by now you get the picture and can guess what these leaves look like.

33. This is the equation for photosynthesis. This is the process by which plants change energy from light into glucose to feed themselves. As they then go on to feed all the animals and people of the world and produce oxygen as a by-product this is a pretty important job. Maybe give your spider plant a grateful pat next time you're passing its dusty windowsill.

34. This is the equation for respiration. This is the cellular process that occurs in all living organisms where glucose is used to make energy, usually by combining it with oxygen. Also a pretty impressive feat, we think you'll agree. Perhaps next time you are considering a tattoo, these two spectacular sums would be good candidates?

35. c) These are all intimate parts of a flower. Anthers are an element of the plant's male part, the stamen. They produce and contain pollen. The pistil is the female part of the flower made up of the stigma, style and ovary. The style is the long stalk that holds up the stigma and the stigma's job is to receive pollen, either from the plant's own stamen or from a different plant (possibly delivered by a helpful bee). This pollen travels down the style to the ovary where it fertilises the plant, leading it to produce seeds which grow into lovely plant babies.

36.

Kingdom	Animal
Phylum	Chordata
Class	Mammalia
Order	Primate
Family	Hominidae
Genus	Homo
Species	Homo sapiens

37. b) Spectacles, testicles, wallet and watch . . . No, the real list of your vital ingredients is: brain, larynx, bronchi, lungs, heart, liver, gall bladder, spleen, stomach, pancreas, small intestine, large intestine, kidneys, appendix, genitals, skin. All present and correct? Phew.

38. a) The pigment chlorophyll is continually being produced in the summer, but when autumn arrives and the days become shorter and everyone just feels a little more melancholy and chilly, production slows down and eventually stops. This unmasks the carotenoid and anthocyanin pigments and creates the wondrous display of yellow, orange, brown and red leaves that make autumn worthwhile.

39. Plasma, corpuscles, erythrocytes, leucocytes, thrombocytes, phagocytes, lymphocytes, antibodies.

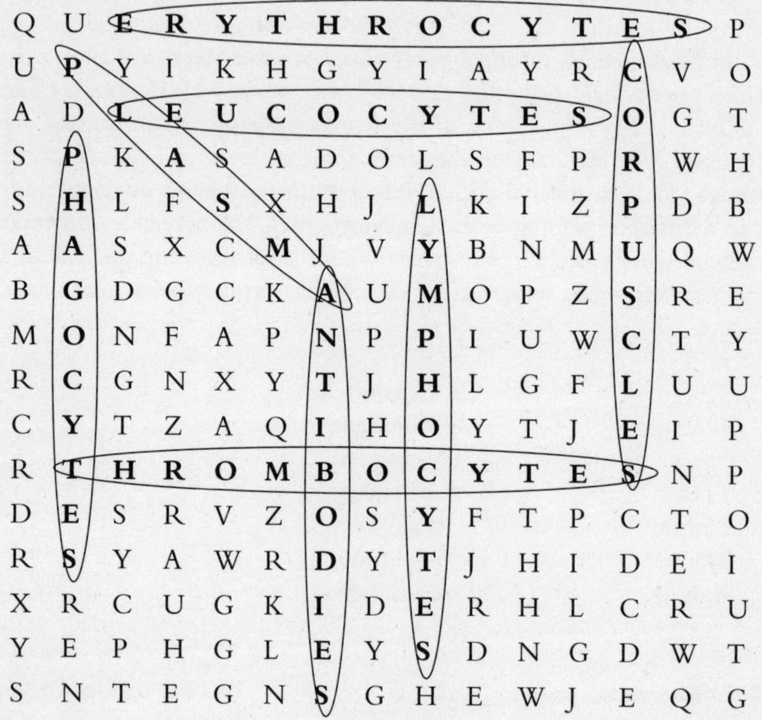

40. b) The endocrine system is made up of glands that secrete hormones which stimulate processes such as growth, saliva and sweat production, fertility and digestion. In threatening scenarios the endocrine system stimulates the adrenal glands to produce greater quantities of adrenalin which prepares the body for physical exertion, be it brawling in the aisles or running for the hills.

41. a) and c). Aqueous humour is the nutrient-filled fluid located in front of the lens and vitreous humour is the clear jelly that sits behind the lens. Mmm, delicious!

42.

Cerebrum	Senses, speech, thought, memory
Brainstem	Digestion, blood pressure, breathing
Cerebellum	Muscular activity
Hypothalamus	Body temperature, sleep, hunger, thirst
Pituitary Gland	Growth, water balance

43. a) Yes, the blue-blood theory is a myth perpetuated by school textbook diagrams (which also might make you think that your blood has little arrows swimming in it pointing out the direction of flow). Although your veins might appear blue, the blood inside is still red, albeit a darker shade. The presence of oxygen in blood cells makes their haemoglobin molecules turn bright red. When the oxygen leaves the cells, as the blood helpfully delivers it to the organs, the haemoglobin turns darker.

44. b) The genome is a complete set of genetic instructions also known as the 'book of life'. In 2003 the Human Genome Project, of which Craig Venter's company Celera Genomics was a major part, finished identifying the sequence of every human gene. It sequenced around three billion letters of molecular code. The interpretation of the code is still in its early stages but it is anticipated that it will lead to advances in medicine and biotechnology.

45. b) This five-metre length of gut is responsible for absorbing the nutrients of your supper. It would probably love you more if you ate fish and rice every now and then. Just a thought.

46. b), c) and d). The somatic nervous system comprises nerves that send information from your CNS to your effectors, the parts of your body that perform actions (muscles, glands). The sensory nervous system comprises nerves that transfer information from your sensory receptors (skin, taste buds, ears, nose, eyes) to the CNS. The autonomic nervous system stimulates effectors to carry out crucial unconscious actions like breathing, hormone release and digestion.

47. a) The corpora cavernosa are the two chambers running along inside the penis that fill up with blood to produce an erection. Next time you are planning an evening of seduction and dirty talk, impress your partner by referencing them.

48. c) DNA is the body's genetic instruction manual. It tells our bodies how to grow and repair themselves. It is present in the cells of nearly all living things and in most humans it is tucked away neatly in the forty-six chromosomes that are found in the nuclei of our cells.

49. c) Right back to Hippocrates' time, willow bark has been used in pain-relieving medicines. Today aspirin is one of the most widely used drugs across the world. It has been used to lower blood pressure for decades and recent research has suggested that it may also have anti-carcinogenic properties.

50. a) or b) You can argue until you're blue in the face, it's unlikely you're going to come to a definitive conclusion. Give yourself a point for trying.

HOME ECONOMICS

Gone are the days when a double Home Ec. period meant the chance to turn your attention away from Maths and towards rustling up the perfect pineapple upside-down cake. These days the subject is as much about calorie counting, the body mass index and charting our carbon footprint as it is about creating a stupendous chicken chow mein. But in a world that is moving ever and ever faster, while our riches seem to get fewer and fewer, we can take great comfort in the fact that simple things can bring us vast pleasures too, and enjoy reminding ourselves that our grandmothers may have had the upper hand when it comes to mending and making do. So in this stimulating section of our scrutiny and study, we'll take a tour from the basics of home health to the finer points of crockery identification, and we'll be asking you to identify bogus energy efficiency tips as well as rediscover the lost art of carving . . . So please have your knives sharpened, your pinnies on and your dusters to the ready, it's time to awaken your inner domestic god.

1. The fine art of carving was, until recently, as essential a part of a gentleman's education as a knowledge of horsemanship, swordsmanship and dancing. In the old days, carving was a rite. With impressive, leisurely dignity, the host set about dismembering the fare, with the result that the first person served was just about ready for pudding before the careful carver had lopped off his own meat – one always serves oneself last, of course.

So, what are the first essentials for carving?

a) A clean cutting board and serving tray.
b) A steel pan and an emery stone.
c) A good carving knife and fork.
d) A damp cloth close by to mop up pesky spills.

2. If you should ever have occasion to carve a suckling pig, how should the pig be served?

a) With the nose separated from the body.
b) With the head separated from the body.
c) With the legs and ribs removed.
d) With just the ribs removed.

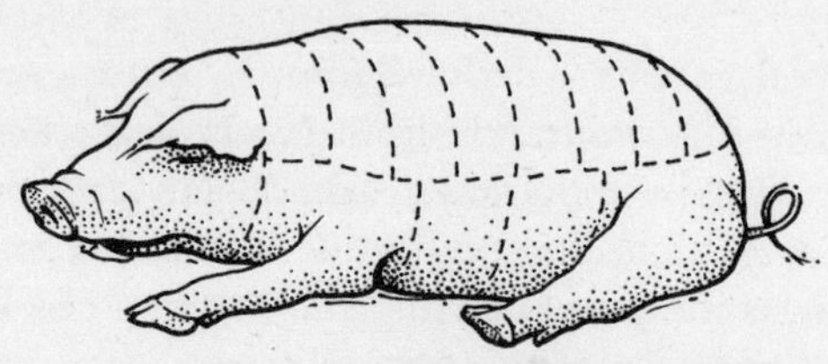

3. Even the most spotlessly clean homes are at times visited by pernicious pests. Simple and effective precautions and remedies are usually all that is needed to control them and an additional knowledge of their habits helps you get the measure of your particular tiny enemies. Name the verminous interlopers described below:

a) These neat and well-organised insects are harmless and will enter a house in a steady stream in search of food and then immediately return to their nests, which are outside. The best way to repel them, therefore, is by destroying their homes with boiling water, painting sticky tanglefoot across doorsteps and sprinkling borax (found in health-food shops) across their routes indoors.
b) This small, round, dark brown insect is relatively harmless, though it has a thoroughly unpleasant reputation largely due to its name and because it feeds on the blood of animals and humans. Like most household pests, it prefers dirt to cleanliness and dark to light. It thrives at temperatures above 13°C and when it lays eggs, it applies a cement-like serum to them to hold them in their resting places, which means getting rid of them involves a lot of scrubbing with a stiff brush.
c) Broad and oval-shaped, these brown and white hairy devils will fly into the house during spring and summer and attack any animal fibre (carpets, wool, feathers, hair) and lay their eggs. They are often found in trunks, as well as behind skirting boards and underneath floorboards.

d) This unpleasant insect is thought to have made its way into Britain during the sixteenth century by way of the cargo of a merchant ship. At first it was found only in and around seaports, but soon enough it spread inland and now appears frequently in large numbers in the kitchens and sculleries of old houses. Why? Well, it thrives in a warm, damp atmosphere, hates light, and makes its home in wall cavities, cracks and crevices, so the best way to prevent it is to keep your kitchen scrupulously clean and in good repair.

e) Unlike most other insects, this pest has evolved into a variety of different types which are peculiar to different hosts. They can only live on their specific hosts and are carriers of various types of fever (most notoriously trench fever which they spread very effectively during the First World War, as well as typhus). When their presence on a person has been identified, the ones affected must be isolated and their clothing and bedding must be washed at high temperatures.

4. Which is the only fish that yields 'real' caviar?

a) Sturgeon
b) Salmon
c) Whitefish
d) Mullet

5. Home Economics lessons used to be about how to make an apple crumble, change a light bulb or turn your leftover lentil soup into a tasty Indian curry by adding rice and a few spices. But now the home is an extension of the planet, and our environmental concerns have a rightful place in the running of our households. Of course, saving resources will also save you money, so even if you are a climate-change denier, there are still personal gains to be had by thinking about your carbon footprint.

a) Which is more energy-inefficient:

Driving a 13-miles-per-gallon (mpg) four-by-four rather than the average 22 mpg car for one year OR leaving the fridge door open for six years?

b) Which is longer:
The cumulative distance travelled by an average twenty items of fresh food in a shopping basket, or half the distance to the moon?

c) Which is worse:
Eating an organic apple from New Zealand, or a Fairtrade apple from South Africa?

d) Which is better:
Washing dishes by hand, or using a dishwasher?

6. Can you find the names of the SIX classes of nutrients in the word search below?

C	T	X	L	N	E	Q	V	R	X	A	J	N	G	J
G	A	P	S	L	E	I	S	L	A	R	E	N	I	M
F	Q	R	O	D	T	D	I	K	B	N	Z	P	J	E
L	D	H	B	A	I	D	T	S	H	E	U	N	K	P
P	G	A	M	O	M	P	X	L	D	D	C	X	X	N
C	O	I	E	J	H	X	I	J	N	F	Y	S	M	V
C	N	T	Y	S	R	Y	K	L	Y	F	V	D	P	N
S	O	Z	J	X	F	U	D	Z	D	N	E	B	R	N
S	Q	W	W	W	W	D	K	R	N	O	Q	L	O	R
M	W	Z	S	T	F	R	W	P	A	X	C	F	T	E
Z	X	C	L	S	L	O	H	X	A	T	I	K	E	T
L	X	M	A	W	I	Q	K	H	M	W	E	V	I	A
B	M	L	R	Y	O	D	X	H	R	T	P	S	N	W
W	E	R	X	J	Y	V	C	V	P	C	D	P	S	X
M	D	I	U	A	J	I	B	R	H	D	X	L	C	J

7. Everyone knows that different ovens have different temperaments and a thirty-minute spell in your own cooker can produce a perfectly buoyant Victoria Sponge where half an hour in your mother's oven will create a burnt biscuit. One step in the right direction towards accurate stove-wrangling is the ability to convert between different temperature measures. Gas marks correspond to specific temperatures, now measured in Celsius, but based on your immediate, instinctive knowledge, match the gas mark number to the description of the temperature they invoke.

6 Cool
9 Fairly hot
3 Warm
5 Very hot
2 Fairly hot

8. Back in the sixteenth century the humanist scholar and author of *A Handbook on Manners for Children,* Erasmus, had firm views on table etiquette ('What you cannot hold in your hands you must put on your plate') and there's no reason why it shouldn't be at the forefront of our minds now in the twenty-first. Test your table manners by answering true or false to the statements below.

a) The proper way to eat bread in a restaurant is to break a piece using your fingers, use the butter knife to put butter on the side of your bread plate, then use your own butter knife to butter your piece of bread.
b) Assuming you are right-handed, the proper way to use a knife and fork involves placing the fork in your left hand with the prongs facing up and manoeuvring your food with the knife, in your right hand, on to your fork. Once the food is on the fork, put the knife down, place your fork in your other hand, prongs facing up, and eat.
c) The fish knife, that funny little bent thing, can also be used when serving fruit for pudding.
d) When pausing during a meal, lay your utensils on your plate together with the fork prongs facing up at the ten o'clock position and the handles at four o'clock to indicate that you are not finished. When you have finished your meal, place your knife and fork in an X shape with the fork prongs facing down to signal that you are finished.

9. Thought to have originated in Asia, the onion was (like the cabbage) an object of worship by the idolatrous Egyptians 2,000 years before the Christian era and remains a key base flavouring for many, many dishes. But on their own they also make a tasty, simple soup which even the most dunderheaded of cooks would have to work at to mess up. Below are the key ingredients from three official onion soup recipes and one that has been bastardised with a rogue ingredient. Which is the group of items which will NOT render you a beautiful broth?

a) Onions, butter, salt, pepper, cream, stock, water.
b) Onions, butter, salt, pepper, rice flour, powdered sugar, flour, water.
c) Onions, butter, salt, pepper, flour, consommé, scaled milk, grated Swiss cheese, dried French bread, full-bodied red wine, water.
d) Onions, butter, salt, dry mustard, soy sauce, thyme, white pepper, dry white wine, water.

10. Still on the subject of onions, which of the following is NOT a trick to prevent your eyes from watering while chopping onions?

a) Run your wrists under cold water.
b) Put a spoon in your mouth whilst chopping.
c) Keep onions in the fridge for an hour before you chop them.
d) Chop with a very blunt knife.

11. Long before the advent of chemically induced, commercial cleaning products, our grannies made do with a few simple natural products to keep their houses, clothes and bodies spick and span, so there is no reason why these natural solutions can't be used in your home. Cheap and good for the environment, match the potion to the product:

a) Lemon juice	Brass and copper shiner
b) Vinegar	Glass cleaner
c) Olive oil and lemon juice	Fabric softener

d) Baking soda	Furniture polish
e) Baking soda and vinegar	Surface cleaner
f) Rubbing alcohol, vinegar and water	Toilet cleaner

12. The same can be said for beauty products. Long before L'Oreal and Crème de la Mer convinced us that we needed to spend hundreds of pounds to look like Kate Moss, the pantry was the place to look for effective homemade and natural cosmetics. Again, match the potion to the product, then try at home.

a) Lemon juice	Hair conditioner
b) Baking soda, salt, glycerin and peppermint	Baldness-combater*
c) Chilli	Facemask
d) Teabags	Skin rejuvenator
e) Mayonnaise	Toothpaste
f) Egg whites	Sunburn

13. While we have yet to find a recipe for natural lipstick (unless you want to try staining your lips with food colouring which *was* recommended to us by a man selling cosmetics in the beauty department at Barneys, New York . . .), here's some food for thought: a regular lipstick wearer (81 per cent of women) ingests roughly how much lipstick during the course of her life?

a) 400 grams
b) 250 grams
c) 1 kilogram
d) 1000 grams

14. The sun is past the yard-arm and the cocktail hour is upon us. If you avail yourself of four parts Rye or Bourbon, one part Italian Vermouth, then stir (don't shake) these with ice and pour into a glass

* See, chaps? This section isn't just for the ladies . . .

holding the proverbial cherry or, preferably, a twist of lemon, what would you be about to sip?

a) A dry Manhattan
b) 2:1 Manhattan
c) A sweet Manhattan
d) 4: 1 Manhattan

15. The wearing of clean clothing and the care of garments is of such enormous, global importance that the order and meaning of washing symbols have been formalised so that all countries now use the same ones, relieving everyone of every poor excuse they have for not being able to understand the washing instructions on the tags of their clothes no matter where they are or where their clothes were made. What do the following symbols mean?

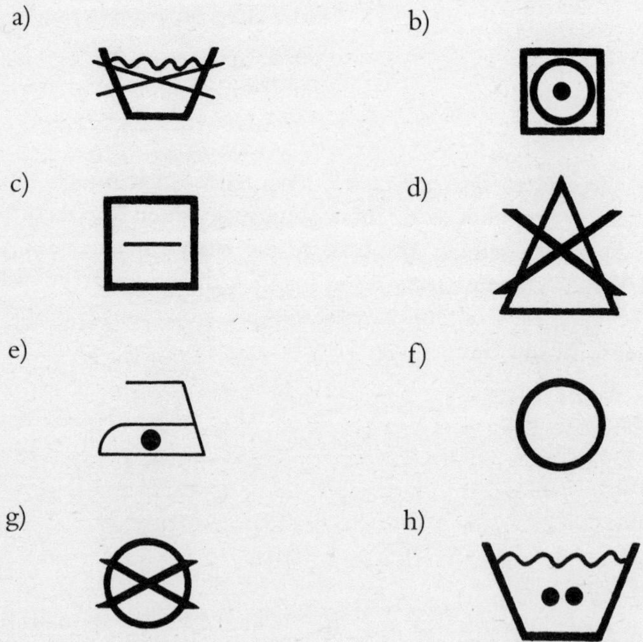

16. Elsie Widdowson (1906–2000) was an English nutritionist who, in collaboration with her longtime research partner, Robert A. McCance, guided the British government's Second World War food-rationing programme. Spurred by the government's concerns about the effects of the heavy rationing necessitated by the outbreak of the war, the pair did extensive research into the effects of dietary deprivation, eventually determining that a basic diet of which three staple foods was sufficient?

a) Oats, kale and carrots.
b) Potatoes, apples and spinach.
c) Bread, potatoes and cabbage.
d) Bread, cabbage and courgettes.

17. We are living in a material world: can you solve the following fabric riddles?

a) I am made from the fleece of sheep. I am relatively weak, yet exceptionally absorbent; I hold in body heat and dye well. I prefer to be dry-cleaned, though I will tolerate a hand wash. I like mothballs, but cannot be wrung. What am I?
b) I come from the flax plant and am best in spring and summer weather. I am strong and absorbent, but I wrinkle like mad! I also deteriorate at the slightest hint of mildew, I tend to shrink when washed in water and – despite my reputation for being refined and luxurious – I am rather coarse. What am I?
c) I am elastic, yet I also tend to pill. I don't wrinkle, I'm super strong, I love being washed in a machine, I can take the tumble-dryer, and I am enormously versatile. Still, I'm often paired with other fabrics and play an accompanying role as a lining or masquerade for other, more expensive fabrics. What am I?
d) I too am made from plants, and the crops used to produce me are very sensitive to insects and sunlight. There are many ship sails in my past, though the last few decades have been good to me and I am now hugely popular in high-street fashion. I can be used for workwear or summerwear; I shrink unless treated and I need to be ironed while damp. What am I?

18. Many UK households involve children and the economics of infants could take up another whole chapter. It is generally held to be environmentally unfriendly to have babies but here's hoping yours will grow up to invent a perfectly clean, safe, sustainable fuel or a super new C5 lookalike. Until then it's worth considering the number of disposable nappies discarded every day in the UK (the vast majority of which end up in landfill). What is this number?

a) 1 million
b) 8 million
c) 3 million
d) 9 million

19. Sourdough, or, to call it by its more funky name, 'wild yeast bread', is leavened by natural fermentation that occurs when the natural yeasts from the air or the grain combine with enzyme-enhancing bacteria. In a process which is miraculous to observe, these cultures grow slowly given the right temperature, digesting the starches and changing the pH and allowing the wild yeasts to feed, which causes the dough to rise. Hundreds of years ago, before packaged yeast, bakers kept a pot of live culture in a bowl of flour and water which they let sit for several days. Like a beloved pet, the culture was 'fed' with new water each day and stirred regularly, so the yeast remained alive and active. Making yeast has become popular again among bread lovers and bakers alike. When growing it, how does one know when it's time to mix the yeast with the flour and start baking?

a) The wild yeast grows so large it overflows the bowl.
b) A distinct smell, much like the scent of burnt sunflowers, arises from the yeast.
c) The yeast begins to bubble when stirred.
d) The yeast grows a harmless green fur which simply needs to be skimmed off.

20. Moving from the kitchen to the great outdoors, the following are recipes for various gardening potions. Based on the descriptions of what they are, can you tell what they are used for?

a) Mixing equal parts of borax and icing sugar makes an excellent ____.
b) Boil 100g (4 oz) of cigarette ends (200g or 8 oz if filter tips) in a gallon of water for half an hour, strain the clear brown liquid

through a nylon stocking and use as one part in four with water to kill ____. Add 25g (1 oz) of soap flakes to a quart of the mixture against ____ ____.

c) Add one dessertspoonful of carbolic acid to a gallon of cold water and stir in 50g (2 oz) of soapflakes to make a spray against ____ on roses, peas, or anything else in the garden that has it.
d) Dissolve 85g (3 oz) of copper sulphate in a gallon of hot water in a plastic bucket, leaving it overnight because copper sulphate dissolves slowly. Stir 100g (4 oz) of slaked lime into a gallon of cold water and mix the two. Bingo! You have a ready-made, inexpensive and terribly effective ____.

21. Alcoholic drinks served, and ingested, prior to a meal are called ____ and alcoholic drinks served, and partaken of, following a meal are called: ____.

22. The following garden vegetables are high in minerals and vitamins: asparagus, cabbage, carrots, peas, potatoes and tomatoes.

Which, per 100g (raw), has . . .

a) the most vitamin C?
b) the least protein?
c) the most riboflavin?
d) the highest calorie content?
e) the most water?
f) the least fat?
g) the most vitamin A?
h) the least carbohydrates?
i) the least niacin?

23. Make your granny proud by exposing some of these hand-sewing technique tips as false and verifying some as true!

a) Cut thread at an angle, using sharp scissors. Never break off or bite the thread – this frays the end, making it difficult to pass through the eye of the needle.
b) Needle choice: A long needle is best for short, single stitches, such as padding stitches; a short needle is best for long or multiple stitches, such as basting.

c) Twisting and knotting can be a problem in hand sewing with any thread. For best results thread the needle with the end cut from the spool and wax the thread before starting to sew.
d) Backstitching is one of the least versatile of the hand stitches and is only useful when repairing seams.

24. Which of the following is one of the five 'mother sauces' of French cooking, from which hundreds of other sauces are derived?

a) *Sauce espagnole*
b) *Sauce soubise*
c) *Sauce verte*
d) *Sauce tartare*

25. An apple a day not only keeps the doctor away but could also extend your lifespan, according to recent research. Arrange the following kinds of scrumptious superfruit according to their blossoming periods.

Cox's Orange Pippin, Gascoyne's Scarlet, Beauty of Bath, Cox's Pomona, Crawley Beauty, Sunset, Gravenstein, Edward VII, Blenheim Orange, White Transparent, Early Victoria, Tydeman's Late Orange, Ribston Pippin, Court Pendu Plat, Adams Pearmain

Early	**Mid-season**	**Late**

b) Now identify which apples are palatable and mark them with an 'E' for eating and mark those more suitable for cooking with a 'C'.

26. Whether you prefer yours from the sea or the rocks, sodium chloride is omnipresent in British kitchens. Besides making foods delicious, there are more than 14,000 uses for salt. Many of these were for keeping things spick and span around the home before the advent of modern chemicals and cleaners, and these 'old' uses are still valid today and a lot cheaper than using more sophisticated products. Some of them have been listed below: can you separate the truths from the falsehoods?

a) Salt is a great weed killer.
b) Poaching eggs in salted water helps set the egg whites.
c) Apples, pears and potatoes dropped in cold, lightly salted water as they are peeled will prevent browning.
d) A little salt added to cake icings prevents them from sugaring.
e) Salt tossed on a grease fire on the stove or in the oven will smother flames.
f) Salt is a great drain-clearer. Pour a strong salt brine down the kitchen sink drain regularly to eliminate odours and keep grease from building up.
g) Adding a pinch of salt to milk will keep it fresh longer.
h) To prevent mould on cheese, wrap it in a cloth dampened with saltwater before refrigerating.
i) Mix one part salt to two parts baking soda after pulverising the salt in a blender or rolling it on a kitchen board with a tumbler before mixing. It whitens teeth, helps remove plaque and it is healthy for the gums.

27. A calorie is:

a) The percentage of trans-fats found in foods per gram of protein.
b) The scientific term for unhealthy foods.
c) The amount of heat that will raise the temperature of 1 gram of water from 14.5° to 15.5°C.
d) A shy breed of golden pheasant found only in the Welsh Marches.

28. Be Prepared. If there's one thing your scout and girl-guide days will have taught it's how to face any situation head on. So for all those times when you find yourself in a pickle by the dockside, it's very important that you know your knots. Match the names of the knots below to the knots themselves:

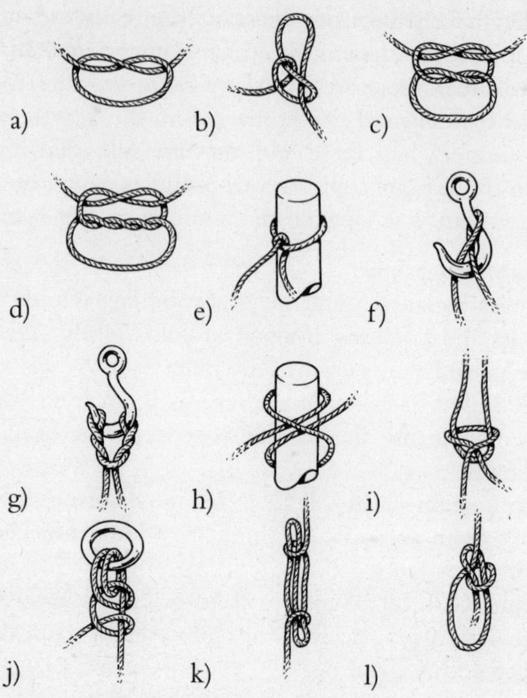

29. Given our persistent precipitation (and given that we are an island), it seems strange to think that Britain's water is such a precious resource. But our huge appetite for it (the UK water industry collects, treats and supplies about 18 billion litres of water per day) still creates shortages. Which of the following are NOT effective ways of conserving water in and around your household?

a) Washing dishes in a bowl rather than under a tap.
b) Using the half-load programme on dishwashers and washing machines.
c) Taking a bath rather than a shower.
d) Removing the trigger nozzle from your hosepipe.
e) Watering your garden in the cool of the early morning or evening.
g) Refraining from using garden sprinklers.

30. Not all dishes have names that accurately describe what they are and if you are a picky eater, a vegetarian or someone who simply likes to know what exactly you are ingesting, you'll need to be familiar with the contents of these delicacies.

a) A Scotch woodcock is ____
b) Bombay duck is ____
c) Devils on horseback are ____
d) Angels on horseback are ____
e) A pig in a blanket is ____
f) Laverbread is ____
g) Mannish water is ____

31. The object of First Aid is to save lives, and a working knowledge of some basic techniques could save you and yours in the event of household fires, rogue electrics, burst pipes or other ordinary accidents that can occur in the home. Do you know your safety stuff?

ACROSS

2. One condition associated with internal haemorrhage (6)
4. A St John's arm sling gives support to the whole arm and is useful for wounds to the ____ (8)
7. One of the two main methods of artificial respiration (7)
9. Mustard, salt, sodium bicarbonate and water make for an excellent ____ (6)
11. Inhalant to ease congestion (10)
12. To soothe irritation caused by mosquito bite, you can apply this common vegetable (5)
13. A ____ can be treated with hydrocortisone cream (4)

DOWN

1. Sunstroke occurs when the sun's rays fall directly on the head or the ____ (5)
3. When dealing with bleeding from a wound, apply direct pressure, raise the affected limb above the level of the heart. It is no longer recommended to apply a ____ in these situations unless as a last resort (10)
5. For best results, remove splinters and thorns with a small ____ (7)
6. The degree of burn indicated by blistering (6)
8. A temporary condition of unconsciousness (8)
10. To get rid of an insect in the ear ____ it out with olive or castor oil (5)

32. It takes years of experience and study to become an expert in the marks on English pottery and porcelain: the marks of the most famous English firms alone run into the hundreds and some have used a dozen or more during the course of their long histories. Still, it's good to have a basic understanding of some of the most ubiquitous, if for no other reason than to be able to determine whether your own porcelain and pottery are authentic, and it's crucial that one never looks a fool when watching *Antiques Roadshow* in company (though the seasoned collector would never place *too* much importance on the marks alone). Here are four examples of some English marks. Can you match them to their makers?

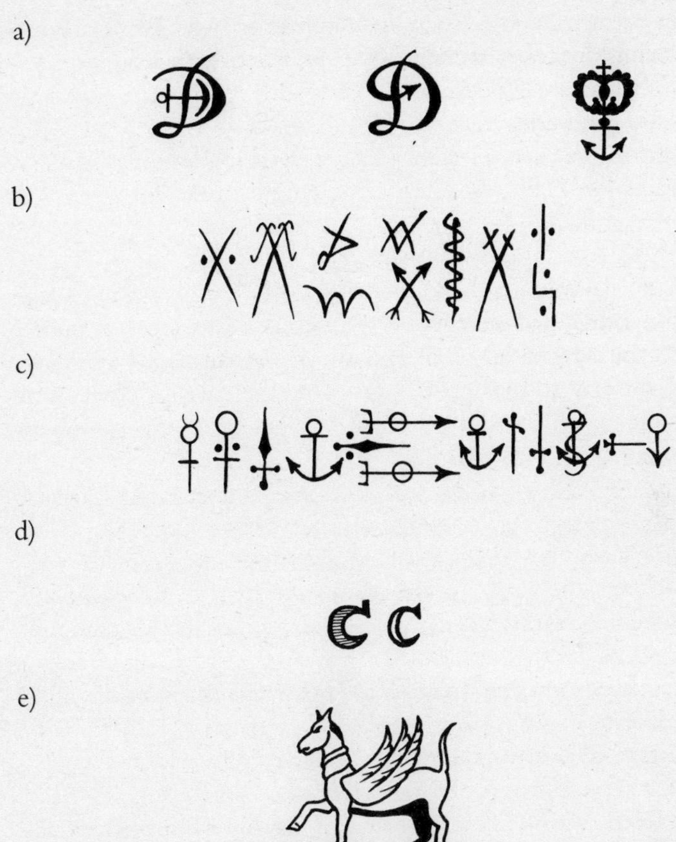

33. It has become usual to disregard wedding anniversaries before the twenty-fifth, though many of the earlier ones have special names. What are they for the following number of years of matrimonial bliss?

a) One
b) Five
c) Ten
d) Fifteen
e) Twenty
f) Twenty-five
g) Fifty
h) Sixty

34. By long custom, certain foods are eaten in a particular way. Which of the following delicacies should NOT be eaten with a fork?

a) Cakes and patisseries
b) Asparagus
c) Ice-creams
d) All of the above

35. It is sometimes said that letter writing is a lost art, but perhaps now – with the advent of email and social networking – it is more important than ever to make sure you know the rules of correspondence. Can you match the correct form of sign-off to the appropriate kind of letter?

'Yours as ever', 'Yours affectionately', 'Yours sincerely', 'Yours faithfully', 'With love', 'Yours truly', 'Yours affectionately', 'As ever'

a) 'Dear Sir, Your advertisement in today's *Times* interests me and I should like to apply for the post.'
b) 'Dear Mary, We are so happy that you have done John the honour of consenting to be his wife.'
c) 'Dear Helen, May I call you that? For we have heard so much about you from Peter, and we feel we know you already!'
d) 'Dear James, As your uncle, I am delighted to see that you have achieved your ambition and received a First. Well done!'
e) 'Dear Susan, Betty told me the good news. How perfectly lovely! I'm sure there was never such a perfect girl born!'
f) 'Dear Henry, It was wonderful to read of your new appointment in the paper this morning. What a long time it seems since we were shinning up apple trees in short trousers together!'
g) 'Dear Mrs Smith, What a lovely present! Thank you both so much. You have been so clever, for the china is just the same colour as our new dining-room curtains.'
h) 'My dear Mrs Pearson, My husband and I were so shocked to read of your sad loss in this morning's papers.'

36. What do the numbers on this four-panelled door represent?

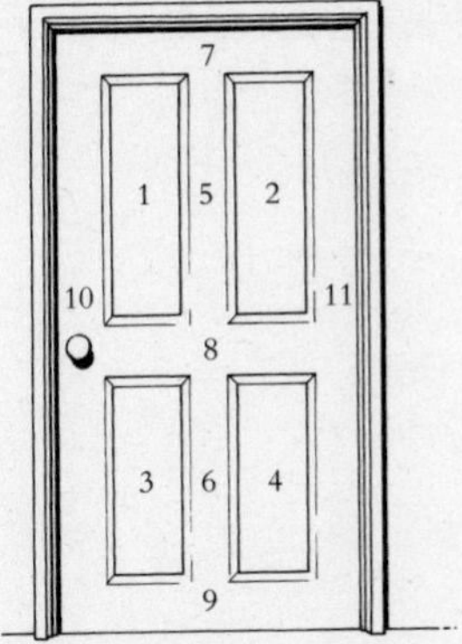

37. 'What separates two people most profoundly is a different sense and degree of cleanliness.' Wise words from philosopher Friedrich Nietzsche that you should call to mind when considering whether you really need to wash your hair tonight. See where you stand on Nietzsche's spectrum by answering the following cleaning riddles:

a) What children's toy prevents 'fur' in kettles?
b) What sort of stains are removed by boiling spoons for two or three minutes in the water in which the eggs have been cooked?
c) What fatty substance, when rubbed on waxed wood furniture, removes heat stains?
d) Four or five medium-sized and sliced onions in a bucket of cold water left to stand overnight do what to the room in which they are placed?
e) What kind of nut kernel, when cut in half and rubbed over scratches on furniture, reduces their unsightly appearance considerably?

38. It's amazing how much smarter a person and a household can look if their clothes and trimmings have been properly looked after. Many linen and cotton fabrics are dressed with a stiffening material during manufacture. Sometimes the stiffening will last the lifetime of the garment, but sometimes it is removed during the normal washing process and must be renewed to restore the fabric to its sprightly upstanding best. This is known as 'starching'. Which of the following items of clothing and household linen need regular starching?

a) Underwear
b) Net curtains
c) Table linen
d) Bed linen
e) The cuffs of men's shirts
f) Baby clothes
g) Stiff collars
h) Handkerchiefs

39. Much essential kitchen equipment has a deliberately descriptive name to make life in the kitchen as easy as possible, yet sometimes different items appear to do the same things. Which item in the following lists doesn't belong with its sister utensils?

a) Lemon zester, vegetable peeler, olive pitter
b) Cake tester, cake wire, metal skewer
c) Strainer, skillet, colander, sieve
d) Steamer, crock-pot, slow cooker

40. Name FOUR knitting and purl stitch patterns that begin with **B**; THREE that begin with **C**; TWO that begin with **W**; and ONE that begins with **K**.

41. Although Britain is officially a 'metric' country, we haven't completely done away with imperial equivalents. Wrangling between London and Brussels to rid the UK of 'pints' of milk and beer, 'pounds' of butter and road signs which indicate how many more 'miles' to Birmingham has been going on for years and led to Europe's Industry Commissioner ruling that the imperial system can be used in conjunction with metric measurements, which means we Brits need to be bilingual when following recipes and apothecaries' instructions. And we also need to know which forms of measurements measure which sorts of things.

a) Millimetres, centimetres, inches, yards and miles are metric and imperial measurements for ____.
b) Square centimetres, acres, square inches and hectares are metric and imperial measurements for ____.
c) The imperial version of a hectolitre is a ____ and both measure ____.
d) Milligrams, grams, kilograms and tonnes are ____ measures of ____.

42. The method of visual communication and signalling using flags, often from high towers (although nothing should stop you from trying it from your kitchen window), to create messages read by telescopic sightings is called:

a) Semaphore
b) Morse code
c) Sign language
d) Telegraphy

43. Match the names and letters of the flag signs to the signs themselves:

'V', 'X', annul, rest, attention

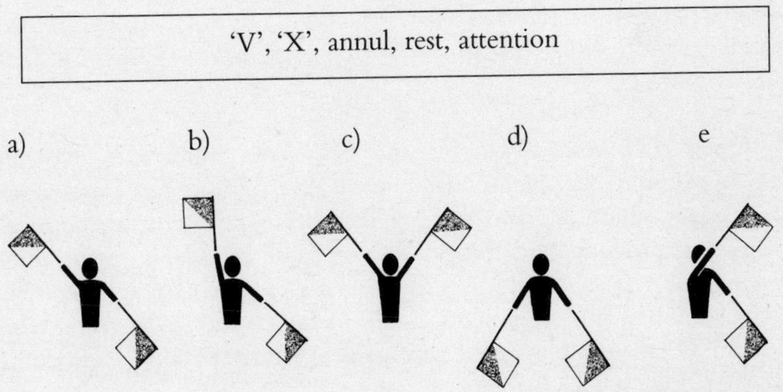

44. The life of a gardener is one in tune with the seasons and the weather. As we all know there is a time for sowing and a time for reaping. Which kitchen-garden vegetables can be identified based on the dates given for their proper planting and harvesting?

carrots, endive, savoy, winter spinach, swede, asparagus, kale, celery, runner beans, cauliflower, broad beans and shallots, beets and ridge cucumber, parsnip, spring cabbage, broccoli

Date for sowing	Harvesting time	Vegetable
February–March	July	________
February–March	September–November	________
March	August–December	________
March	September–December	________
March–May	October–June	________
March–July	June–October	________
April	May–June	________
April	July–September	________
April	October–March	________
April	November–May	________
May	July–October	________
June	October–January	________
July	March–June	________
July	September–March	________
August	October–March	________

45. Open your nearest window and take a deep breath of fresh air. Recent research has shown that indoor air is almost ten times more toxic than outdoor air, mainly due to hazardous and synthetic chemicals in cleaning products and things like the flame retardants in furniture, solvents and petroleum additives. While most products are now required to label any harmful ingredients, it falls to the consumer to know what they are. What horrible-sounding chemical names are these innocuous acronyms standing in for?

a) TBT
b) POPs
c) VOCs
d) PVC
e) MDF

46. What kind of tea do Italians swear by as a remedy for babies suffering from colic and sleeplessness?

a) Fresh mint
b) Peppermint
c) Fennel
d) Camomile

47. Many types of needles are made for hand sewing, each for a specific purpose. These vary according to eye shape (long or round), length (in proportion to eye), and point (sharp, blunt, ball-point, or wedge). Can you match the type of needle to the type of sewing they are used for?

milliners, cotton darners, sailmakers, sharps, tapestry needles, ball-points, curved needles, glovers, chenilles, betweens, double longs, yarn darners, calyx-eyes, crewels, beading needles

General hand sewing	**Needlecraft**	**Darning**	**Heavy-duty sewing**

48. i. Name the countries these puddings are associated with . . .

a) Tiramisù
b) Kheer
c) Chè
d) Black Forest Cake
e) Kissel
f) Sachertorte
g) Mochi
h) Baklava
i) Polvorón

ii. . . . and then select which ones you could serve to your lactose-intolerant guests.

49. Most folk are fond of honey but are deterred from apiarist ambitions by fear of the difficulties and dangers associated with the little beasts. Below are some commonly asked questions. Using your innate knowledge of the subject, can you help shed light on these beginners' doubts by circling the correct answer?

a) Is beekeeping a skilled job? YES/NO
b) Is it dangerous? YES/NO
c) Can a woman be as good a beekeeper as a man? YES/NO
d) Must one have a large garden to keep bees? YES/NO
e) Must one grow special flowers for the bees? YES/NO
f) Is it safe to obtain bees from a man in a pub? YES/NO
g) Are some strains of bees better tempered than others? YES/NO
h) Does one need to feed bees? YES/NO
i) Do I need to take out insurance in case my neighbours get stung? YES/NO

50. We certainly wouldn't expect you to be able to answer any questions about how to fix your car in this day and age, but do you know your way around your car's engine? This will help you look intelligent when your mechanic is pointing to things and explaining how costly they are. Use the words below to make sense of the following sentences.

above, drains, beside, top, attaches

a) The air filter and PVC hose are at the ____ of the engine.
b) The valve spring and water pump are ____ the fan belt.
c) The gas pump is ____ the gas line.
d) A spark plug cover ____ a spark plug cable to a spark plug.
e) The exhaust pipe ____ the exhaust manifold.

HOME ECONOMICS ANSWERS

1. c) While b) are also useful, and d) nearly always a good idea, one cannot carve without a carving knife and fork. They are, to be sure, essential.

2. b)

3. a) Ants. b) Bed bugs. When the infestation is mild, it should be possible to get rid of them by scrubbing down a room with carbolic soap and hot water and washing carpets, bedclothes and furniture, though with more serious infestations it's wise to call your local council. c) Carpet beetles. Keep your woollens in well-fitting drawers and cupboards to prevent them from getting in and vacuum up any larvae or beetles you find. They don't like borax so you could dust it over areas in which you suspect they are lurking (with due caution and respect for this chemical). If things get serious you might need to call in professionals. d) Cockroaches (also known as black beetles). Cockroaches are virtually indestructible and are often said to be the only creatures that would survive in the event of a massive nuclear holocaust. Killing them with toxic insecticides is an efficient, yet environmentally harmful, method of destruction. We recommend the more natural approach which involves the wearing of a strong workboot and the stamping of a foot upon them with force. e) Lice. Head lice are the most common type and can be picked up easily from human hairs clinging to the backs of seats on public vehicles. They can be removed with special shampoos and careful combing, though we also recommend a mixture of equal parts of paraffin and olive, linseed or cottonseed oil to pull lice away from hair. The most important thing to know about lice is that any insects removed from the hair by hand should be dropped into a fire or very hot water and never killed by squishing them between your fingers as that can result in the spread of louse-borne epidemics. And yes, we do permit you to enjoy the spit and crackle as they expire, but not too much.

4. a) Caviar is, by definition, a product processed from the eggs of sturgeon, which are any of about twenty-five species of fishes of the family Acipenseridae (subclass Chondrostei), native to the temperate waters of the Northern Hemisphere. Grades are named for the types of sturgeon from which the eggs are taken: *beluga*, the largest, is black or grey; the smaller *osetrova* is greyish, grey-green, or brown; *sevruga*, the smallest, is greenish black. The roe of other fishes, such as salmon or whitefish, are sometimes dyed and sold under the label of 'caviar' but are impostors and not worthy of the name.

5.

a) Driving the four-by-four.
b) Half the distance to the moon, but only just! The 'food miles' travelled by the twenty items averages 100,000 miles (160,934 kilometres) while half a journey to the moon is a mere 119,400 miles (192,200 km) away.
c) For the simple reason that it travels a lesser distance, the Fairtrade apple from South Africa is less harmful to the planet. Also, they are grown by South African farmers who are part of the Thandi Initiative which encourages joint ownership and empowerment by improving local social capital. Still, the best apples to eat are UK apples, even if they are not organic. Aside from the food miles they don't burn, if the demand for the UK's many kinds of apples diminishes, the loss of our orchards will seriously affect biodiversity.
d) If used correctly, most likely the dishwasher. As only 27 per cent of British homes have a dishwasher, it is safe to guess that the remainder get by with the good old-fashioned method of washing up by hand, leaving us to assume that dishwashers are inessential, energy-hungry, environmentally unfriendly and expensive appliances that take the same amount of time to load and unload as a spot at the draining board with the Fairy liquid. But modern dishwashers use substantially less water and

equal (or smaller) amounts of energy than washing by hand. One 2003 study from the University of Bonn found that British and Germans averaged 63 litres per set of dishes. Compare this to the 20 litres that the average dishwasher uses, even with pre-soaking and rinsing added in, and the seemingly evil appliance looks less menacing than it first appears.

6. Carbohydrates, proteins, lipids, vitamins, minerals, water.

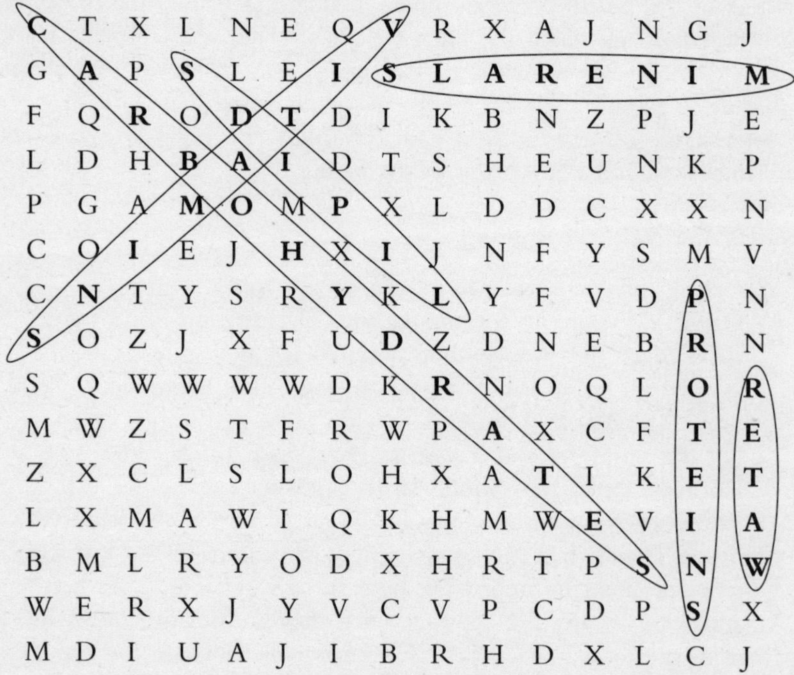

7. 6 = Fairly hot (200°C), 9 = Very hot (240°C), 3 = Warm (160°C), 5 = Fairly hot (190°C), 2 = Cool (150°C)

8. a) True. Using the communal butter knife to butter one's own bread is simply *not done*. What if you'd already taken a bite of your bread and your germs jumped on the knife and, by proxy, got on to someone else's piece of bread? However, it's perfectly fine to use your fingers to break off a piece of bread from a baguette or to lift a piece of bread from a basket because an even more important table manner than the correct use of the bread knife is washing your hands before you eat.

b) False. The dinner knife should not be thought of as a kind of cattle prod with which one pushes food on to the dinner fork (which equally should not be thought of as a kind of shovel) and should remain in the right hand while the fork is ferrying food into your mouth.

c) False. Tempting as it is to double-up utensils and save on the washing up, fish knives are smelly and would interfere with the flavour of any other foods.

d) False. The X shape, prongs down, indicates that you are still eating while the ten/four o'clock angle with prongs up says that you are finished.

9. c) While no recipe can be officially 'wrong' and dry red wine in an onion soup would perhaps not make it completely unrecognisable, it would taste rather vile. Take it from us: we sampled the goods. For a terrific and easy onion soup, we recommend the recipe based on the ingredients of option a) as told to us by Mrs Beeton. You'll need 6 large onions, 60g of butter, salt and pepper to taste, 150 mls of cream and just over a litre of stock. Chop the onions, sauté them in the butter and stir occasionally, but do not let them brown. When tender, add the stock and let it simmer for an hour and a half. Strain the soup, add seasoning and boiling cream and serve four people a delicious warm and wintery treat!

10. d) When you chop an onion, you break the walls of the cells and release their juices which – once in the air – can sting the eyes, but the sharper the knife, the fewer the number of broken cells. Various master and sous chefs swear by the three other suggestions.

11.

a) Lemon is a great substance to clean and shine brass and copper.

b) Vinegar can be used as a fabric softener. Add ½ cup of vinegar to the rinse cycle in place of store-bought fabric softener. Vinegar has the added benefit of breaking down laundry detergent more effectively and can be especially helpful for people who have sensitive skin.

c) Mix 1 cup olive oil with ½ cup lemon juice and you have an excellent furniture polish for your hardwood furniture.

d) In addition to its deodorising functions, baking soda can be used to scrub surfaces in much the same way as commercial abrasive cleansers.
e) Baking soda and vinegar works well as a toilet cleaner as the foam it makes gets under the rim of the toilet bowl nicely, the baking soda functions as a scrub and the vinegar as a disinfectant.
f) Combining 1 cup of rubbing (isopropyl) alcohol, 1 cup of water and 1 tablespoon of white vinegar makes a very effective glass cleaner. Why? Mixing isopropyl alcohol and white vinegar together makes a quickly evaporating spray, which also comes in handy when giving a nice shine to hard tiles and chrome.

12.

a) Lemon juice is great for the skin because it contains high levels of alpha hydroxy acids, which should be a familiar term to anyone who has looked at the ingredients of an anti-ageing product. Alpha hydroxy acids are an entire family of acids, which can be derived from fruit, milk or sugar, which rejuvenate skin in a variety of ways, from bleaching freckles to erasing lines to exfoliating dead skin cells to combating scars and spots. Alpha hydroxy acids are used in the very trendy chemical peels and plain old lemon juice has tons of 'em. Rub the juice on your face before bed, ignore the stickiness, and see instant results.
b) 6 teaspoons of baking soda, ⅓ teaspoon salt, 4 teaspoons glycerin and 15 drops peppermint will give you the cleanest-feeling teeth of your life if you mix the ingredients thoroughly to achieve a toothpaste consistency.
c) Chilli beats baldness. No, really! A US study showed that eating chilli peppers and soybeans may stimulate hair growth. Some people even try to stimulate hair follicles by rubbing chilli on the scalp.
d) Everybody knows that soaking two teabags in warm water and placing them over the eyelids for twenty minutes is good for tired or puffy eyes, but soaked teabags are also good for treating sunburn.
e) It's messy, but putting mayonnaise in your hair and letting it sit for thirty minutes will leave it feeling shiny and tangle-free for days.
f) Using egg whites as a thirty-minute facemask tightens pores like nobody's business.

13. c) and d) Just testing your conversion skills . . .

14. d)

15. a) Do not machine wash, i.e. wash it by hand only and don't wring it out. b) Tumble dry allowed at minimum temperature (appropriate for polyester, nylon and acetates). c) Dry flat (appropriate for acrylics, cashmere and loose knitwear). d) Do not bleach. This sign usually accompanies wools and silks. e) The ironing symbol lets you know that the garment is safe to iron, and the dots indicate the temperature. In this case the one dot means cool iron at 110°C max (i.e. acrylic, nylon, acetates and polyester). f) The circle is the dry-cleaning symbol and the empty circle means articles are cleanable in all normally available dry cleaning solvents. g) Do not dry-clean. Obviously . . . h) Wash at 40°C.

16. c) Before the war, Widdowson and McCance conducted experiments to investigate how the body metabolises certain elements, using themselves as guinea pigs. Not all their experiments went according to plan. While researching strontium, they injected strontium lactate into their veins and, when nothing happened, decided to increase the dose. Less than an hour later they began to feel extremely ill, with intense headaches, raging fever and aching backs and limbs. Nevertheless, they were able to show that the body rids itself of strontium slowly and that about 90 per cent of it is excreted through the kidneys. They eventually worked out that bread, cabbage and potatoes contained all the nutrients for healthy survival. For three months Elsie and a number of her companions ate nothing else, and, to test their fitness following this bleak regime, went on a rigorous course of cycling and mountain climbing.

17. a) Wool; b) Linen; c) Nylon; d) Cotton

18. b) The average baby using disposable nappies produces one tonne of nappy waste during its two-and-a-half years in nappies and for every pound we spend on the nappies, the taxpayer spends 10p on their disposal.

19. c)

20. a) Ant killer. Though borax is a poison, it was used in baby powders for years, and it is now much safer than commercial pesticides for use against ants in the house. Once mixed with icing sugar, it should be sprinkled where ants are found. And because ants eat each other's droppings (sharing, as it were, a common digestive system), ants that take the borax bait home can destroy a nest without risk to anything else. b) Caterpillars and cabbage caterpillars. Nicotine has served British gardeners well for the past century against caterpillars and though it is a powerful poison, it is not a persistent one. (DDT was found in the fat of Antarctic penguins after only a bare twenty years of use, but Captain Scott's expeditions found none of the nicotine that had been used all over the world for 150 years. Nicotine breaks down in about four days although cigarettes are, of course, more deadly to humans than any pesticide.) c) Mildew. For a weaker mixture, which is more effective against aphids on roses, dissolve 50g (2 oz) of the carbolic soap used for washing dogs in a gallon of hot water and spray when cool. d) Fungicide.

21. An alcoholic beverage served prior to a meal to stimulate the appetite is an *apéritif*, while an alcoholic beverage served after a meal to stimulate digestion is a *digestif*.

22.

a) Peas (40 milligrams)
b) Tomatoes (0.85 grams)
c) Potatoes (0.035 milligrams)
d) Peas (81 kcal)
e) Tomatoes (93.76 grams, which is almost as much as iceberg lettuce [95.89 grams])
f) Potatoes (0.10 grams, which is a far cry from the fat in potato crisps: 34.60 grams . . .)
g) Carrots (28,129 IU, compared to only 133 IU in cabbage and (gasp!) 0 IU in potatoes)
h) Asparagus (4.54 grams)
i) Cabbage (0.300 milligrams)

23.

a) True.
b) False. A short needle is best for short stitches and a long needle is best for long stitches.
c) True.
d) False. Very false! The back stitch can do all sorts of things, including securing the beginning – as well as the end – of a row of stitches, sometimes in place of a knot in garment areas where a knot could leave an indentation after pressing, for hand-under-stitching, topstitching and hand-picking zippers. And there are many variations of backstitch, although each is formed by inserting the needle behind the point where the thread emerges from the previous stitch.

24. a) *Sauce espagnole* is a simple brown sauce made from beef or veal stock. The four other 'mother sauces' are *sauce velouté*, a light stock-based sauce, *sauce béchamel*, a white sauce (all three of these are *roux*-based), the two basic emulsified sauces, *hollandaise* and *mayonnaise*, and the oil and vinegar-based *vinaigrette*.

25. **Early**: Adams Pearmain (E), Gravenstein (E), White Transparent (C), Beauty of Bath (E) and Ribston Pippin (E); **Mid-season**: Blenheim Orange (E), Early Victoria (C), Tydeman's Late Orange (E), Cox's Orange Pippin (E) and Sunset (C); **Late**: Gascoyne's Scarlet (C), Edward VII (C), Court Pendu Plat (E), Cox's Pomona (C) and Crawley Beauty (C).

26.

a) True. Salt is a desiccant. It absorbs nearby available moisture. Salt deposited on a plant results in 'exosmosis' and causes the water in the leaf to move out of the leaf. The areas of the leaf which are affected will look brown and burnt. Salt in the soil will dry out plant roots and damage the plant's ability to soak up moisture and nutrients. While this can damage landscaping in areas affected by sea spray or by road-salt run off, it can be used in selectively killing weed species by placing a strong salt solution directly on the weed targeted for elimination.
b) True.
c) True.

d) True.
e) True. Never use water to extinguish a grease fire: it will only spatter the burning grease.
f) True.
g) True.
h) True.
i) True.

27. c) The calorie, a unit of heat or energy, has undergone a few definitions, the first of which was the amount of heat required at a pressure of 1 standard atmosphere to raise the temperature of 1 gram of water 1° Celsius. Since 1925 this calorie has been defined in terms of the joule, the definition since 1948 being that one calorie is equal to approximately 4.2 joules. Because the quantity of heat represented by the calorie is known to differ at different temperatures (by as much as 1 per cent), it has consequently been necessary to define the temperature at which the specific heat of water is to be taken as 1 calorie. Thus the '15°C calorie' (also called the gram-calorie, or small calorie) was defined as the amount of heat that will raise the temperature of 1 gram of water from 14.5° to 15.5°C, which is equal to 4.1855 joules. In more colloquial language, dieticians use it to mean the 'kilocalorie' when measuring the calorific, heating, or metabolising value of foods. Although government publications now often provide energy counts in kilojoules and kilocalories, calorie is still the most commonly used food energy unit around the world.

28. a) Overhand knot; b) Slipknot; c) Square knot; d) Surgeon's knot; e) Half hitch; f) Blackwall hitch; g) Cat's paw; h) Clove hitch; i) Sheet bend; j) Fisherman's bend; k) Sheepshank; l) Bowline

29. b), c) and d). Despite their promise, the half-load option on washing machines and dishwashers is rarely economical with water or energy when half full. A five-minute shower uses about one third of the water of a bath and attaching a nozzle to your hosepipe controls the flow so you use less water.

30. a) A Scotch woodcock is not a roasted piece of Scottish fowl, but a savoury treat of creamy, soft scrambled egg on toast with anchovy fillet on top. b) Bombay duck (or bummalo) is a dried, marine lizardfish from Southern Asia usually eaten as an accompaniment to curry. c) Devils on horseback are prunes wrapped in bacon. (Using 10 prunes, with their stones removed, 5 rashers of streaky bacon halved widthways and 1 tbsp of olive oil, preheat the over to 200°C/400°F/Gas mark 6, wrap half a rasher around each prune and secure it with a cocktail stick. Then place on to a baking tray and drizzle over the oil. Cook in the oven for ten minutes, or until the bacon is crisp, serve and enjoy!) d) Angels on horseback are oysters wrapped in bacon, usually served as an appetizer. e) Pigs in blankets are sausages wrapped in bacon. f) Laverbread is not bread at all – it's a Welsh dish made of stewed seaweed. g) Mannish water is a Jamaican goat stew with a reputation for being an aphrodisiac . . .

31.

32. a) Chelsea-Derby. No, not a race involving the plumed and perfumed of the King's Road; in fact, around 1745, the manufacture of porcelain was begun at the Chelsea Works. The best period runs from 1750 until 1765. In 1770, the factory was bought and operated side by side with the Derby Works. b) Worcester. The Worcester factory began production in 1751 and in 1788 became known as the Royal Worcester Porcelain Works. The Flight and Barr period then covered the years between 1783 and 1840. In 1786, a second and independent venture was begun by former employee Robert Chamberlain and the two factories were amalgamated in 1840. c) Bow. The first recorded porcelain of Bow (New Canton) dates from 1744 and the factory closed in 1776. d) Caughley (Salopian). A factory for the manufacture of porcelain was started here in 1772 and continued production until 1814, when it was transferred to Coalport. e) Rockingham. A factory was opened for the production of pottery in 1765.

33. a) First year: paper; b) Fifth year: wood; c) Tenth year: tin; d) Fifteenth year: crystal; e) Twentieth year: china; f) Twenty-fifth year: silver; g) Fiftieth: gold; h) Sixtieth: diamond. The first year is also sometimes known as cotton and the second: paper, the seventh: wool, the twelfth: leather or silk and fine linen, the thirtieth: ivory or pearl, the fortieth: ruby or wool, the forty-fifth: silk. All very helpful when you're choosing anniversary presents.

34. b) Asparagus should *always* be eaten with the fingers. Why? We don't know, but those who prefer to cut off the edible part of the stalk, dip it into butter and then eat it with a fork, rather than dipping the stalk into the melted-butter sauce, biting it off and placing the remainder of the stalk on the rim of the plate, are often cast out of society. Cakes and patisseries should be eaten with a small fork and ice-creams must *only* be eaten with the fork which is usually brought on to the table with the ice-cream plate.

35. a) 'Yours faithfully' should end a letter of application for a job, or indeed any letter that opens with 'Dear Sir'. b)'Yours affectionately' is an appropriate sign-off for a letter of congratulation and c) would also be right for someone the writer has not yet met, for instance a letter from a forthcoming mother-in-law to her future daughter-in-law. d) 'Yours truly' works well for a letter to someone from a younger generation, especially if a congratulation is in order, where e) 'As ever' is a nicely personal ending to a letter of congratulation to someone you know only casually, or through someone else. f) 'Yours as ever' makes for a solid camaraderie between men, g) 'With love' is appropriate on receiving a gift or after being a guest at a party, and, while all letters of condolence are difficult, h) 'Yours sincerely' will often help to lift the sorrow of the bereaved person, not emphasise it.

36. The proper sequence of painting operations. When painting doors, remove the handle and finger plates and wedge the door three-quarters of the way open. Doors vary considerably in design, but if yours is of the panelled variety, paint the panels and mouldings first (indicated by numbers one through four), and then the flat sections for best results.

37. a) Kept inside a kettle, a stone marble of the kind used in children's games, will prevent the kettle from becoming coated in fur. b) Egg stains on egg spoons. c) Either margarine, butter or a little bit of olive oil. d) Clear paint smells by morning. e) A Brazil nut.

38. b), c), e) and g) (net curtains, table linen, the cuffs of men's shirts and stiff collars) should be starched if you have any house-pride at all (and plenty of spare time).

39. a) Olive pitter. The other utensils are used for peeling, not pitting. b) Cake wire. This is a handy gadget for cutting cakes evenly, quickly and simply, but does not belong with the cake tester and the metal skewer, both of which can be used to test the doneness of a cake. c) Skillet. We tried to slip you up with alliteration into believing that 'colander' was the odd one out, but obviously a strainer, colander and sieve are all used to separate food items (usually solids from liquids), whereas a skillet is a flat-bottomed pan used for frying. d) Steamer. A crock-pot is simply a patented name for one kind of slow cooker, which is an electric pot that cooks food slowly at a relatively low temperature. A steamer is simply a containment system which channels its sealed steam to cook foods.

40. B: Basketweave, basketweave II, box stitch and broken rib. C: Checks & ridges, chevron and close checks. W: Windmill and woven stitch. K: King Charles Brocade.

41. a) Length; b) Area; c) Gallon/volume; d) Metric/mass

42. a) Semaphore is the system of the international maritime signals flags which operate through an alphabet, though a few individual flags have specific meanings.

43. a) Annul; b) 'V'; c) Attention; d) Rest; e) 'X'

44.

Date for sowing	Harvesting time	Vegetable
February–March	July	Broad beans and shallots
February–March	September–November	Parsnip
March	August–December	Cauliflower
March	September–December	Celery
March–May	October–June	Broccoli
March–July	June–October	Carrots
April	May–June	Asparagus
April	July–September	Beets and ridge cucumber
April	October–March	Savoy
April	November–May	Kale
May	July–October	Runner beans
June	October–January	Swede
July	March–June	Spring cabbage
July	September–March	Endive
August	October–March	Winter spinach

45. a) Tributyltin is used in many synthetic floor coverings. A suspected EDC (endocrine-disrupting chemical), it prevents mould, mildew and bacteria in floor coverings and some fabrics, but contains organotin compounds that can find their way into the body through the skin. b) Persistent Organic Pollutants are carbon-based chemical compounds that are the products and by-products of heavy industry and chemical (particularly petrochemical) manufacturing. Found in many plastics, pesticides, coolants and transformer lubricants, some of the worst POPs were banned in the seventies yet traces of them still show up in Arctic polar bears, even in the breastmilk of Inuit mothers. It is assumed that everybody on the planet has traces of POPs in their system and they can cause cancer, as well as damage to the reproductive and immune systems of people and animals. c)

Volatile organic compounds are also EDCs and are mostly found in paint, especially gloss paint. The VOC content is now listed on paint labels, but it's safe to assume that any VOC is a bad thing. It causes nose and throat problems, headaches, allergic skin reactions, nausea, fatigue and dizziness. d) Polyvinyl Chloride, made of PVC-u (an unplasticised polyvinyl chloride) is one of the world's most popular forms of plastic. In the home, the kind of vinyl floor covering that became popular during the Second World War as a rubber substitute is made of PVCs. It may sound quaint, but linoleum is a much more friendly alternative for easy-to-wipe floors. PVC windows, which are billed as 'low maintenance', are manufactured using a variety of POPs. e) Our love affair with Medium Density Fibreboard may be coming to an end. This simple 'alternative' to wood is made of wood dust bonded together by formaldehyde-based glue, a suspected carcinogen, but perhaps even more frightening is the danger the dust particles can cause when cutting MDF. Warning stickers now advise consumers to wear a mask when sawing MDF, but do you really want to live with something that is dangerous to inhale? Remember asbestos? All very cheery.

46. d)

47. General hand sewing: Sharps, betweens, milliners, ball-points and calyx-eyes. This group of hand needles is used for general-purpose sewing and most are sharp with a size range sufficient to accommodate most fabric weights. **Needlecraft**: Crewels, chenilles, beading and tapestry needles. This group of hand needles is used for a variety of art and needlecraft purposes, such as embroidery, needlepoint and decorative beading. **Darning**: Cotton darners, double longs and yarn darners. These needles vary in length and diameter to accommodate most darning and mending jobs. **Heavy-duty sewing**: Glovers, sailmakers, curved needles. These needles do what the packet says: heavy sewing jobs. Both the glover and the sailmaker have wedge-shaped points to pierce vinyl, plastic, leather and leatherlike fabrics in such a way that holes resist tearing. Curved needles are used on upholstery, braided rugs or lampshades – anywhere too awkward for a straight needle.

48. i) a) Tiramisù: Italy; b) Kheer: South Asia; c) Chè: Vietnam; d) Black Forest cake: Germany; e) Kissel: Eastern Europe; f) Sachertorte: Austria; g) Mochi: Japan; h) Baklava: Turkey; i) Polvorón: Spain. ii) While many of these sweeties taste good because they contain whipped cream (black forest cake and sachertorte), mascarpone (tiramisù), or some kind of flour/wheat/milk/sugar combo (polvorón, kheer), chè, kissel, mochi and baklava are all dairy-free. Chè is made of beans cooked in water and sweetened with sugar, kissel is a fruit soup created from sweetened juice and thickened with arrowroot, corn or potato starch, mochi is mostly glutinous or sweet rice with traditional Japanese sweets (such as wagashi and mochigashi), and baklava is made of sweet pastry layers filled with chopped nuts and sweetened with honey. Delicious!

49. a) Yes. But reasonable skill is not difficult for anyone to acquire. b) No (barring allergies and accidents, of course). c) Yes. In fact, one's gender does not come into play in beekeeping at all. Not at all. d) No. e) No. The bees will forage for a distance of up to two miles from their hive. f) Yes. g) Yes. Always make enquiries as to this before purchase. h) Yes, though only occasionally when the season is so bad and they cannot amass enough honey to see them through the winter and early spring a little syrup is required. i) It's a good idea in these litigious times.

50. a) The air filter and PVC hose are at the top of the engine. b) The valve spring and water pump are above the fan belt. c) The gas pump is beside the gas line. d) A spark plug cover attaches a spark plug cable to a spark plug. e) The exhaust pipe drains the exhaust manifold.

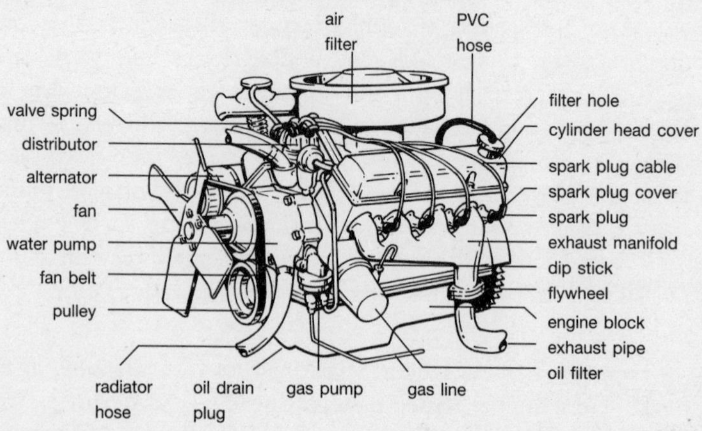

RELIGIOUS EDUCATION

Though Karl Marx somewhat snidely called organised religion the opiate of the masses (rather than football, as Terry Eagleton claimed more than 150 years later), there's no denying that it has shaped, shifted and had a seismic effect on the course of man's journey through history. From the petrifying practices of the Ancient Mayans (children needed to watch their backs when a new temple was going up) to the more outlandish claims of the modern day, celebrity-endorsed Scientologists (space opera anyone?), religion has been a key part of human society since its very beginnings. Indeed, some might say it's our thirst for a narrative, for a story to shape and make sense of the why, what and when of our quintessence of dust that has powered history since the dawn of time. And some of the practices, beliefs and tenets of the world's religions are as gripping and extraordinary as any fiction. To be ignorant of them is to miss out. On a more prosaic level, in our ever-increasingly cosmopolitan societies you're just as likely to chat to your greengrocer about yoga as you are to your neighbour about Yom Kippur. It would be very rude to be unable to sort your Shintoism from your Shi'ites, and your Jainism from your Jehovah's Witnesses. So eyes down, pencils ready, and please do keep an open mind.

1. If you overheard a man on a bus describing 'a deistic sort of polytheism', which of the following faiths would you think he was talking about?

a) Mayan religion
b) Baha'i faith

c) Epicureanism
d) Deism

2. To get you started on this wide-ranging and complex subject we will begin with a holy mix and match. Match the correct person or deity with the religious movement they are most associated with:

Saint Ignatius de Loyola	Rastafarianism
Joseph Smith, Jr	Conservative Judaism
Amaterasu	Egyptian Religion
Alī ibn Abi Talib	Shī'ism
Zacharias Frankel	Wicca
Abu Bakr	Shinto
Gerald Brousseau Gardner	The Jesuit Order
Neith	Sunnī Islam
Haile Selassie I	Mormonism

3. Like Martin Luther and John Calvin, this group was made up of serious, tough-minded fellows. Unlike Luther or Calvin, they pulled up stakes and moved to Massachusetts. Who were they?

a) The Plymouth Brethren
b) The Mennonites
c) The Puritans
d) All of the above

4. It seems John was a very popular name in Jesus's day: there is a very large number of them among the saints. But do you know what professions they took before adopting general saintliness? Using the clues, which will help you determine which John is being referred to, find what the principle Johns of Christianity's jobs were before they were famous . . .

ACROSS

1. Born in Portugal in 1495; died at Granada in 1550 (7)
4. 'Of the Cross' (4)
5. Martyr associated with another Paul mentioned in the canon of the Roman Mass (7)
9. Popular medieval English saint who ordained the Venerable Bede (6)
10. Egyptian hermit (9)
11. Beheaded by Henry VIII for treason two weeks before Thomas More got the chop (8)

DOWN

2, 8 Founder of the Priests of the Blessed Sacrament in Paris (5, 6)
3. Played an influential part in healing divisions in the Franciscan order (8)

6. One of Christ's twelve apostles (9)
7. Of whom Christ said: 'Among those who are born of women there is not a greater prophet' (8)
8. See 2 down

5. The ancient religious figure Abraham is probably most famous for getting a bit knife-happy with his son Isaac. However, his significance stretches far beyond this story and he is a key figure in several religious movements. The oldest three Abrahamic religions are:

a) Daosim, Sikhism and Shamanism
b) Buddhism, Islam and Hinduism
c) Judaism, Christianity and Islam
d) Christianity, Judaism and Jainism

6. Can you match up the meanings with the names of some of the most prominent women in the Bible?

bee, princess, cow, 'the mother of all things', weasel, from 'to judge', lily, ewe

Leah
Deborah
Eve
Dinah
Rachel
Sarah
Susanna
Huldah

7. The Jamaican nationalist Marcus Garvey (1887–1940) espoused a doctrine of black exceptionalism that considered Africans to be the superior race, inspiring the creation of which Afrocentric Protestant sect?

a) Seventh-day Adventist
b) Athlicanism
c) African Orthodox Church
d) Nation of Islam

8. Which of the following is NOT a paraphrased example of one of the great Italian theologian Saint Thomas Aquinas's 'five ways' of understanding the existence of God, espoused in his *Summa Theologica* (1265–73)?

a) Everything does stuff, even things with no brains. Therefore something must be telling us all what to do.
b) Everything is finite, yet everything wants to be immortal. Therefore there must be something that makes death not only possible, but essential.
c) Everything comes from somewhere, so there must be something that existed before everything else and created everything else.
d) Something causes everything to move. Who can it be?
e) Everything has or does something to varying degrees and the standard by which we measure these must derive from a larger ideal.
f) Everything seems to be designed for something, which proves it's not all some random jumble – that something, or someone, had a master plan.

9. Buddhism is a religious philosophy based on the teachings of the rotund prince and deep thinker Siddhartha Gautama, the Buddha, and practised primarily in Asia. The Buddha's teachings were at first transmitted orally, resulting in varying interpretations and the establishment of eighteen different Buddhist schools of thought. Can you find the names of EIGHT forms of Buddhism in the word search below?

P A I G O J Z M I V H N K K V

W U H W R G A D N A Q A W D N

V W R B O H E M M J J T T T V

Y Q P E A C A T G R H E K F N

T K E Y L T B J B A W B Y S E

I N A Q V A I P L Y Y I Z Z Z

O N Q Y S Q N M U A Q T G D C

A O J Q L G G D A N G Y R E A

F T H E R A V A D A M I H Q Q

T P H J V P R I W I E U T X G

Q E N E R I H C I N Y I Y Y Y

R F N H P V W X X P O Z R U A

Y B B E U Q N A I P V U B G O

A T L D T E C B T C W M N U B

P N Y E Z Q P L V M P B Q H S

10. Which prominent US statesman, president and founding father famously said: 'The legitimate powers of government extend to such acts only as are injurious to others. But it does me no injury for my neighbour to say there are twenty gods, or no god', and was much more likely to comment on the quality of French wine than matters to do with transubstantiation?

a) Thomas Jefferson
b) John Adams
c) James Madison
d) Abraham Lincoln

11. The sixteen countries listed below count Islam as either their dominant – or one of their dominant – religions, yet only eight countries have large populations of Shi'a muslims, in addition to Sunni muslims. Which are the eight Shi'a-inclusive countries?

Brunei, India, Albania, Indonesia, Lebanon, Bangladesh, Jordon, Turkey, Yemen, Maldives, Afghanistan, Bahrain, Azerbaijan, Saudi Arabia, Macedonia, Mongolia

12. Circle the correct spellings of these commonly misspelt/misspelled places/people/rituals/names.

Calaphs/Caliphs	Jianism/Jainism
Bar Mitzah/Bar Mitzvah	Feng Shiu/Feng Shui
Messiah/Mesiah	Solomon/Soloman
Yahweh/Yaweh	Sikh/Sihk
Pranamaya/Pranayama	Bah'ai/Baha'i
Dali Lama/Dalai Lama	Confucious/Confucius
Judaic/Judiac	Synagogue/Synogogue
Bhagadav Gita/Bhagavad Gita	Eucherist/Eucharist
Taoism/Toasim	Yom Kippur/Yon Kippur
Lao-Tzu/Tao Lzu	Deuteromony/Deuteronomy

13. What is the current title for the person who was, until the fourth century, known as the Bishop of Rome?

a) Antipope
b) Swiss Guard
c) Priest
d) Pope

14. There are just under 300 people who have held the office of pope or antipope (an antipope is not a pope-hater but rather someone who claims to be pope at the same time as a legitimate pontiff). How many of these were 'Clements'?

15. Which Clement was the illegitimate son of the fifteenth-century Florentine leader Giuliano de' Medici and was brought up by his uncle, Lorenzo the Magnificent?

16. You know the tenets, the dietary restrictions, the festivals, the history, the practices of these religions and spiritual movements inside out. But do you know what their names mean? Match the translations to the spiritual paths they refer to:

Islam	'The Practice of the Wheel of Dharma'
Santería	'Way of the Kami'
Shintõ	'Way of the Guru'
Jainism	'To conquer'
Kabbalah	'Surrender'
Gurmat	'Way of the Saints'
Falun Gong	'Tradition'

17. Put the following religions in order from oldest to youngest:

Islam
Buddhism
Christianity
Judaism
Hinduism
Sikhism

18. Which American traditional gospel song tells the story of Exodus 7 (in which Yahweh commands one of his followers to deliver the people of Israel from Egypt and parts the waters of the Red Sea so the Israelites can pass) referring the story to American slavery, with Israel standing in for African-American slaves and Egypt and the Pharaoh representing the slavemaster?

a) 'Amazing Grace'
b) 'Precious Lord, Take My Hand'
c) 'We Shall Overcome'
d) 'Go Down, Moses'

19. Though it's not a religious event, over one sixth of the people in the world celebrate Chinese New Year. The Chinese use the Lunar calendar for their festivals, which is made up of a cycle of twelve years, each of them being named after an animal much like our own astrological signs. Can you name all twelve animals that make up the Chinese zodiac?

20. Can you guess which religious festival is being alluded to based on the clues below?

a) A five-day festival starting on the thirteenth day of the dark half of the lunar month Ashvina to the second day of the light half of Karttika.
b) An eight-day festival, beginning on the twenty-fifth day of Kislev.
c) A four-day festival beginning on the tenth day of Dhu'l-Hijja.
d) A three-day festival occurring the day after Holi.
e) A forty-day festival which begins six-and-a-half weeks before Easter.

21. In which year did the popular and still much-admired 'King James' version of the Bible appear as an 'authorised edition to be read in the churches'?

a) 1611
b) 1612
c) 1116
d) 1721

22. The thirty-nine books of what is called the Old Testament (or Old Covenant) were originally written in:

a) Aramaic
b) Latin
c) Hebrew
d) Greek

23. The 114 chapters that make up the *Qur'an* were originally written in:

a) Sumerian
b) Sanskrit
c) Arabic
d) Aramaic

24. Much like a *Choose Your Own Adventure* book, most religions have their very own creation myths, which provide an astounding array of possibilities about how we got here and why life is the way it is.

a) If you believe that the universe was made by Waheguru, chances are you are a ____.
b) If you believe that God created the world in six days and rested on the seventh, chances are you are ____.
c) If you believe that the world was created by a creator deity who made an egg bearing two pairs of twins who, at maturation, were meant to be androgynous (the most perfect creatures), chances are you are a ____.
d) If you believe that in the beginning of time there was no light or darkness, just emptiness and that into this emptiness, two gods appeared – Ranginui, the god of the sky, and Papatuanuku, the goddess of the earth – and that when they appeared so did the sky and the earth and they embraced so closely that the earth and the sky were joined together and had six children, one of whom was called Tu, the god of war, who in turn created people, chances are you are a ____.

25. '*Adah*' means what in Islamic law?

a) Complete submission to the will of Allah, the fundamental tenet of Islam
b) Muslim jurisprudence (the science of determining the exact meaning of canon law)
c) A religious duty to fight religious wars
d) A local custom that can be recognised as a law

26. Ever feel like you aren't taking enough of a stand for what you believe in? Prepared to be burned on a flaming wheel for your principles? Here are eight martyrs who suffered the ultimate penalty for their faith. Match the dates of their demises to the beatified.

1532, 1252, 1900, *c*.620, 249, 1885–87, 680

a) The year Saint Apollonia (patron saint of dentists) had her teeth knocked out before jumping into a fire when she refused to renounce her faith during the reign of Emperor Philip.
b) Execution of the Martyrs of Uganda, forty-five Anglican and Roman Catholics killed during the persecution of Christians under Mwanga, the ruler of Buganda.
c) Assassination of Saint Peter Martyr (also known as Peter of Verona) by the heretical Christian sect, the Cathari.
d) The 'Boxer Rebellion', a mass killing of thousands of foreigners and Chinese Christians by martial art devotees who thought they could become immune to bullets and swords through calisthenics and diet and were provoked by Christian missionaries.
e) The beheading of Saint Dymphna by her own father after she refused to marry him.
f) The slaying of al-Husayn ibn Alì, grandson of the Prophet Muhammad and son of Alì (the fourth Islamic caliph) and Fàtima, daughter of Muhammad, for refusing to recognise the legitimacy of the Umayyads after his father's assassination.
g) The year Solomon Molcho (Diogo Pires), the son of Portuguese or Spanish Jews who had been forced to convert to Christianity, was burned at the stake for trying to convince the Portuguese that an Arabian adventurer called David Reubeni was the messiah and for refusing to convert to Christianity.

27. The *Book of Hours* is a Christian devotional book which was very popular in the Middle Ages and is one of the most common types of illuminated manuscript (a handwritten book that has been decorated with gold or silver, brilliant colours, elaborate designs or miniature pictures) that survives. Developed for lay people who wanted to incorporate elements of monasticism into their devotional life, the book is an abbreviated form of the breviary and contains (among other things) a calendar of church feasts, an excerpt from each of the four gospels, a litany of saints and an office for the dead, usually written in Latin, though there were many English translations available. In addition to helping Christians get closer to God, the *Book of Hours* can also be held responsible for:

a) The increased literacy of women and children
b) The increase of interest in book collecting and ownership
c) An increase in social rivalry as determined by whose *Book* was more beautifully (and expensively) produced
d) All of the above

28. Over the centuries, many texts have been banned by religious authorities. Can you name the country these books below are (or were) banned in, and the religious dispositions they offend?

a) *A Feast for the Seaweeds* by Haidar Haidar (1983)
b) *Alice's Adventures in Wonderland* by Lewis Carroll (1865)
c) *Borstal Boy* by Brendan Behan (1958)
d) *The Diary of Anne Frank* by Anne Frank (1947)
e) *Jinnah of Pakistan* by Stanley Wolpert (1984)
f) *Uncle Tom's Cabin; or, Life Among the Lowly* by Harriet Beecher Stowe (1852)

29. Which philosopher and theologian of the Roman Catholic church, who has been the subject of an earlier Religious Education question, claimed (rather dishearteningly) that laws are moral obligations that originate in the mind of God and terminate in the mind of man?

a) Saint Thomas Aquinas
b) Albertus Magnus
c) Roger Bacon
d) Saint Ignatius de Loyola

30. This question is as tricky as Gomukhasana (cow-faced pose). Though its practical aspect does play a more central role than its intellectual component, Yoga is not just an exercise regime for Notting Hill types.

Rather it's one of six orthodox systems of Indian philosophy and holds that spiritual liberation comes when the self is freed from the bondage of matter. This liberation is reached only after mastering the eight stages of yoga, the first seven of which are listed below, though in scrambled form. By unscrambling the letters and spelling out their proper names, use the letters in the numbered boxes below and feel your own sense of ecstasy arrive by naming the eighth stage: the precondition for attaining Yoga's ultimate reality.

MAYA	☐☐☐☐ (box 3 = 3rd letter)
NIAYMA	☐☐☐☐☐☐ (box 7 = 2nd letter)
NAASA	☐☐☐☐☐ (box 1 = 2nd letter)
NAYPAARAM	☐☐☐☐☐☐☐☐☐ (box 4 = 5th letter)
TAAPAHRAYR	☐☐☐☐☐☐☐☐☐☐ (box 6 = 7th letter)
DAANAHR	☐☐☐☐☐☐☐ (box 5 = 1st letter)
HAADYN	☐☐☐☐☐☐ (box 2 = 6th letter)

☐☐☐☐☐☐☐
1 2 3 4 5 6 7

31. Before we say goodbye to Yoga, you must master the second stage of this question by matching the eight stages of yoga to the dispositions they cultivate. And we'll give you a hint: the first two stages are ethical preparations; the following two are physical; the final three are mental. (To give you a hint about stage number five would make the question too easy . . .)

yama	'breath control'
niyama	'restraint'
asana	'holding on'

pranayama	'withdrawal'
pratyahara	'self-collectedness'
dharana	'observance'
dhyana	'seat'
samadhi	'concentrated meditation'

32. Which Roman emperor said, on his deathbed (as a joke): '*Vae, puto deus fio*' ('Oh dear, I think I'm becoming a god') and was immediately accorded deification.

a) Titus (79–81 CE)
b) Vespasian (69–79 CE)
c) Augustus (31 BC–14 CE)
d) Claudius (41–54 CE)

33. For some, telepathic activity, UFO-spotting, polygamy and mass suicide are more preferable ways of expressing devotion than boring old prayer, fasting and adherence to some old-fashioned holy text. The practitioners of the former are said to be members of sects or cults, which are often rich repositories for novelistic material. Which of these cults are real and which are the figments of a writer's imagination?

a) Chen Tao was a cult holding many strange UFO-related beliefs (including the assumption that spaceships disguised as clouds would land on earth and, for the small sum of about $40,000 made payable to their leader Hon-Ming Chen, one could gain passage aboard). In 1997 Chen claimed that at 12:01 on 15 March God would appear on Channel 18 on TV stations across America.
b) Heaven's Gate was another UFO-loving cult which advocated extreme self-renunciation to the point of castration. Leader Marshall Applewhite was convinced that the Hale-Bopp comet's passing was an opportunity to hitch a ride with a spacecraft in the dust trail. However, reaching this spaceship involved death by asphyxiation, claiming the lives of over thirty-five members.
c) The Elohimites were a sect of sun-worshipping, free-love

practising alien-watchers based on Lanzarote who claimed to have perfected the art of cloning. Not only could they save cells cryogenically, but they also found a way to allow personality and memory to be passed intact from generation to generation. They believed that these exact DNA replicas of people would go on to inhabit the world for ever, even in a post-apocalyptic landscape ravaged by global warming and nuclear war.

d) NICE, the National Institute for Co-ordinated Experiments, was a British body of so-called scientists dedicated to reorganising civil society along strictly scientific lines by first taking over the university town of Edgestow before hitting up all of England and then the grand prize: world domination by controlling the media, the economy and the government. The new social rules included 'remedial treatment' (whatever that is) for prisoners, vivisection for those whose moral senses needed 'dulling', and the full elimination of 'useless' and 'obsolete' people who slowed down the quest for the efficient conquest of nature.

34. Karma, the law by which good or bad action informs the future circumstances of a person in the cycles of birth, death and rebirth, is a central belief of Hinduism and Buddhism. Which other religion's theological discourse and practice is also dominated by the concept of karma?

a) Hare Krishna
b) Jehovah's Witnesses
c) Jainism
d) Both a) and c)

35. Catholicism, that decisive spiritual force in the history of Western civilisation, has over 1.1 billion followers. That's more than the number of *all* other Christians combined and more than *all* Buddhists or Hindus. Within this amalgam of followers are many converts. Which of the following British writers made the switch?

Graham Greene
W. Somerset Maugham
Muriel Spark
Frederick Rolfe
Ernest Dowson
William Golding

Evelyn Waugh
Ford Madox Ford
Wilfred Owen
Coventry Patmore
Beryl Bainbridge
Elinor Brent-Dyer
Thomas Hardy
Kingsley Amis
C.S. Lewis
G.K. Chesterton
J. R. R. Tolkien
Siegfried Sassoon
Iris Murdoch
Georgina Fullerton
Edmund Crispin
Mary Wesley
Margery Allingham
H.G. Wells
John Galsworthy
Arnold Lunn

36. What is the name of the group of Russian religious dissenters who refused to accept the liturgical reforms imposed upon the Russian Orthodox church by the patriarch of Moscow, Nikon, and became separated from the Church after 1666?

a) The New Mongols
b) The Old Believers
c) Rasputinites
d) The Ivanists

37. Below are the names of eleven sacred mountains, but for whom are they sacred?

Mount Kailash
Mount Ararat
Mount Sinai
Mount Moriah
Mount Tabor
Mount Arunachala
Mount Olympus
Mount Fuji
Mount Tlaloc
Adam's Peak
Mount Katahdin

38. Christ's twelve disciples were a real motley crew. Answer the questions below about this famous team.

a) What is the name of the first disciple, and what is he also known as?
b) Who was his brother?
c) Which one was a tax inspector?
d) Whose sons were the two Jameses?
e) Thaddaeus was also known as?
f) What is the full name of the disciple who betrayed Jesus?

39. In Juan de Juanes' famous painting *The Last Supper* (*c.* 1560), Judas Iscariot has been equipped with an object so that he can be instantly recognised, by the viewer, as the traitor among Christ and his disciples. What is the object?

a) A money pouch
b) A wafer
c) A wash-pan
d) A crucifix

40. Continuing with the subject of religion and art, which of these statements about Islamic art are true, and which are not?

a) Islamic art is restricted to religious work.
b) People do not appear in specifically religious art.
c) A Muslim artist will not attempt to replicate nature as it is, but tries to convey what it represents.
d) Geometry is a common feature of Islamic art, but has no spiritual significance.
e) Islamic art is intended to be the mirror of Islamic culture and its world view.
f) Islamic art discourages the aesthetic influence of other cultures and religions.

41. Roman Catholicism has a reputation for the extreme veneration of relics, i.e. any object that has been in contact with a saint, including their body parts. What are the governing Islamic, Buddhist and Hindu attitudes to relic worship?

42. Most religions are associated with one or a number of texts. Match the religions (and the one non-religion) with the (or one of) the texts they adhere to:

Confucianism	*The Divine Principle*
Deism	*Al-Naqd al-Khafi* (*Copy of the Secret*)
Scientology	Thomas Paine's *The Age of Reason*
Seventh-day Adventists	*Zend-avesta*
Unification Church	Bonpo canon
Zoroastrianism	*The Communist Manifesto*
Gnosticism	*Analects*
Bön	*Gospels* and *Acts*
Atheism	Christian Bible
Druze	*Dianetics*

43. Which member of the Royal Family is reportedly worshipped as the incarnation of a spirit who emerged from a volcano by members of the Yaohnanen tribe on the island of Tanna in southern Vanuatu?

a) Prince Andrew
b) Prince William
c) Princess Anne
d) Prince Philip

44. Dietary laws and religious custom often go hand in hand (except within Christianity, which appears not to have developed any food rules). Such laws can range from a simple restriction to the exclusion of an entire food group to a fetishisation of one particular item or the banning of particular things during certain festivals. Below are some descriptions of various kinds of food customs. Can you figure out what the missing words are?

a) The laws of food and custom are a prevalent part of Hinduism that function also as an index to social standing. For instance, only ____ are permitted to eat 'pakka', foods that usually include ____ (clarified butter), which is not only expensive but is thought to promote health and virility, and they must also avoid all meat and accept neither cooked food nor water across caste lines.

b) Hasidism abides by the dietary laws of Judaism (no animals that chew their cuds or have cloven feet, like pigs or horses; no fish without ____ or shellfish, no animal blood, no creatures that creep and no fowl enumerated in the Bible, including vultures, hawks or owls) but imposes the further restriction that all preparation, manufacture, handling and selling of food must only be done by someone from the Hasidic community. Anything less is deemed ____.

c) Many of the dietary regulations for Muslims outlined in the *Qur'an* reflect Mosaic Law in forbidding consumption of the ____ of any animal, the flesh of swine or of animals that are found dead, food that has been offered or sacrificed to idols and alcohol of any kind. Like 'kosher', ____ is a term which designates a permissible action or object and in relation to food, it denotes a specific way in which an animal must be slaughtered, a technique intended to effectively drain the body of the animal's blood, resulting in more hygienic meat.

d) The Kofyar are a population of about 50,000 in central Nigeria who gained much notoriety when the American anthropologist Robert McCorkle Netting began observing them in the early 1960s for his groundbreaking book *Hill Farmers of Nigeria* (1968). ____, explained Netting, plays such a central role in their lives that Kofyar men seem to 'believe that man's way to god is with ____ in hand'.
All social relations among the tribe are accompanied by its consumption, and fines are levied in payments of it. (It should be said, however, that theirs is weak in alcoholic content and is quite nutritious. Furthermore, they rarely consume the European stuff and never drink distilled liquor.)

45. Match up the religious movements with the dates they were founded AND the names of their founders (or, in one case, the place of origin).

Christian Science	1965	Zeno
Aladura	1879	Mary Baker Eddy
Confucianism	*c.* 550 BCE	Phineas P. Quimby

Eckankar	*c.* 1918	Confucius
Jehovah's Witnesses	6th–5th century BCE	West Nigeria
New Thought	19th century	Lao-Tzu
Stoicism	*c.* 300	John Paul Twitchell
Taoism	1879	Charles Taze Russell

46. Who is Senuna?

a) An ancient British goddess
b) An ancient Norse goddess
c) The daughter of Hera and Zeus
d) The Aramaic name for the Virgin Mary's mother

47. It's an indisputable fact that people's passionately held religious beliefs can lead to misunderstandings and brutal conflicts. Can you unscramble the words below to find six religious wars?

a) Ibgeanlsian Dreuacs
b) Rüetsmn Nlrleibeo
c) Intpgia Nroleilbe
d) Ttleab fo Donmarum
e) Rwlfeo Rsaw

48. In the Roman Catholic church priests are supposed to be celibate, in emulation of Jesus's celibacy. However, this difficult principle has not always been honoured, even by the highest church officials. Which of these popes had children?

Pope St Hormisdas
Pope Hadrian II
Pope Alexander VI
Pope Paul III
Pope Benedict XVI

49. Animals have always played a large part in religious worship (think of Ganesh, the elephant-human who holds such a central role in Hinduism). Which of the following religions worships their chief angel through the figure of a peacock?

a) The First Church of Jesus Christ, Elvis
b) Shamans
c) The Yazīdī
d) Bronze Age Greece

50. Complete the following sentence:

A Bar Mitzvah is a Jewish ritual and family celebration commemorating the religious adulthood of a ____ on their ____ birthday and a Bat Mitzvah is a Jewish ritual and family celebration commemorating the religious adulthood of a ____ on their ____ birthday.

꩜ RELIGIOUS EDUCATION ꩜ ANSWERS

1. c) Epicureanism, founded in Athens in *c.* 300 BCE, is based on the metaphysical and ethical doctrines of Epicurus (341–270 BCE,), a Greek philosopher, and holds that gods do exist, but take no notice of us insignificant humans. Its primary texts are the 'Letters' and *Principal Doctrines* of Epicurus. The Mayans were very much a polytheistic people, worshipping many gods, including Itzamná, Kukulcán, Bolon Tzacab and Chac, all of whom were spiritually active in the world. The Baha'i faith, founded in 1863 by Bahã Ullãh in Tehran, takes the very open position of believing in a singular god who has revealed himself progressively through major world religions, and straight-up Deism subscribes to the tenet that reason is the basis for all knowledge, but believes there is only one God who is loftily not very interested in the world.

2. Saint Ignatius de Loyola (1491–1556) founded the Society of Jesus, commonly known as the Jesuit Order, with five associates in Paris in 1534.

Joseph Smith, Jr is credited with the organisation of the Mormon Church at Fayette, New York in 1830, when he published the *Book of Mormon*.

Amaterasu is a Shinto sun goddess. Shinto is an organised mythology stemming from a simple worship of nature and an insistence on physical and ritual purity, which was formed in Japan prior to 645 CE. After the introduction of the rival religion Buddhism, this combination of nature-worship, ritual and ancestor-honouring was given the name of 'Shinto' to distinguish it from the imported Indian religion.

Alì ibn Abi Talib was the first imam (leader) of the Shī'a Muslims, and a cousin of the Prophet Muhammad.

Zacharias Frankel founded Conservative Judaism. Born in 1801, Frankel's ideas about Judaism inspired a religious movement that seeks to conserve essential elements of traditional Judaism while allowing for the modernisation of religious practices in a less radical sense than that espoused by Reform Judaism. He broke with modernising extremists after a series of Reform conferences in Germany between 1844 and 1846.

Abu Bakr founded Sunnī Islam. The death of the Prophet Muhammad in 632 CE created confusion in the nascent Muslim community, because he hadn't named his successor. After a heated discussion by the senior members of the community, Abu Bakr was selected as the first caliph (or 'ruler'). However, he was not universally embraced and the confusion did not end with his accession, as tribes all around Arabia broke out in open revolt. Known as the 'Wars of Apostasy', the rebellions were not subdued until the end of 633. One of the two major branches of Islam, the other being Shī'ism, the Sunnis recognise the first four caliphs as Muhammad's rightful successors.

Gerald Brousseau Gardner (1884–1964) founded Wicca. Wicca is a predominantly Western movement whose followers practise witchcraft and nature worship and who see it as a religion based on pre-Christian traditions of northern and western Europe. Gardner was a retired British civil servant who spent most of his career in Asia, where he became familiar with a variety of occult beliefs and magical practices. Most controversial to outsiders is that Wiccans call themselves *witches*, a term that many identify with Satanism. As a result, Wiccans are continually denying any connection with Satan or devil worship. Wiccans have also attempted to establish ties with other polytheistic (Hindu) and nature-oriented (Native American) religious communities.

Neith was an ancient Egyptian war goddess who was the patroness of the city of Sais in the Nile River delta and worshipped as early as predynastic times (*c.* 3000 BCE). Her principal emblem was a pair of crossed arrows shown against the background of a leather shield.

Haile Selassie I founded Rastafarianism. Though Bob Marley can be credited with popularising this religion, many (though not all) Rastas believe that the Ethiopian emperor, His Imperial Majesty Haile Selassie I (crowned in 1930) is the Second Coming of Christ who returned to redeem all black people. The movement takes its name from the emperor's pre-coronation name, Ras Tafari, and began in Jamaica in the 1930s. Adopted by many groups around the globe, it combines Protestant Christianity, mysticism, and a pan-African political consciousness.

3. c) The Puritans. Having grown discontented with the Church of England, the Puritans were a branch of dissenters who escaped persecution from church leadership and the king by fleeing to America, mostly to New England. What many of us remember about them is reflective of the modern definition of the term 'puritan' and not of the historical account. Firstly, they were not a small, marginal cult. In England many of their persuasion sat in Parliament and as they emigrated and formed individual colonies in America, their numbers rose from 17,800 in 1640 to 106,000 in 1700. Secondly, the witchcraft trials did not appropriately define their methods of living for the hundred years that they formed successful communities. What it did show was the dangers of their self-imposed isolation (religious exclusiveness was the foremost principle of their society) and the degree to which their persecution informed their fears about their own self-preservation.

4.

5. c) Abraham was the first of the Hebrew patriarchs, the earliest biblical character who is delineated clearly enough to be correlated within world history and a figure revered by the three great monotheistic religions – Judaism, Christianity and Islam – which trace their common origin to him. Judaism regards itself as the religion of the descendants of Abraham's grandson Jacob, Christianity began as a sect of Judaism and reveres Abraham as an example of great faith in God, and within Islam he is known as an important prophet (called Ibrahim) through whom God revealed his will, and an ancestor of the Arab people.

6. Leah means cow; Deborah means bee; Eve means 'the mother of all things'; Dinah comes from 'to judge'; Rachel means ewe; Sarah means princess; Susanna means lily; Huldah means weasel

7. c)

8. b) Saint Thomas's arguments for the existence of God are a little more refined than our descriptions have them, but can be summarised as the argument for motion; the argument for possibility and necessity; the argument from design; the argument from efficient causes; and the argument from gradation of being. Death, in other words, doesn't come much into it. Aquinas wasn't completely original in his theory and based his 'five ways' on Aristotle's own arguments for God, most specifically his conception of the 'unmoved mover' or the 'uncaused cause'.

9.

Amitabha: as related in the *Sukhavati-vyuha-sutra*s, many ages ago a monk named Dharmakara made a number of vows, the eighteenth of which promised that, on his attaining buddhahood, all who had faith in him and who called upon his name would be reborn in his paradise. Having accomplished his vows, Dharmakara reigned as the buddha Amitabha in the Western Paradise, called Sukhavati, the Pure Land. **Mahayana**: a movement that arose within Indian Buddhism around the beginning of the Common Era and became, by the ninth century, the dominant influence on the Buddhist cultures of Central and East Asia, which it remains today. In contrast to the stricter Theravada tradition, it is the Buddhism of ordinary people and holds that Buddhahood is attainable, in principle, by everyone. **Nichiren**: also known as the Lotus Sect, this is one of the largest schools of Japanese Buddhism named after its founder, the thirteenth-century militant prophet and saint, Nichiren. **Pure Land**: one of the most popular forms of Mahayana Buddhism in eastern Asia today, it believes that rebirth in Sukhavati is ensured for all those who invoke Amitabha's name with sincere devotion. **Theravada**: the oldest Buddhist school which claims to perpetuate the authentic teachings of the Buddha according to the scriptures of his early followers, and a major form prevalent in Sri Lanka, Burma, Thailand, Laos and Cambodia. **Tibetan**: also called Lamaism, this is a Mahayana school derived primarily from Indian traditions. **Vajrayana**: a form of Tantric Buddhism that developed in India and neighbouring countries, notably Tibet. In the history of Buddhism it marks the transition from Mahayana speculative thought to the enactment of Buddhist ideas in individual life. **Zen**: an amalgam of Mahayana Buddhism with Taoism. Zen is the way of enlightenment through meditation and simple living.

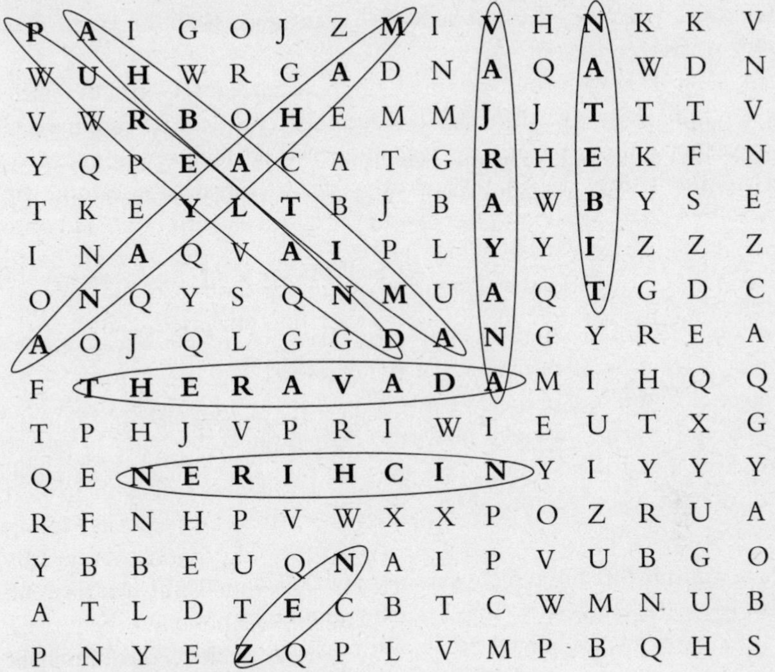

10. a) Thomas Jefferson (1743–1826), from his book *Notes on the State of Virginia* (1783). In a letter written in 1815, Jefferson examined the other side of the matter, declaring that the interference of the church in affairs of state, under the guise of political sermons, was equally menacing. 'The mass of human concerns, moral and physical, is so vast, the field of knowledge requisite for man to conduct them to the best advantage is so extensive, that no human being can acquire the whole himself, and much less in that degree necessary for the instruction of others. It has of necessity, then, been distributed into different departments, each of which, singly, may give occupation enough to the whole time and attention of a single individual. Thus we have teachers of languages, teachers of mathematics, of natural philosophy, of chemistry, of medicine, of law, of history, of government, etc. Religion, too, is a separate department, and happens to be the only one deemed requisite for all men, however high or low.'

11. India, Lebanon, Turkey, Yemen, Afghanistan, Bahrain, Azerbaijan, Saudi Arabia.

12. Caliphs, Bar Mitzvah, Messiah, Yahweh, Pranayama, Dalai Lama, Judaic, Bhagavad Gita, Taoism, Lao-Tzu, Jainism, Feng Shui, Solomon, Sikh, Baha'i, Confucius, Synagogue, Eucharist, Yom Kippur, Deuteronomy.

13. d) Regarded as the successor of St Peter (head of the Apostles), and God's representative on earth, the pope is the head of the Roman Catholic Church, though the job title varies to include: Vicar of Jesus Christ, Successor of the Prince of the Apostles, Supreme Pontiff of the Universal Church, Patriarch of the West, Primate of Italy, Metropolitan Archbishop of the Province of Rome, Sovereign of the State of Vatican City, Servant of the Servants of God. The title *pope* or *papa* is officially used only as a less solemn style.

14. Seventeen, three of which were 'antipopes' (Clements III (1080–1100), VII (1378–94) and VIII (1423–29) who, in an effort to erase them from the historical record, Stalin-style, had the numbers following their names allocated to their successive Clements (the new Clement III was pope from 1187–1191, VII from 1523–1534 and VIII 1592–1605).

15. The 'new' Clement VII (1523–1534), whose real name was Giulio de' Medici. He is the famous pope who refused Henry VIII his divorce from Catherine of Aragon.

16.

Islam means 'surrender'. Founded by Muhammad in Arabia in the early seventh century CE, the Arabic word 'islam' means 'surrender', specifically the surrender of the will to the one God.

Santería means 'Way of the Saints' in Spanish. Brought to Cuba by the people of the Yoruban nations of West Africa, the name 'The Way of the Saints' comes from the correspondences made by some devotees between the Yoruba deities called *orishas* and the saints (*santos*) of Roman Catholic piety. Many contemporary practitioners refer to the tradition as 'the religion of the *orisha*s' or the 'Lukumi religion,' after the name by which the Yoruba were known in Cuba.

Shintõ means 'Way of the Kami'. Based on the worship of spirits known as *kami*, Shinto has no founder and no official scripture, though its mythology is collected in the *Kojiki* ('Records of Ancient Matters') and *Nihon shoki* ('Chronicles of Japan'), written in the eighth century CE.

Jainism means 'to conquer'. From the Sanskrit verb *ji* (which means 'to conquer'), Jainism is a religion of India established between the seventh and fifth centuries BCE, the core belief of which is *ahimsa*, or non-injury to all living things.

Kabbalah means 'tradition'. This school of thought with a Hebrew name is based on a series of esoteric Judaic teachings concerning the relationship between an eternal divinity and a finite humanity. It began in the twelfth century and has always been essentially an oral tradition.

Gurmat means 'Way of the Guru'. This Punjabi term is what Sikhs call their faith. According to Sikh tradition, Sikhism was established by Guru Nanak (1469–1539) and subsequently led by a succession of nine other Gurus.

Falun Gong means 'The Practice of the Wheel of Dharma'. The sudden emergence of this controversial Chinese spiritual movement founded by Li-Hongzhi in 1992 was a great concern to the Chinese government, which viewed Falun Gong as a cult. The teachings of Falun Gong draw from the Asian religious traditions of Buddhism, Taoism, Confucianism and Chinese folklore as well as those of Western New-Age-movements, and its adherents exercise ritually to obtain mental and spiritual renewal.

17. Hinduism (*c.* 1800 BCE); Judaism (*c.* 1500 BCE); Buddhism (between 600–400 BCE); Christianity (*c.* 100); Islam (*c.* 610); Sikhism (*c.* 1500)

18. d) 'When Israel was in Egypt's Land,/Let my people go,/Oppressed so hard they could not stand,/Let my people go. (Chorus): Go down, Moses,/Way down in Egypt's Land./Tell ol' Pharaoh,/Let my people go.' The lyrics and music to 'Go Down, Moses' are anonymous, though it is widely assumed that the hymn was first written and performed as a rallying anthem for the Contrabands (slaves who fled to join the Union army) at Fort Monroe sometime before July 1862. In 1958, Louis Armstrong recorded a now-famous version of it and William Faulkner's *Go Down, Moses* (1942), a book of interwoven stories about exploitation on a plantation, was named after the hymn. 'We need not always weep and mourn,/Let my people go,/And wear these slavery chains forlorn,/Let my people go' is the final verse.

19. Rat, Ox, Tiger, Rabbit, Dragon, Snake, Horse, Goat, Monkey, Rooster, Dog and Boar. We are currently in the Year of the Rabbit, which began on 3 February 2011 and marked the start of year 4709 on the Chinese Calendar. The rabbit is said to be affectionate, gentle and to have strong family ties. It is caring and peace-making with many friends, and dislikes being the centre of attention. Sound like your year thus far?

20. a) Diwali. The festival of lights is the most popular of all the festivals in South Asia. It is an occasion for celebrations by Hindus as well as Jains and Sikhs in late October and November. b) Hanukkah, the Jewish 'Festival of Lights', occurs in December and marks the restoration of the temple by the Jewish rebels, the Maccabees, in 164 BCE. c) Eid al-Adha is the Festival of Sacrifice, which marks the culmination of the hajj (pilgrimage) rites at Minā, Saudi Arabia, near Mecca, and is celebrated by Muslims throughout the world. d) Hola Mahalla is the Sikh festival of military exercises and mock battles, together with religious discussions and devotional music, at the city of Anandpur Sahib. Holi, of course, is the Hindu spring festival celebrated throughout North India on the full-moon day of the month of Phalguna in February and March. e) Lent commences on Ash Wednesday in Western Christian churches and on the Monday of the seventh week before Easter in Eastern churches. Lent is the season marking the time Jesus spent in the wilderness and many Christians imitate his fast by giving something up, be it chocolates, chips or cigarettes.

21. a) By the time of James I of England and VI of Scotland's accession to the throne in 1603, the variety of translations of the Bible available reflected more the religious and social turmoil of the previous century than a scholarly desire for pluralistic interpretation. After James I proclaimed, 'I profess I could never yet see a Bible well translated in English . . . I wish some special pains were taken for a uniform translation', forty-seven scholars laboured in six groups at three locations for seven years, utilising previous English translations and texts in the original languages. The new translation was intended to be conceived of not only as a document of political and theological compromise which could unite Christians in their beliefs, but also as a text that would openly refer to and incorporate previous translations. The KJV, if you want to call it by its nickname, is celebrated for the poetry of its language. It begins sonorously with the lines from Genesis: 'And the earth was without form, and void; and darkness [was] upon the face of the deep. And the Spirit of God moved upon the face of the waters. And God said, Let there be light: and there was light.'

22. c) The Old Testament was first written in Hebrew, even though Hebrew was so unfamiliar to the Palestinian Jews in the first century that even in synagogues the scriptures had to be paraphrased! It was then translated into Aramaic, the assumed language of Jesus and his immediate circle. The twenty-seven books of the New Testament were thought to have been written in Greek for the Greek Christians of the first century, and from Greek were translated into the Latin 'Vulgate' by Jerome, an early Christian leader (though Jerome returned to the original Hebrew for his 405 translation of the entire Old Testament as he was dissatisfied with the Greek version) and many fourteenth-, fifteenth- and sixteenth-century bibles (including the Wycliffe and Rheims-Douai) were translated from his Vulgate edition.

23. c) One of the most important qualities of the *Qur'an* as a sacred text (and one that marks it out as being categorically different from its great rival in exclusivity, the Bible) is that it was written in the exact same sacred and liturgical language as that of its historical and contemporary readers.

24. a) Sikh. Sikhs believe the universe was made by Waheguru (God) who created the earth and all forms of life on it by uttering a single word. b) Either Christian or Jewish. For Christians, the story of creation is found in the first two chapters of the Book of Genesis in the Bible; for Judaism accounts of creation are found in the first two chapters of the book of Genesis in the Torah. c) A member of the Dogon peoples of west Africa. The myth states that within the creator's egg were two pairs of twins, each pair consisting of one male and one female, who would be born androgynous. But before they were born, one of the twins desired to control creation and broke from the egg carrying a part of the egg with him, from which he created an imperfect world. d) Maori.

25. d) '*Adah*' is a local custom that is given special consideration by judicial authorities to be regarded as lawful, even when it conflicts with a principle of Sharia law. For instance in parts of India many Muslims adopt children, which is forbidden by canon law. Communities often decide themselves which *adahs* can be recognised by religious courts.

26. a) 249; b) 1885–87; c) 1252; d) 1900; e) *c.* 620 (she was fifteen at the time of her death); f) 680; g) 1532.

27. d) Alongside a love of God, it is true to say that many people adore beautiful things and the autonomy that comes with being literate.

28. a) *A Feast for the Seaweeds* was banned in Egypt, Gaza and other Arab states in 2000 on the grounds that it didn't 'agree with the teachings of Islamic Sharia'. b) *Alice's Adventures in Wonderland* was banned in China in 1931 for portraying animals as being as intelligent as humans. (According to the Governor of Hunan Province, 'Animals should not use human language.') c) *Borstal Boy*, Brendan Behan's autobiographical prison memoir, was banned on publication in Ireland for its critique of both the Republic and the Catholic Church. d) *The Diary of Anne Frank* remains (at the time of writing) banned in Lebanon for its favourable portrayal of Jews, Israel and Zionism. Several other books that may be seen to portray Jewish people in a favourable light have also been banned in Lebanon, including some by Philip Roth, William Styron and Thomas Friedman. (We wonder if Woody Allen's films are available . . .) e) Academic and historian Stanley Wolpert's biography of Mohammed Ali Jinnah, the founder and first governor of Pakistan, was banned in that country for its account of the Indian Muslim's appetite for whisky and forbidden pork. Pressure was put on Wolpert by his publisher to simply exclude any mention of Jinnah's indulgences and avoid the ban, but Wolpert refused to change anything. The ban was lifted in Benazir Bhutto's first term, and the book is now in print in Pakistan and India. f) *Uncle Tom's Cabin; or, Life Among the Lowly* was famously banned in the US during the Civil War for its position against slavery, but was also banned in Russia by Nicholas I due to the idea of equality it presented, and for its 'undermining religious ideals'.

29. a) From 'Treatise on Law', Aquinas' analysis of how laws are formalised from customs which is found in the first section of part two of the sadly incomplete *Summa theologiae* (1265 or 1266–73).

30.

yama
niyama
asana
pranayama
pratyahara
dharana
dhyana
samadhi

31. *Yama* (restraint, i.e. abstinence from stealing and lying), *niyama* (observance, or being clean, austere and devoted to God), *asana* (seat, which denotes a series of exercises to make one's body supple and flexible), *pranayama* (breath control, which consists of exercises to stabilise breathing), *pratyahara*(withdrawal, or control of the senses), *dharana* (holding on, or the ability to focus on one thing for extensive periods of time), *dhyana* (concentrated meditation), *samadhi* (self-collectedness).

32. b) Vespasian famously restored peace and order to an empire in disarray following the death of the famously unpopular Nero, so it was fitting that *pax* ('civil peace') should be a principle motif on his coinage, but amid his earnest accomplishments he also cultivated a bluff manner, characteristic of the humble origins he liked to recall, and had a hearty sense of humour, as evidenced by his final words.

33. a) Real. Chen Tao ('True Way') was one of the most recent and highly publicised of the 'new religions' in Taiwan. Unfortunately for Chen, God did not appear on everyone's TV set at the predicted time and the cult all but disbanded in 1998. b) Real. Heaven's Gate was a San Diego-based cult from the 1990s that had a number of different names over the years, including Human Individual Metamorphosis, Bo and Peep, and Total Overcomers Anonymous. c) Fictional. The Elohimites are a cult at the heart of Michel Houellebecq's 2003 novel,

The Possibility of an Island, though they are very much based on the real cult the Raëlians, with whom Houellebecq spent some time. The Raëlians, founded by journalist Claude Vorilhon in the French provincial town of Clermont-Ferrand, are also free-love UFO-worshippers who gained notoriety when one of their leaders announced in 2002 that they had successfully cloned the world's first human. d) Fictional, though it's easy to see aspects of some very real social agendas in this. NICE is at the centre of C. S. Lewis's 1945 novel *That Hideous Strength: A Modern Fairy Tale for Grown-ups*. Its ultimate reality includes not just the doing away with undesirables, but also all organic (i.e. flawed) life. Quite nicely, an earthquake ruins the NICE headquarters causing the deaths of most NICE personnel and liberating many of the caged animals upon which they were conducting experiments.

34. d) Hare Krishna is the Western interpretation of the popular sixteenth-century Bengali yoga tradition. Adherents believe that humans are eternal spiritual beings trapped in a cycle of reincarnation and that it is possible to change one's karma by practising extreme forms of yoga (or through the much easier method of reciting the Lord's holy names, Krishna and Rama, hence their love of chanting). In Jainism, the recommended method for eliminating the results of karma is to lead an ascetic life.

35. The most famous is perhaps Graham Greene, whose conversion, in 1926, was largely to do with his wife's faith. Dame Muriel Spark took the plunge in 1954 when she was in her mid-thirties; Evelyn Waugh, whose awakening is very much represented in *Brideshead Revisited* (1945), in 1930. Ford Madox Ford (having already changed his name) saw the light at the age of nineteen while his grandfather's contemporary Coventry Patmore made the move in 1862. No one knows exactly how old Dame Beryl Bainbridge was because her date of birth is undetermined (it's either 1932 or 1934, so averaging it out to 1933 would have her sixteen when she converted. Also unknown is whether she ever practised her newly found faith . . .). Children's writer Elinor Brent-Dyer converted in 1930, G. K. Chesterton in 1922, Frederick Rolfe in 1886 and the poet Ernest Dowson in 1892. J. R. R. Tolkien's mother converted in 1900 when he was only eight, so we can assume that's when his devotion took hold, Siegfried Sassoon shortly after his seventy-first birthday in 1957, Georgina Fullerton in 1846 and Mary Wesley sometime after 1945. Finally, the British skier and writer Sir Arnold Lunn turned his back on Protestantism only two years after he wrote some very public criticisms of Catholicism, in 1934.

36. b) In the seventeenth century, Russia was still using the liturgical books that were around at the time of the conversion of Rus to Christianity in 988 CE: literal translations from the Greek into Old Slavic and later, manuscript copies of those translations that were sometimes inaccurate, obscure and further mutilated by the mistakes of the scribes. Patriarch Nikon wanted to reform these old texts and sign off on a definitive new one, but this proved to be difficult because there was no agreement as to what – or where – the ideal or original text was. To simplify everything, he decided to follow exactly the texts and practices of the Greek Church as they existed in 1652, the beginning of his reign, and to this effect he ordered the printing of new liturgical books following the Greek pattern. The reform, obligatory for all, was supported by Tsar Alexis Romanov, but opposition to Nikon was led by a group of Muscovite priests, notably the archpriest Avvakum Petrovich. Even after the deposition of Nikon (1658), who eventually broached too strong a challenge to the Tsar's authority, a series of church councils officially endorsed the liturgical reforms and anathematised the dissenters. Several of them, including Avvakum, were executed. Today between 500,000 to a million 'Old Believers' exist in Russia, which is no mean feat, given how unsympathetic the Soviets were to religion.

37. Mount Kailash is a great mass of black rock soaring to over 6,705 metres (22,000 feet), and a holy mountain in western Tibet sacred to Buddhism, Hinduism, Jainism and the shamanic religion of Bon-po.

In the Judeo-Christian region of the Middle East there are four primary sacred mountains: Mount Ararat in eastern Turkey, the traditional landing place of Noah's ark; Mount Sinai in the Sinai peninsula, the peak where Moses received the Ten Commandments; Mount Moriah (or Mount Zion) in Israel, where lies the city of Jerusalem and the Temple of Solomon; and Mount Tabor in Israel, the site of the transfiguration of Jesus.

Mount Arunachala, in Tamil Nadu, a state in southern India, was the home and retreat of Indian sage Sir Ramana Maharshi (1879–1950) who venerated the mountain as the embodiment of the god Shiva, one of the three gods in the Hindu Trinity. It is said to bestow enlightenment and moksha (liberation from reincarnation) to the pilgrim who circumambulates its base.

Mount Olympus is traditionally regarded as the heavenly abode of the ancient Greek gods and the site of the throne of Zeus. It seems to have originally existed as an idealised mountain that only later came to be associated with a specific peak. The *Illiad* and the *Odyssey* offer little information regarding the geographic location of the heavenly mountain and there are several peaks in Greece, Turkey and Cyprus that bear the name Olympos. The most favoured mythological choice is the tallest mountain range in Greece, the Olympos massif, 60 miles (100 km) southwest of the city of Thessaloniki in northern Greece with the highest peak – Mytikas – reaching a whopping 2,918 metres (9,573 feet).

Mount Fuji (*Fuji-san*) is the highest mountain in Japan, rising to 3,775 metres (12,388 feet). Visible from Tokyo on a clear day, the beautiful cone-shaped mountain is located west of the city, surrounded by lakes in a national park. It is named for the Buddhist fire goddess Fuchi and is sacred to the Shinto goddess Sengen-Sama, whose shrine is found at the summit. It is the holiest of Japan's 'Three Holy Mountains'.

Mount Tlaloc rises 4,125 metres (13,533 feet) above sea level and lies about 47 miles (75 km) east of Mexico City near the borders of the states of Puebla and Tlaxcala. It is probably the highest archaeological site in the Mexican Republic. In the Aztec religion it was believed that the god Tlaloc lived upon, or within, this mountain where great stores of clouds, mist, rain and snow were kept. On the summit are the remains of half-ruined buildings as well as an Aztec shrine where ceremonies, among them human sacrifices, were carried out.

Jutting sharply skyward from the lush jungles of southwestern Sri Lanka is the 2,243-metre (8,015-feet) peak of Sri Pada, also known as the 'Holy Footprint' of Buddha or Shiva, or Adam's Peak, depending on your faith. This mountain has the unique distinction of being sacred to the followers of Buddhism, Hinduism, Christianity and Islam.

Mount Katahdin, in Baxter State Park, Maine, lies 144 miles (232 km) northwest of Millinocket, in Piscataquis county. The Penobscot Indians gave the mountain the name Katahdin which means 'The Greatest Mountain' and it was believed by the local Native Americans to be the home of the storm god, Pamola, 'an eagle-like monster with a large head and the body and feet of an eagle, who feeds on moose and lives on the top of the mountain in the clouds, ready to tear to pieces anyone who should climb to the summit'. Its highest point is 1,606 metres (5,269 feet).

38. a) Simon/Peter. He was given his second name by Jesus as it means 'rock' and Jesus nominated him to be the 'rock on which I build my church'. Simon Peter is regarded as the first pope; b) Andrew; c) Matthew; d) Zebedee and Alphaeus; e) Judas, son of James and also John, so as not to confuse him with Christ's betrayer; f) Judas Iscariot

39. a) The pouch is either the common purse which held the money of Jesus and his disciples, which wouldn't be that odd as Judas Iscariot was the 'treasurer' of the group, but as all the other disciples have halos above their heads with their names just visible, the pouch more likely contains the payment Judas received for his betrayal. The scene shows the group just after they have learned that there is a traitor among them.

40. a) False. Islamic art includes all the artistic traditions in Muslim culture, including crafts and decorative arts, which have full 'art' status. b) True. c) True. Islamic art focuses on the *spiritual* representation of objects and beings, and not their physical qualities. d) False. Geometry *is* a common feature of Islamic art, but its use is thought to reflect the language of the universe and to help the believer reflect on life and the greatness of creation. For example, because circles have no end they are infinite and therefore remind Muslims that Allah is infinite. e) True. f) False.

41. Like Christianity, Islam has had a cult of relics associated with its founder and with saints, but the use of relics has had no official sanction. Indeed Muslim theologians have frequently denounced the veneration of relics and the related practice of visiting the tombs of saints as conflicting with the Prophet Muhammad's insistence on his own purely human, non-divine nature and his stern condemnation of idolatry and the worship of anyone other than God himself. Buddhism, on the other hand, has remained enthusiastic about relics ever since (as tradition tells us) the cremated remains of the Buddha (d. *c.* 483 BCE) were distributed equally among eight Indian tribes in response to a demand for his relics. Though it partakes in the worship of images, Hinduism has no such practice, either because it regards the physical world and its attributes as an illusion, or perhaps because it has no founder, so no cult has grown up in relation to sacred objects relating to one being.

42.

Confucianism – *Analects*
Deism – Thomas Paine's *The Age of Reason*
Scientology – *Dianetics*
Seventh-day Adventists – Christian Bible
Unification Church – *The Divine Principle*
Zoroastrianism – *Zend-avesta*
Gnosticism – *Gospels* and *Acts*
Bön – Bonpo canon
Atheism – *The Communist Manifesto*
Druze – *Al-Naqd al-Khafi* (*Copy of the Secret*)

43. d) Ever since Prince Philip visited the island in 1974, the Yaohnanen have revered him as the human incarnation of their ancestral spirit and a 'cargo cult' (a kind of religious movement that grew up in the Pacific islands during the Second World War when US military planes dropped supplies by parachute which were assumed to have come from supernatural sources) has grown up around him. After his visit, the people sent the Prince a traditional club as a gift and were sent back a framed picture of him holding the club, which has now become a religious icon. Vanuatu is also home to the cargo cult of John Frum, a mysterious figure who is believed to have been an American serviceman who told the tribe that they would be rewarded if they resisted the Christian missionaries in the 1930s or '40s. After the Second World War the islanders saw their homeland transformed by the aircraft, jeeps, refrigerators and Coca-cola belonging to the American troops and ever since then 15 February has been John Frum Day, when followers assume he will return.

44. a) Brahmans, ghee; b) fins or scales, unkosher; c) blood, halal; d) beer, beer

45. Christian Science was founded in 1879 by Mary Baker Eddy. Aladura was founded in *c.* 1918 in west Nigeria. Confucianism was founded in the 6th–5th century BCE by Confucius. Eckankar was founded in 1965 by John Paul Twitchell. Jehovah's Witnesses were founded in 1879 by Charles Taze Russell. New Thought was founded in the 19th century by Phineas P. Quimby. Stoicism was founded in *c.* 300 BCE by Zeno. Taoism was founded in *c.* 550 BCE by Lao-Tzu.

46. a) Senuna was a Celtic goddess who continued to be venerated into the Roman period, but fell out of favour and was forgotten for 1,500 years until the discovery of her shrine in Suffolk in 2003. Welcome back, Senuna!

47. a) The Albigensian Crusade, 1209–29, was a series of military campaigns led by Pope Inncocent III against the Cathars.

b) Münster Rebellion. After the city of Münster, Germany, came under Anabaptist rule for eighteen months, Protestants and Catholics united to end the crazy apocalyptic regime in 1534–5.

c) The Taiping Rebellion in China of 1850–64 left some 20 million people dead. It was the result of warfare waged by an illegal Protestant missionary cult led by Hong Xiuquan. In his own version of Christianity, he placed a lot of importance on the wrathful aspects of the Old Testament and denounced the divine pretensions of the imperial offices of the Qing dynasty.

d) Battle of Omdurman, 1898. The Mahdi was a self-proclaimed redeemer of the Islamic world and the Mahdists rose to prominence in Sudan during the successful Sudanese wars. When he died in 1885 his disciple Abd Allāh succeeded to the temporal rule, but following initial victories, his forces were gradually hunted down by Anglo-Egyptian armies and almost entirely destroyed.

e) Flower Wars. The name given to a series of battles fought by the Aztecs and others in pre-Columbian central America, perhaps to generate victims for human sacrifices.

48. All of them! Except, of course, Pope Benedict XVI who is the current Pope. Pope St Hormisdas (514–523) was the legitimate father of Pope St Silverius (536–537). Hormisdas was married, fathered Silverius, then widowed, then became pope, so this was all above board. Pope Hadrian II (a.k.a. Adrian II, 867–872) had a wife and daughter still living when he was pope who were murdered by another ecclesiastical/aristocratic faction during Hadrian's papacy. Although the issue was political no one seems to have been much troubled by their potentially controversial existence. Pope Alexander VI (Rodrigo Borgia) had lots of mistresses and children, including Cesare Borgia, Lucrezia Borgia and the less sexy Giovanni (father of St Francis Borgia), and Gioffre Borgia. St Francis Borgia was a leading Jesuit, and canonised, despite being the illegitimate grandson of a pope. Pope Paul III (1534–1549) had several children, made one of them Duke of Parma (where the family continued to rule until 1731), and made two of his grandsons cardinals.

49. c) The Yazīdī is a religious sect found in parts of Iraq, Syria, Armenia, the Caucasus region and Iran. Many of their rituals are conducted in the utmost secrecy and they have kept themselves strictly segregated from the people among whom they live. The chief divine figure of the Yazīdī is Tawsi Melek ('Peacock Angel') and is worshipped in the form of a peacock.

50. A Bar Mitzvah is a Jewish ritual and family celebration commemorating the religious adulthood of a **boy** on his **thirteenth** birthday and a Bat Mitzvah is a Jewish ritual and family celebration commemorating the ritual adulthood of a **girl** on her **twelfth** birthday.

THE ARTS

Think of 'the Arts' and the image that may come to mind is of a young man or woman with artistic pretensions, shut high up in a damp Parisian garret and agonising over his or her romantic entanglements with the help of an Alexandre Dumas paperback and the strains of Josephine Baker wafting from a gramophone ... But the arts – art, drama, dance, music and film – play a key role in the development of human civilisation and therefore, of course, should not be dismissed. And they're full of gossip and intrigue, too – our celebrity-obsessed, *Heat* generation is no new thing: creative types, aside from producing era-defining works of art, have always been willing to show a dark side too. In this section you'll find out who did what at history's most badly behaved dinner party, discover if the palatable pudding the Pavlova really was named after a famous ballerina, and separate your clavichord from your harpsichord.

1. Which play, about a train-wreck of a family, was locked up at publisher Random House's New York offices with specific instructions that it neither be performed, nor published, for twenty-five years after the playwright's death, a wish that was broken by his wife (to whom the play was dedicated) and first performed only three years after the playwright's death on 2 February 1956 in Stockholm, the city that had granted him the Nobel Prize for Literature in 1936 (he subsequently went on to win a posthumous Pulitzer Prize)?

a) *Le Malentendu* by Albert Camus
b) *Who's Afraid of Virginia Woolf?* by Edward Albee
c) *Look Back in Anger* by John Osborne
d) *Long Day's Journey into Night* by Eugene O'Neill

2. On 18 May 1922, a wealthy British couple living in Paris named Sydney and Violet Schiff, took it upon themselves to hold a dinner party at the Majestic Hotel to bring together the good and the great from the modernist arts scene. It was a bold move, with some extraordinary behaviour exhibited by the guests, most of whom had never met one another. They included James Joyce, Pablo Picasso, Marcel Proust, Igor Stravinsky and Serge Diaghilev. Stravinsky's ballet *Le Renard*, performed by Diaghilev's Ballets Russes, had just opened that night in Paris and everyone was on edge. Perhaps that's why the party was a *complete disaster.* Based on what you know of the luminaries listed above, can you identify the antics with the artist?

> ____ arrived drunk, wanted to talk about 'dukes' and 'chambermaids' and later fell asleep slumped over the table. ____ arrived late and, having taken a healthy dose of adrenalin before the party, complained throughout about a pain in his stomach and ate nothing. Proust told ____ that he loved Beethoven, who replied that he detested Beethoven and turned away. ____ snubbed the occasion by deliberately violating the dress code, wearing a Catalan headband around his forehead and glowering. ____ had been in charge of the guest list . . .

3. Which of the following is an artistically famous Neolithic town in Anatolia?

a) Çatalhüyük
b) Nunavet
c) The Great Ziggurat of Ur
d) Dur Sharrukin

4. The following ballet dancers all defected from their countries of birth. Can you fill in the blanks to answer from where they left and where they defected to?

America, United Kingdom, America, Cuba, Soviet Union, Mexico, Soviet Union, China, America, Cuba, Canada, Soviet Union, America

Rudolf Nureyev: ____ to ____ in 1961.
Octavio Martin: ____ to ____ in 2005.
Mikhail Baryshnikov: _____ to ____ in 1974.
Li Cunxin: ____ to _____ in 1981.
Natalia Makarova ____ to ____ through ____ in 1970.
Cervilio Amador: ____ to ____ in 2004.

5. Which of the following films DID NOT win an Academy Award for Best Foreign-Language Film?

a) *The Counterfeiters* (2007)
b) *Z* (1969)
c) *Rashomon* (1951)
d) *Slumdog Millionaire* (2008)
e) *The Secret in Their Eyes* (2009)
f) *Mephisto* (1981)
g) *Indochine* (1992)

6. True or false?

a) On 3 January 1969, the Greek-born sculptor Takis (Panayotis Vassilakis) went to the Museum of Modern Art in New York City and attempted to remove one of his sculptures, *The Machine*, from the Museum's exhibition, contending that, as the artist, he had the right to control the exhibition and treatment of his work whether or not he had sold it.

b) During the late 1960s, there was a great deal of interest in 'Body Art' in both Europe and the United States. In such work, the body of the artist was the central element in the work and was used in extremely dangerous ways. For example, the American artist Charles Burden shot himself in the arm with a .22 caliber bullet in *Shoot*(1971) and had himself 'crucified' with nails in his hands on to the back roof of a Volkswagen in *Transfixed* (1974).

c) In the 1940s and 1950s, a group of British artists who called themselves 'Eveandadam' created a series of land art pieces that involved deliberately dumping lorryloads of asphalt into main streets throughout Manchester, Bristol, Cardiff and London at scheduled times, planting non-native species of trees and fauna (including Australian gum trees, which require eighty-five times as much water as any native British tree and can create drought conditions) throughout parts of the Pennines, and bulldozing 'scars' on the sides of Scottish Munros as a statement about the consequences of various kinds of industrial pollution. The leader of 'Eveandadam', an Irish woman called Niamh Shaughnessy, was sentenced to life imprisonment for 'crimes against nature' when she confessed to having no interest in environmental issues and claimed Eveandadam was inspired by sheer 'boredom'.

d) In Venice in 1573, Paolo Veronese was tried before the Tribunal of Inquisition on charges of having introduced unacceptable figures into a religious painting called *The Feast in the House of Levi*, executed for the Refectory of S. S. Giovanni e Paolo. The judges required Veronese to 'improve and change his painting' within three months of the trial and decreed that if he did not 'correct the picture' he would be liable to penalties imposed by the Holy Tribunal. However, Veronese did not change the picture; instead he changed its title to *Feast in the House of Simon*, thereby satisfying the Inquisition.

7. Exercise your musical muscles with this crossword:

ACROSS

2. Number 48 on *Hit Parader*'s list of the 100 Greatest Heavy Metal Singers of All Time (5)
7. Gaelic disco (7)
8. A small, sneaky, extra note printed in tiny type and not counted in (5,4 words)
11. Sung by a soloist in a concerto (7)
12. Jazz style that rhymes with 'hip-hop' (5)
15. Not the sequence of single tones (7)
16. Czech composer, born 1841, who believed that African-American and Native American music should be used as a foundation for the growth of American music (6)

DOWN

1. *The Well-Tempered*_____ (7)
3. Of a symphony (9)
4. Yiddish folk music (7)
5. Leisurely (6)
6. 'Redemption Song' (8)
9. Another name for A-sharp (1,4)
10. C+C Music____ (7)
13. Got 'lost' with John Lennon (3,4)
14. German for 'song', but not German for 'deceived' (4)

8. Père Ubu is a central figure in the surrealist plays of which French playwright, who was under five feet tall and enjoyed riding his bicycle around Paris with two revolvers tucked in his belt and a carbine across his shoulder which he fired to warn people of his approach?

a) Alfred Jarry
b) Jean Genet
c) Eugène Ionesco
d) Samuel Beckett

9. Can you match the films with the genre they belong to?

Annie Hall (1977)	B-movie
The Big Sleep (1946)	Mockumentary
The Snorkel (1958)	Documentary
Faster, Pussycat! Kill! Kill! (1965)	Romantic comedy
This is Spinal Tap (1984)	Musical
The King and I (1956)	Film noir
Shoah (1985)	Hammer film

10. In Frida Kahlo's painting *Fulang-Chang and I*, Fulang-Chang refers to:

a) A city in China
b) Her husband, Diego Rivera
c) An empty mirror
d) A monkey

11. Of course you are more than confident in your knowledge of the great operas, but do you know from which country they originate?

Siegfried, La Vida Breve, The Rake's Progress, Carmen, The Queen of Spades, The Cunning Little Vixen, Peter Grimes, The Devils of Loudun, King Roger, Porgy and Bess, La Bohème, Háry János, Salome, Pelléas et Mélisande, The Consul, Rusalka, Riders to the Sea, Madama Butterfly, Duke Bluebeard's Castle, Goyescas

Italy	Germany	Russia	England	Poland
Hungary	**America**	**Spain**	**France**	**Czechoslovakia**

12. In the 1964 television special, *Rudolph the Red-nosed Reindeer*, produced in stop motion animation by Rankin/Bass and directed by Larry Roemer and Kizo Nagashima, which reindeer is Santa's ninth reindeer's father?

a) Dasher
b) Donner
c) Blitzen
d) Comet

13. We have some extraordinary eponyms for you here. Are these things really named after these particular people?

a) Pavlova – the delicious meringue cake topped with cream and fruit – was named after the Russian ballerina Anna Pavlova (1885–1931) who is remembered for being prima ballerina at the Russian Imperial Ballet at age twenty-one, her roles in

Giselle and *The Dying Swan* and the formation of her own ballet company in 1914.

b) Morris dancing, the traditional English dance performed in the open air by costumed men wearing bells and carrying sticks, which often illustrates a legend or portrays an activity, was named after William Morris, the English designer, craftsman, poet and socialist.

c) Leotards, the all-in-ones worn for dancing, were named after Jules Léotard (*c.* 1839–1870), the French acrobatic performer who invented the flying trapeze in 1859.

d) Axel – a jump with one and a half turns in the air in figure skating – was named after Axel Hägerström (1868–1939), the Swedish philosopher who founded the Uppsala school of philosophy, which espoused phenomenological and conceptual analysis and rejected metaphysical suppositions and subjectivism, and who was a huge fan of figure skating.

14. The Arts is a wondrously wide-ranging subject, encompassing creative endeavours in a panoply of disciplines. Can you identify who or what is being described below?

a) Started as a thirty-minute radio play broadcast in 1947, was panned by a critic when it opened in 1957 ('Coincidence is stretched unreasonably') and after its 1,998th performance became Britain's longest-running straight play?
b) Built with funds from the success of *The Beggar's Opera* (1728); burned down on 24 February, 1809?
c) Playwright who died on his birthday?
d) The site of the first permanent playhouse in the USA, built in 1716?
e) As told from the Nurse's point of view, used by Bertolt Brecht as an exercise for actors in his company, the Berliner Ensemble?
f) The 'Shakespeare of Spain' (whose funeral lasted nine days . . .)?
g) When an actor who collapses into uncontrollable laughter during a rehearsal or performance, he or she is ____.
h) The prototypical Greek theatre, situated on the south side of the Acropolis in Athens, in which all extant classical Greek plays were first presented?

15. Which of the following is NOT the title of a Surrealist magazine?

a) *Minotaure*
b) *La Révolution surréaliste*
c) *October*
d) *Documents*

16. Can you identify the Madonna albums based on the last four track listings?

a) 'Holiday', 'Think of Me', 'Physical Attraction', 'Everybody'
b) 'Dress You Up', 'Shoo-Bee-Doo', 'Pretender', 'Stay'
c) 'Rain', 'Why's It So Hard', 'In This Life', 'Secret Garden'
d) 'The Power of Good-bye', 'To Have and Not To Hold', 'Little Star', 'Mer Girl'

17. Match the year to the event listed below.

1941, 1999, 1964, 1978, 1997, 1999, 1953, 1899, 1957, 1903, 1973, 1962

a) In what year did Audrey Hepburn win an Academy Award for best actress in the film *Roman Holiday*?
b) In what year was the UK ban on the film *The Texas Chainsaw Massacre* lifted?
c) In what year was Swedish director Ingmar Bergman's film *The Seventh Seal* released?
d) In what year was Alfred Hitchcock born?
e) In what year did the Sundance Film Festival begin?
f) In what year was *The Great Train Robbery*, a twelve-minute film made by Edwin S. Porter and widely acknowledged to be the first film to achieve temporal continuity from one shot to the next (i.e. the first 'motion picture'), released?
g) In what year did George Lucas begin writing the story behind his film *Star Wars*?
h) In what year was James Cameron's epic, disaster film *Titanic* released?

i) What is the year of Marilyn Monroe's death?
j) What is the year of Richard Burton and Elizabeth's Taylor's *first* marriage?
k) In which year did *Citizen Kane* (nominated for nine Academy Awards) fail to win the Oscar for Best Picture?
l) In what year was the Pierce Bronson and Rene Russo *re-make* of the 1968 film *The Thomas Crown Affair* (which originally starred Steve McQueen and Faye Dunaway) released?

18. Which famous painting by Pablo Picasso had a hole punched in it by its owner as he was auctioning it in 2006?

a) *The Dream*
b) *Portrait of Dora Maar*
c) *Blue Roofs*
d) *Boy with a Pipe*

19. Match the character to the correct George Bernard Shaw play:

Joan	*Pygmalion*
Lady Britomart	*Saint Joan*
Centurion	*Pygmalion*
Vivie	*Saint Joan*
Don Juan	*Major Barbara*
The Archbishop	*Androcles and the Lion*
Walpole	*The Doctor's Dilemma*
Doolittle	*The Apple Cart*
Magnus	*Man and Superman*
Higgins	*Mrs Warren's Profession*

20. Which of the following is NOT considered an official dance form?

a) Martial arts
b) Jitterbug
c) Both a) and b)
d) Ice dance

21. Fill in the blanks with the words below and call yourself Maestro!

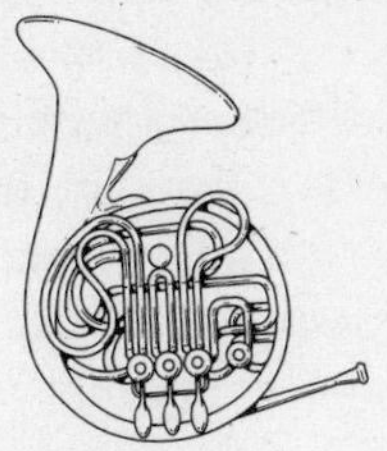

French horns, idiophones, English horn, piano, viola, octaves, oboe, treble clef, drums, membranophones, percussion, virginal, tubas, harpsichord, alto clef, clavichord, baritone, notation, saxophone, eight, piccolo, trombones, Bösendorfer, clarinet, cymbals, French horn, bassoon, euphonium, contrabassoon, woodwind

The _____ section of a Romantic orchestra usually includes three flutes, three clarinets, three oboes, one _____, one _____ _____, and a _____ in E-flat. In addition to the _____, there are two other double-reeded woodwinds, the _____ and its counterpart, which sounds an octave lower, the _____. The _____ is a woodwind but is not part of an orchestra. The brass section usually consists of three to four trumpets and _____, four to eight _____ _____, and one or two _____, whose _____ is in the bass clef. A woodwind quintet is comprised of four woodwind instruments and one _____ _____, whose notation is in the _____ _____. In a symphonic, brass or marching band, there is usually another brass instrument that looks like a small tuba and sounds like a trombone, either a _____, which has three valves, or a _____, which has four or five valves. The _____ is a stringed instrument with proportion similar to a violin but with a longer body length and a darker tone and its notation is in the _____ _____; the modern _____ has eighty-eight keys and seven _____, though the Austrian piano of _____ can span _____ octaves, and is both a keyboard stringed instrument as well as a member of the _____ family, of which there are two groups: _____, in which the instrument's own substance vibrates to produce sound, such as _____, and _____, which emit sound by the vibration of a stretched membrane, such as _____. Henry VIII, who was an accomplished musician, wrote music for – and played upon – the _____ and also the oldest member of the _____ family, the _____.

22. Cubism is an early twentieth-century movement in the visual arts that challenged conventional depictions of three-dimensional objects and became one of the seminal movements in art history which set the stage for abstract art. Centered mainly in France, its pioneers included Pablo Picasso and Georges Braque and it was given the name Cubism after:

a) A hostile critic who picked up on Henri Matisse's description of Braque's images as 'cubes' and derisively critiqued Braque's 1908 work *Houses at L'Estaque* as being composed of cubes.
b) Picasso declared that the 'cube' was the most perfect shape.
c) Marcel Duchamp went on holiday to Cuba.
d) Paintings that were drawn from cubes in simplified colour schemes of nearly monochromatic scale were seen as the only shapes with which not to distract the viewer from the artist's primary interest, which was the structure of form itself.

23. The aunt of which contemporary Hollywood movie star and famous silver fox was a leading pop and jazz singer who graced the cover of *Time* magazine in 1953 and starred in several films, most notably *White Christmas* (1954), with Bing Crosby?

a) George Clooney
b) Brad Pitt
c) Keanu Reeves
d) Paul Giamatti

24. Match the following plots, described in limericks, to the plays they pertain to:

a) Though not true sisters they are quite insane
And predict a general will be thane,
Soon enough it is true
But his wife remains blue
And jealousy, rage and murder then reign.

b) Intended to be something quite funny
A family has run out of money!
And must sell their turf
To a former serf
Which is sad, as the rich then feel crummy.

c) A very successful company
Suddenly files for bankruptcy
Because of fraud
The books were flawed
The economy then tanks immensely.

d) Stymied by his own career frustration
Enraged by his son's procrastination
A man loses the plot
And the rest of his lot
And dies with a bad reputation.

e) Over the course of two days
Men kill time in a number of ways
They discuss salvation
Give in to urination
To keep the horrible silence at bay.

25. Who was the influential American dancer, teacher and choreographer of modern dance, whose ballets and other works were intended to 'reveal the inner man'?

a) May O'Donnell
b) Martha Clarke
c) Martha Graham
d) Robin Howard

26. All the things listed in column A relate (somehow) to one thing in column B. What is related to what, and why?

A	B
Gregorian chant	Wales
Bayreuth Festival	Japan
B-Boy Park	flute
Lyre	*Tapestry*
Counterpoint	Wagner
Philip Glass	Roman Catholic Church
Kora	Greek theatre
Carole King	do
Maxixe	Baroque era
Gong	Brazil
Morriston Orpheus Choir	Malinke

27. It's all in the family . . . Can you fill in the blanks with the Renaissance celebrities and paintings below?

Pietro Perugino, 'The Annunciation with Two Kneeling Donors', Giorgio Vasari, Masaccio, 'Adoration of the Child with St Bernard', Sandro Botticelli, Filippino Lippi, Lorenzo de' Medici, Lucrezia Buti, Domenico Ghirlandaio, Fra Filippo Lippi, 'Adoration of the Child'

According to the Renaissance biographer _____, the Carmelite, Renaissance friar _____, whose work was heavily influenced by the painter known as _____ and includes _____ (*c.* 1440s) and _____ (*c.* 1463), had an affair with a nun, _____, and fathered the Renaissance painter _____, whose work includes _____ (1483) and who was employed, along with _____, _____, and _____, on the frescoed decoration of _____'s Spedaletto villa.

28. i. Below are the beginnings of a notoriously well-known and oft-quoted speech from a notoriously well-known and oft-quoted play by a notoriously well-known and oft-quoted playwright. Can you figure out what it is by unscrambling the clue words and using the circled letters to fill in the blanks?

TAEBIERC
POSPORRE
DARLINSO
AEETCH
LIRGOEN
BOANQU
LANAICB
VIALO
AGOI
LAHMET

_ _ _ _ _ _ _; _ _ _ _ _ _; _ _ _ _ _ _ Y M _ _; _ _ N D
M _ Y _ U _ _ _ _ S

ii. Now, before we bid 'a long farewell to all [their] greatness', can you match the characters above with the plays they feature in?

Othello, The Tempest, Twelfth Night, The Tempest, Much Ado About Nothing, King Lear, Macbeth, Macbeth, Hamlet, As You Like It

29. 'Egghead Weds Hourglass' was *Variety*'s 1956 headline after which high-profile marriage?

a) Lana Turner and Lex Barker
b) Humphrey Bogart and Lauren Bacall
c) Cary Grant and Betsy Drake
d) Arthur Miller and Marilyn Monroe

30. Some artists aren't just talented with the pencil or paintbrush but also have a way with words. Match the quotation to the artist who proclaimed it:

Frank Lloyd Wright, Salvador Dali, J.M.W. Turner, Pablo Picasso, Chuck Close

a) 'On this day I was to suffer one of the most harrowing experiences of my life because I turned into a fish! The story is well worth retelling.'
b) 'Painting is a strange business.'
c) 'Any house is a far too complicated, clumsy, fussy, mechanical counterfeit of the human body. Electric wiring for nervous system, plumbing for bowels, heating system and fireplaces for arteries and heart, and windows for eyes, nose and lungs generally.'
d) 'Inspiration is for amateurs. The rest of us just show up and get to work.'
e) 'We all know that art is not truth. Art is a lie that makes us realise truth.'

31. Which twentieth-century, *enfant terrible* pianist made two divergent recordings of Bach's *Goldberg Variations*, the first of which forced a revision of the composer's piano music?

a) Glenn Gould
b) Wanda Landowska
c) Vladimir Horowitz
d) Yo-Yo Ma

32. Can you find TEN ballet steps, movements and body positions in the word seach below?

Y	C	P	O	Z	D	T	E	K	W	M	Y	É	G	A	V
P	P	A	N	D	P	F	D	N	C	P	S	P	U	Z	S
H	E	S	B	Y	O	T	E	M	T	I	M	R	T	W	Z
J	H	N	K	R	C	B	M	F	R	R	Y	B	K	X	S
R	Y	D	O	O	I	E	J	B	Q	M	E	H	J	S	Z
T	J	R	Q	O	A	O	Q	A	É	Q	D	C	S	Y	A
R	B	Y	K	E	Z	G	L	P	T	Q	V	I	H	R	F
G	L	I	S	S	A	D	E	E	E	Y	B	T	A	A	M
G	P	R	B	N	D	I	W	K	J	A	Z	B	A	M	T
P	I	R	O	U	E	T	T	E	T	I	E	J	S	I	E
P	T	N	I	W	X	K	B	T	P	S	Y	F	S	E	Y
A	V	Z	U	W	I	R	E	L	Q	L	B	T	E	R	W
Q	W	G	R	U	R	M	X	U	S	F	I	G	M	A	W
C	R	B	K	X	E	F	E	M	C	G	D	É	B	I	D
T	C	Y	T	N	Q	N	X	P	C	N	F	Z	L	E	R
T	Q	Y	T	S	Y	J	S	L	W	P	Q	E	É	F	H

33. Which of the following is NOT a circular, domed, architectural structure?

a) An igloo
b) The Mousgoum tolek
c) The Hagia Sophia
d) The Koricancha Inca temple of the Sun

34. Which of the following plays is NOT considered to be a 'masque'?

a) *The Parliament of Bees* (1641) by John Day
b) *Comus* (1634) by John Milton
c) *The Faithful Shepherdess* (1609 or 1610) by John Fletcher
d) *Hymenaei* (1606) by Ben Jonson

35. Can you name ALL the notes of the octave on the keyboard below? (And yes, that includes sharps and flats, so you should have seventeen notes.)

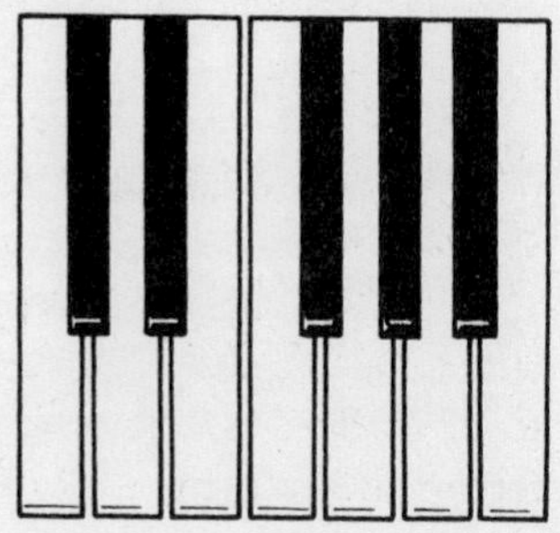

36. In 2006, the illusionist David Copperfield was walking to his tour bus with two of his assistants after a show in West Palm Beach when four teenagers pulled up in a car behind them, pulled a gun out and demanded they hand over their valuables. Copperfield's assistants both produced cash, phones, plane tickets and even a passport. What did David Copperfield do?

a) Performed a magic trick of turning his pockets inside out to reveal nothing in them, even though he was carrying his passport, wallet and phone.
b) Hid behind the two assistants and instructed one of them to perform a magic trick whereby the items handed over were recovered without the robbers knowing.
c) Hid behind the two assistants and let them get robbed.
d) Hypnotised the assailants just as they were about to run off and got the stolen stuff back.

37. There's a lot more to dance than limber limbs and fancy footwork. Can you match the snippet of dance theory to the theorist?

Stéphane Mallarmé, St Basil, Aristotle, Isadora Duncan, George Balanchine, Plato

a) Dance is rhythmic movement whose purpose is 'to represent men's characters as well as what they do and suffer'.
b) 'The ballet is such a rich art form that it should not be an illustrator of even the most interesting, even the most meaningful literary primary source. The ballet will speak for itself and about itself.'
c) The dancer, 'writing with her body, . . . *suggests* things which the written work could *express* only in several paragraphs of dialogue or descriptive prose.'
d) 'Could there be anything more blessed than to imitate on earth the ring-dance of the angels?'
e) 'To sing well and to dance well is to be well educated. Noble dances should confer on the student not only health and agility and beauty, but also goodness of the soul and a well-balanced mind.'
f) Ballet makes dancers move like 'articulated puppets'.

38. What is *Merz*?

a) The fragmented collage style created by Dada artist Kurt Schwitters.
b) The style of photomontage used extensively in the Pop Art movement of the 1960s and 1970s.
c) The schism that the Bauhaus school of design, architecture and applied arts believed existed (and attempted to bridge) between students trained in art and traditional forms of craftsmanship.
d) The manifesto written by the expatriate Russian sculptors Antoine Pevsner and Naum Gabo in 1920 on which the principles of the Russian Constructivist movement was based.

39. Match the film stars with their real names.

David Kaminsky	Margaret Hyra
Charlton Heston	Allen Konigsberg
Demi Moore	Erik Weisz
Harry Houdini	Danny Kaye
Gene Wilder	Michael Shalhoub
Meg Ryan	John Charles Carter
Omar Sharif	Demetria Gene Guynes
Woody Allen	Jerome Silberman

40. We've all got to go some time but not everyone is cheerful enough about their mortality to choose 'Bye Bye, Baby' for their internment or 'Air on a G String' for their cremation. What is the most popular song played at funerals?

a) 'The Wind Beneath my Wings' performed by Bette Midler
b) 'I Will Always Love You' performed by Whitney Houston
c) 'My Way' performed by Frank Sinatra
d) 'Unforgettable' performed by Nat King Cole

41. Can you name the gallery or museum in which the following famous paintings currently hang?

a) *Birth of Venus* by Sandro Botticelli
b) *Young Girl in Green* by Tamara de Lempicka
c) *Fission* by Bridget Riley
d) *Café Terrace at Night* by Vincent Van Gogh
e) *Girl with a Pearl Earring* by Johannes Vermeer
f) *The Kiss* by Gustav Klimt

42. Cast your minds back into the classical era now and decide which of the following options describes the *Didaskalia*:

a) A compilation of Aristotle's lists of the plays produced at the Dionysian festival in Athens.

b) The working title of Sophocles' most famous play, *Oedipus the King*.
c) The name given to denote the three exponents of the form of Greek tragedy: Aeschylus, Sophocles and Euripides.
d) A crane on which a god could arrive or depart in the theatre of Dionysus.

43. With a twirl of your pen, get your brain sautéing and fill in this random dance crossword!

ACROSS

3. Birthplace of Dame Margot Fonteyn (7)
4. Revered type of dancer in Hawaii trained in a sacred venue (4)
5. Type of dance historically showcased at the minstrel show (3)
6. One of the three characteristic formations in an English country dance (5)
7. Ceremonial folk dance (7)
9. A twentieth-century ballroom dance (5)

DOWN

1. A Maori posture dance incorporated into the pre-game ritual of New Zealand's national rugby union team, the All Blacks (4)
2. Western name for the highly sophisticated Middle Eastern dance *raq sharqī* (5,5)
5. First name of popular American dancer, director and choreographer whose surname is Tharp (5)
8. A nineteenth-century ballroom dance (5)

44. In the film *Pulp Fiction*, what Three Stooges movie is Lance watching when Vincent arrives with overdosed Mia?

a) *Meet the Baron* (1933)
b) *Brideless Groom* (1947)
c) *Dancing Lady* (1933)
d) *Hollywood Party* (1934)

45. Hallelujahs and Haikus! Can you guess the Christmas carol using the Haiku clues?

a) Around the Virgin
All is calm and bright and still
The Saviour has come.

b) On a freezing night
A King and his page set out
To dine with the poor.

c) Two plants red and green
Blossom, berry and flower
To celebrate Christ.

d) On a pile of hay
A baby wakes when cows moo
But he doesn't cry.

46. Which Italian Baroque artist spent the last years of his life on the run from a charge of murder after a bar brawl?

a) Michelangelo Buonarroti
b) Guido Reni
c) Michelangelo Merisi da Caravaggio
d) Scipione Borghese

47. True, or false?

a) New Wave is the theory that positions the director of the film as the most important creative figure (well before the author, screenwriter, producer, etc.).
b) Jean-Luc Godard's first feature film *Breathless* (1960) is an example of the kind of film the so-called New Wave directors were making because it prioritises unorthodox production techniques, such as the incessant use of the jump cut (a sudden temporal ellipsis in the middle of a dialogue take) over subject matter or plot.
c) 'The Male Gaze' is a term coined and defined by the American art critic and theorist Rosalind Krauss and presumes that in film women are typically objects as the camera assumes a male position and therefore the viewer's perspective sees women as heterosexual men do.
d) Soviet director Dziga Vertov's *kino-glaz* ('film-eye') theory is based on the belief that the camera is the most dependable and useful tool with which to explore real events in real life and that films should therefore do away with theatrical influences and artificial techniques and work within a new cinematic language based on the realism of the human eye.

48. Which British actor ordered a man out of the National Theatre in June 2005 when his mobile phone went off for the sixth time during a performance of Alan Bennett's *The History Boys*?

a) James Corden
b) Richard Griffiths
c) Michael Gambon
d) Derek Jacobi

49. Much like mathematics, music is language. Below are descriptions of common musical terms, symbols and elements of music theory. Do you know what they are?

a) The five horizontal lines separated by four spaces in music notation is called a _____.
b) The symbol that appears at the beginning of a stave which determines the notes symbolised on the lines is called a _____.
c) 𝅝: This is a _____.
d) All music has a time signature which indicates the rhythm of the piece. A key signature is represented by a fraction, so 4/4 time is an example of _____.
e) The 4 on the bottom determines _____.
f) The horizontal lines that cut through the stave indicate a _____.
g) The 4 on top determines _____.
h) 'Dynamics' is another way of referring to _____.
i) A group of three notes constructed on three consecutive lines or three consecutive spaces with a specific relationship to one another is called a _____.
j) The two types of key signatures are called _____.
k) The note C major is the same note as _____.
l) 𝄻: This is a _____.

50. The term 'paparazzi' is derived from Federico Fellini's 1960 film *La Dolce Vita* because . . .

a) Marcello's friend Paparazzo is a photographer.
b) Sylvia calls Marcello a 'paparazzi' when he won't take no for an answer.
c) Marcello and Emma attend a swank dinner party full of aristos who call people with day jobs 'paparazzi'.
d) None of the above.

THE ARTS ANSWERS

1. d) Is *Long Day's Journey into Night* the most excruciating play about a dysfunctional family ever written? Unfolding over the course of one day, the Tyrone family screech at one another in a symphony of hatred and blame, yet O'Neill's dedication of the play to his wife on the twelfth anniversary of their wedding reads: 'Dearest: I give you the original script of this play of old sorrow, written in tears and blood. A sadly inappropriate gift, it would seem, for a day celebrating happiness. But you will understand. I mean it as a tribute to your love and tenderness . . .'

2. Joyce arrived drunk, wanted to talk about 'dukes' and 'chambermaids' and later fell asleep slumped over the table. **Proust** arrived late and, having taken a healthy dose of adrenalin before the party, complained throughout about a pain in his stomach and ate nothing. Proust told **Stravinsky** that he loved Beethoven, who replied that he detested Beethoven and turned away. **Picasso** snubbed the occasion by deliberately violating the dress code, wearing a Catalan headband around his forehead and glowering. **Diaghilev** had been in charge of the guest list . . .

3. a) Archaeologists estimate that the earliest building period at Çatalhüyük, located near Konya, in south-central Turkey, was about 6,700 BCE to 5,650 BCE. The inhabitants lived in rectangular mud-brick houses probably entered from roof level by a wooden ladder. In addition to a hearth and an oven, houses had platforms for sleeping, sitting or working. Excavation of the religious quarter produced a series of shrines with wall paintings now considered to be exceptionally brilliant examples of Upper Paleolithic art. Nunavet, of course, is an Inuit territory of Canada, and the ancient cities of Ur and Dur Sharrukin existed in what is today modern Iraq.

4. Rudolf Nureyev: Soviet Union to America in 1961.
Octavio Martin: Cuba to Mexico in 2005.
Mikhail Baryshnikov: Soviet Union to Canada in 1974.
Li Cunxin: China to America in 1981.
Natalia Makarova Soviet Union to America through the United Kingdom in 1970.
Cervilio Amador: Cuba to America in 2004.

5. d) *Slumdog Millionaire* won Best Picture in 2008 and, as it's a UK production, wouldn't have been eligible in the foreign-language film category. The other films, come from a) Austria, b) Algeria, c) Japan, e) Argentina, f) Hungary and Germany, g) France.

6. a) True. b) True. c) False. Totally and completely made up, every word of it. d) False. The original title of the painting was *Feast in the House of Simon* which Veronese changed to *The Feast in the House of Levi*, the title which appeared to pacify the Inquisition. Everything else in the statement is true!

7.

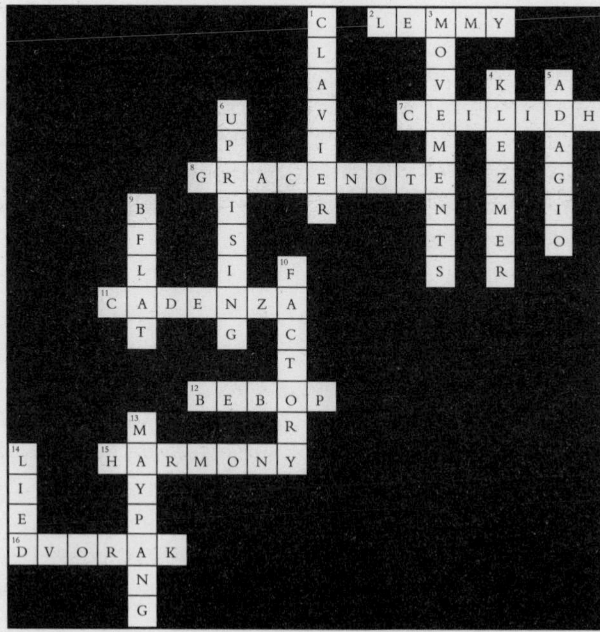

8. a) While Genet, Ionesco and Beckett were also all dramatists of the Theatre of the Absurd, the grotesque character Père Ubu is central to the plays *Ubu roi* (1896) and its sequels *Ubu enchaîné* (1900), *Ubu sur la butte* (1901) and *Ubu cocu* (published posthumously in 1944) by the Pete Doherty of *fin de siècle* Paris, Alfred Jarry (1873–1907).

9. *Annie Hall*: Romantic comedy; *The Big Sleep*: Film noir; *The Snorkel*: Hammer film; *Faster, Pussycat! Kill! Kill!*: B-movie; *This is Spinal Tap*: Mockumentary; *The King and I*: Musical; *Shoah*: Documentary

10. d) This particular self-portrait recalls Renaissance paintings of the Madonna and child, but instead of presenting the customary cherubic infant, Kahlo offers an unlikely protagonist: Fulang-Chang, one of several spider monkeys that she kept as pets. The pet monkeys that frequently appear in her paintings are often interpreted as surrogates for the children she and her husband were unable to conceive. While personal hardship may have played a role in prompting Kahlo's unconventional decision to include her monkey in this self-portrait, many specialists (ourselves included) think her sense of humour is equally evident in the choice.

11. Italy: *La Bohème, Madama Butterfly*. **Germany**: *Salome, Siegfried*. **Russia**: *The Rake's Progress, The Queen of Spades*. **England**: *Peter Grimes, Riders to the Sea*. **Poland**: *King Roger, The Devils of Loudun*. **Hungary**: *Duke Bluebeard's Castle, Háry János*. **America**: *Porgy and Bess, The Consul*. **Spain**: *Goyescas, La Vida Breve*. **France**: *Carmen, Pelléas et Mélisande*. **Czechoslovakia:** *Rusalka, The Cunning Little Vixen*.

12. b) In the film, Sam the Snowman narrates the story of Rudolph, a reindeer who is born with a glowing red nose. His father is Santa's lead reindeer Donner, who feels ashamed and uses a special cover to hide Rudolph's nose so Donner and his wife can send Rudolph to take-off practice a year later without Rudolph being ridiculed by the other yearlings. However, the issue of Rudolph's paternity is up for question in other retellings of the original story by Robert L. May (which makes no mention of Rudolph's parents). For instance in the 2001 film *Rudolph the Red-nosed Reindeer and the Island of Misfit Toys*,

Blitzen is named as Rudolph's father, with Dasher, Comet and Cupid as his uncles. Hmmmmmm . . .

13. a) Yes. b) Sadly, no. The name 'morris' is thought to have originally been 'Moorish dance' and it is widely assumed that the dances derived from the ancient dances of the Moors and were introduced from Spain into England around 1350. c) True. d) False. Hägerström did found the Uppsala school, but we doubt he followed skating. The 'axel' jump was named after Axel Paulsen (1856–1938), a Norwegian figure and speed skater who introduced his jump in Vienna in 1882 at what is generally regarded as the first international championship.

14. a) *The Mousetrap*; b) The Theatre Royal, Drury Lane; c) Shakespeare (23 April, 1564 and 1616, respectively); d) Williamsburg, Virginia; e) the balcony scene from *Romeo and Juliet*); f) Félix Lope de Vega y Carpio (1562–1635); g) Corpsing; h) Theatre of Dionysus.

15. c) Because Surrealism was a movement in both art and literature, surrealist artists were constantly writing stuff and, much like Dada, the history of the movement can be traced through its many journals and reviews. *Minotaure* was published by Albert Skira in Paris from 1933–9. On 1 December 1924, shortly after he published the first Surrealist manifesto which marked his definitive break with Dada, André Breton released the inaugural issue of *La Révolution surréaliste*. With writers Pierre Naville and Benjamin Péret as its first directors, *La Révolution surréaliste* set out to explore a range of subversive issues related to the darker sides of man's psyche with features focused on suicide, death and violence. *Documents* was edited and masterminded by Georges Bataille and published in Paris from 1929 through 1930. It ran for fifteen issues, each of which contained a wide range of original writing and photographs. Given its title and focus, the magazine initially listed an eleven-member editorial board; however, by the fifth issue, Bataille was the only member to remain on the masthead. *October* is an academic journal specialising in contemporary criticism and theory, published by the MIT Press.

16. a) *Madonna*, which is Madonna's first album (1983). The first four tracks are 'Lucky Star', 'Borderline', 'Burning Up' and 'I Know It'; b) *Like*

A Virgin, Madonna's second album (1984), which is the one where she is wearing the craaaaazy frock on the cover. The preceding tracks are 'Material Girl', 'Angel', 'Like a Virgin', 'Over and Over' and 'Love Don't Live Here Anymore'; c) *Erotica*, Madonna's ninth (and artistically adventurous) album of 1992. The earlier tracks are 'Erotica', 'Fever', 'Bye Bye Baby', 'Deeper and Deeper', 'Where Life Begins', 'Bad Girl', 'Waiting', 'Thief of Hearts' and 'Words'; d) *Ray of Light* (1998), her thirteenth album and our personal favourite. Other tracks are 'Drowned World/Substitute for Love', 'Swim', 'Ray of Light', 'Candy Perfume Girl', 'Skin', 'Nothing Really Matters', 'Sky Fits Heaven', 'Shanti/Ashtangi' and 'Frozen'.

17. a) 1953; b) 1999; c) 1957; d) 1899; e) 1978; f) 1903; g) 1973; h) 1997; i) 1962; j) 1964; k) 1941; l) 1999

18. a) *The Dream*(1932). *The Dream* is perhaps the best-known portrait of Picasso's mistress, Marie-Thérèse Walter and in 2006 Steve Wynn, a Las Vegas casino and real-estate developer, accidentally punctured the painting while auctioning it to another collector. 'Look what I've done,' he said. 'Thank goodness it was me.' Both buyer and seller agreed to cancel the sale in light of the damage done and the painting remains with Steve Wynn, who bought it in 1997 from the private collection of Mr and Mrs Victor W. Ganz in New York.

19.

Joan – *Saint Joan*
Lady Britomart – *Major Barbara*
Centurion – *Androcles and the Lion*
Vivie – *Mrs Warren's Profession*
Don Juan – *Man and Superman*
The Archbishop – *Saint Joan*
Walpole – *The Doctor's Dilemma*
Doolittle – *Pygmalion*
Magnus – *The Apple Cart*
Higgins – *Pygmalion*

20. d) Distinguishing dance from other forms of 'patterned movement' can be a controversial undertaking at the best of times. How often have you heard a footballer's movements described as 'balletic'? Yet sport is distinguished from dance because the principles that govern it are not the crucial principles of aesthetic pleasure and self-expression. The same goes for ice skating and ice dancing, where the aesthetic and expressive qualities are important and the movements themselves highly choreographed, yet as the primary purpose of skating is competition, it cannot be defined as an art form. Martial arts, however, can be regarded as dance because the movements of the practitioners are expected to be as refined and as graceful as those in dance and because it is judged solely on those merits. The jitterbug obviously adheres to the highest standards of aesthetic pleasure and self-expression.

21. The **woodwind** section of a Romantic orchestra usually includes three flutes, three clarinets, three oboes, one **piccolo**, one **English horn**, and a **clarinet** in E-flat. In addition to the **oboe**, there are two other double-reeded woodwinds, the **bassoon** and its counterpart, which sounds an octave lower, the **contrabassoon**. The **saxophone** is a woodwind but is not part of an orchestra. The brass section usually consists of three to four trumpets and **trombones**, four to eight **French horns**, and one or two **tubas**, whose **notation** is in the bass clef. A woodwind quintet is comprised of four woodwind instruments and one **French horn**, whose notation is in the **treble clef**. In a symphonic, brass or marching band, there is usually another brass instrument that looks like a small tuba and sounds like a trombone, either a **baritone**, which has three valves, or a **euphonium**, which has four or five valves. The **viola** is a stringed instrument with proportions similar to a violin but with a longer body length and a darker tone and its notation is in the **alto clef**; the modern **piano** has eighty-eight keys and seven **octaves**, though the Austrian piano of **Bösendorfer** can span **eight** octaves, and is both a keyboard stringed instrument as well as a member of the **percussion** family, of which there are two groups: **idiophones**, in which the instrument's own substance vibrates to produce sound, such as **cymbals**, and **membranophones**, which emit sound by the vibration of a stretched membrane, such as **drums**. Henry VIII, who was an accomplished musician, wrote music for – and played upon – the **clavichord** and also the oldest member of the **harpsichord** family, the **virginal**.

22. a) The critic was Louis Vauxcelles who is also credited with naming the French avant-garde movement in painting 'fauvism', a precursor of cubism and abstraction, when he saw some of their paintings displayed in a room that also contained a Renaissance-style sculpture and exclaimed, '*Donatello parmi les fauves!*' (Donatello among the beasts). The movement was short-lived but had a lasting influence on the use of colour in modern art.

23. a) Rosemary Clooney (1928–2002). Born in Maysville, Clooney and her younger sister, Betty, began singing duets on the radio in 1945 and soon became known as The Clooney Sisters, touring with the saxophonist and bandleader Tony Pastor for several years. In 1949 Rosemary moved to New York to embark on a solo career and quickly made a name for herself with her chart-topping rendition of 'Come On-a My House' (1951) and a string of novelty hits followed. Although she was not a trained actor, Clooney's popularity during this period was such that she accepted roles in several films and served as the host of a television variety show *The Rosemary Clooney Show* (1956–57). In 1956, with Duke Ellington and Billy Strayhorn, she recorded the album *Blue Rose*. Though not a popular success when it was released, it was later deemed a jazz classic.

24. a) *Macbeth* (1606–7) by William Shakespeare; b) *The Cherry Orchard* (1904) by Anton Chekhov (note: it is true that Chekhov felt the play was a comedic look at the frivolousness of the aristocracy and the meaninglessness of the emergent bourgeoisie, but most theatre directors – including the two who first staged the play – have insistently read the work as a tragedy); c) *Enron* (2009) by Lucy Prebble; d) *Death of a Salesman* (1949) by Arthur Miller; e) *Waiting for Godot* (1953) by Samuel Beckett.

25. c) Martha Graham (1894–1991) created more than 180 works, from solos to large-scale productions, in most of which she herself danced. She believed that dance, like spoken drama, can explore the inner lives of humans and often choreographed classic tragedies around the moment when characters realise the full extent of their errors. May O'Donnell (1906–2004) was an American dancer who performed with Martha Graham and later founded two dance companies: the San Francisco Dance Theater (1939), and the May O'Donnell Dance Company in New York (1949). Martha Clarke is also an American choreographer who studied with Martha Graham and whose work is extremely emotionally evocative. Robin Howard (1924–89) was a British dance patron who was hugely important in the promotion of modern dance in Britain.

26. Gregorian chant and the Roman Catholic Church. Gregorian chant is liturgical music used to accompany the text of the Roman Catholic mass and the canonical hours.

Bayreuth Festival and Wagner. The composer Richard Wagner settled in Bayreuth in 1872 and the Festival Theatre (*Festspielhaus*) opened in 1876 with the premiere performance of the *Ring of the Nibelungen* cycle. Since Wagner's death in 1883, the festivals have been carried on by his relatives.

B-Boy Park and Japan. B-Boy Park is a Japanese hip-hop festival that takes place annually in Tokyo.

Lyre and Greek theatre. The lyre was perhaps the most commonly used of all ancient Greek musical instruments. It is a stringed instrument shaped like a small harp. The number of strings on a lyre varies, but it usually has between three and twelve; the strings are plucked with a pick in a strumming motion in order to produce sound.

Counterpoint and the Baroque era. Counterpoint – the combination of different melodies which work together with harmonies – became a key feature in the music of the Baroque period (*c.* 1598–1750).

Philip Glass and the flute. The American minimalist composer studied the flute as a child.

Kora and the Malinke. The kora is a harp lute used by the Malinke people of western Africa. Its origins are obscure, but it is traditionally associated with royalty, the ruling classes, or religious practices.

Carole King and *Tapestry*. *Tapestry* is the name of singer/songwriter Carole King's bestselling 1971 album which spent more than 300 weeks on the US charts.

Maxixe and Brazil. Maxixe is a Brazilian dance that was influenced by jazz. It was fashionable (and regarded as sexually provocative) in about 1870–1914, and was the forerunner of the samba.

Gong and do. Gong is the first note of a scale as indicated by a syllable in the Chinese heptatonic scale and 'do' is the first in the Western one (*do, re, mi, fa, so, la, ti, do*).

Morriston Orpheus Choir and Wales. It's always a cliché to say that a Welsh male choir is a popular thing, but the Morriston Orpheus Choir, or the Croeso i safle wê Côr Orpheus Treforys, is arguably one of the most travelled of the Welsh male choirs. Formed in 1935, it enjoys an international reputation as a leading exponent of male choral singing.

27. According to the Renaissance biographer **Giorgio Vasari**, the Carmelite, Renaissance friar **Fra Filippo Lippi**, whose work was heavily influenced by the painter known as **Masaccio** and includes **'The Annunciation with Two Kneeling Donors'** (*c.* 1440s) and '**Adoration of the Child with St Bernard'**(*c.* 1463), had an affair with a nun, **Lucrezia Buti**, and fathered the Renaissance painter **Filippino Lippi**, whose work includes **'Adoration of the Child'** (1483) and who was employed, along with **Sandro Botticelli**, **Pietro Perugino**, and **Domenico Ghirlandaio**, on the frescoed decoration of **Lorenzo de' Medici**'s Spedaletto villa.

28. i. The clue words are all characters from Shakespearean plays: Beatrice, Prospero, Rosalind, Hecate, Goneril, Banquo, Caliban, Viola, Iago and Hamlet. The quote that follows is: 'Friends, Romans, countrymen, lend me your ears' from Act III, Scene ii of *Julius Caesar* (spoken by Mark Antony at the beginning of his funeral oration for Caesar). You will have found this question easier if you read the whole question before attempting to answer, as you were always taught to do at school.

ii. Beatrice: *Much Ado About Nothing*; Prospero: *The Tempest*; Rosalind: *As You Like It*; Hecate: *Macbeth*; Goneril: *King Lear*; Banquo: *Macbeth*; Caliban: *The Tempest*; Viola: *Twelfth Night*; Iago: *Othello*; Hamlet: *Hamlet*

29. d) Miller met Monroe when he went to Hollywood to work on a script about crooked labour leaders in Brooklyn, but dropped out of the project when the labour leaders were changed to communists for *On the Waterfront* (1954). The couple later divorced on 24 January 1961 in Mexico.

30. a) Salvador Dali, from *Diary of a Genius*, July 1952; b) J. M. W. Turner; c) Frank Lloyd Wright, from 'The Cardboard House', 1931; d) Chuck Close, in *Guernica* magazine, July 2010; e) Pablo Picasso

31. a) While Landowska (1879–1959) did once say to a fellow pianist, another Bach specialist, 'Very well, my dear. You continue to play Bach your way and I'll continue to play him *his* way', it was Glenn Gould who recorded his first experimental interpretation of the *Goldberg Variations* in 1955 and his second in 1981. Comparing the two recordings in a CBS interview, Gould admitted to finding the earlier recording, on which he made his name, too 'pianistic' (which was to him a dirty word). The 1981 version comes across as more meditative, more expansive and more introspective, especially as it was made a year before the pianist's death. Horowitz (1903–89) is best known for his performances of Romantic piano works, and Yo-Yo Ma (b.1955) is – as you well know – neither an *enfant terrible*, nor a pianist.

32. Assemblé; battement; brisé; cabriole; entrechat, glissade; jeté; pirouette; plié; arabesque

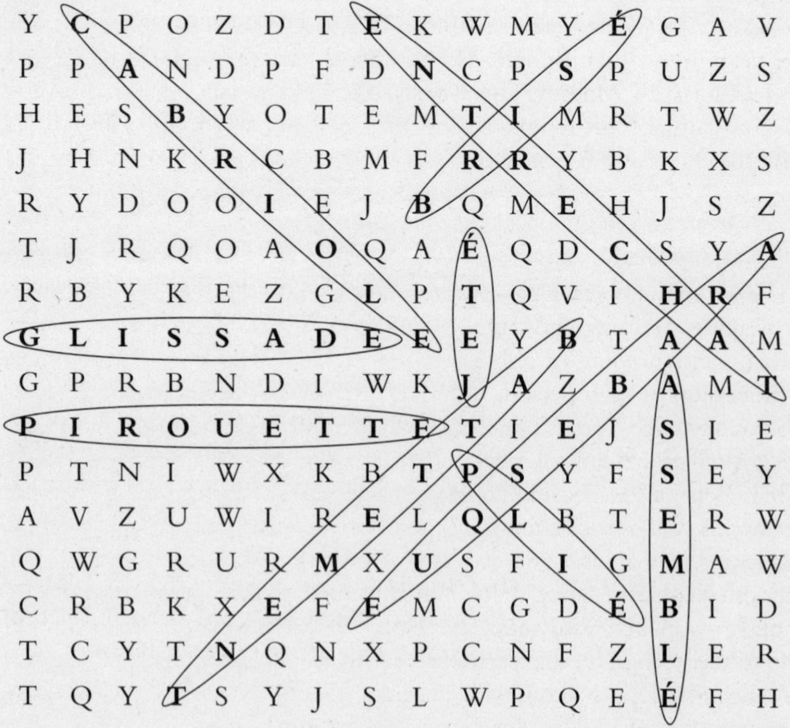

33. d) It seems likely that the dome originated as a roofing method where the absence of suitable timber meant that it was impossible to make a flat roof. First used in much of the Middle East and North Africa whence it spread to other parts of the Islamic world, because of its distinctive form the dome has, like the minaret, become a symbol of Islamic architecture. Igloos (which are also called aputiaks) are the dome-shaped temporary winter home or hunting-ground dwelling of Canadian and Greenland Inuit. The Mousgoum territory lies in the basin of Lake Chad in the far north of Cameroon and their domed hutshells, or 'tolek' have been a source of huge curiosity to architects, explorers and writers alike since the nineteenth century. The ethnologist André Gide wrote in his book *Voyage in the Congo* (1927) that the tolek was: 'A beauty so perfect, so accomplished, that it seems natural . . . The pure curve of its line, which is uninterrupted from base to summit, seems to have been arrived at mathematically, by ineluctable necessity; one instinctively realises how exactly the resistance of the materials must have been calculated.' The Hagia Sophia (also called The Church of the Holy Wisdom) is a domed basilica built in the amazingly short time of about six years in Constantinople. The architects were Anthemius of Tralles and Isidorus of Miletus. The Koricancha Inca temple of the Sun was the most important temple in the Inca Empire, dedicated primarily to Inti, the Sun God. It was one of the most revered temples of the capital city of Cusco, in south-central Peru, but it doesn't have a domed roof.

34. c) A 'masque' is a quasi-dramatic sort of 'skit' where people dress up in disguises and sing and dance before an audience of guests and attendants in a royal court or nobleman's house. The masque could be simply a procession of such persons introduced by a presenter, or it could be an elaborately staged show. The theme of a masque was usually mythological, allegorical or symbolic. Under the Stuarts the masque reached its zenith when Ben Jonson became court poet and endowed the form with great literary, as well as social, force. *The Faithful Shepherdess* is a kind of pastoral tragicomedy that, as far as we know, was oft performed by actors, not random people in fancy dress. *The Parliament of Bees,* published posthumously, is an exquisite masque written as a series of pastoral eclogues about 'the doings, the births, the wars, the wooings' of bees. The masque of *Comus* by John Milton, with music by Henry Lawes, was produced in the great hall of Ludlow Castle, on 29 September 1634.

35.

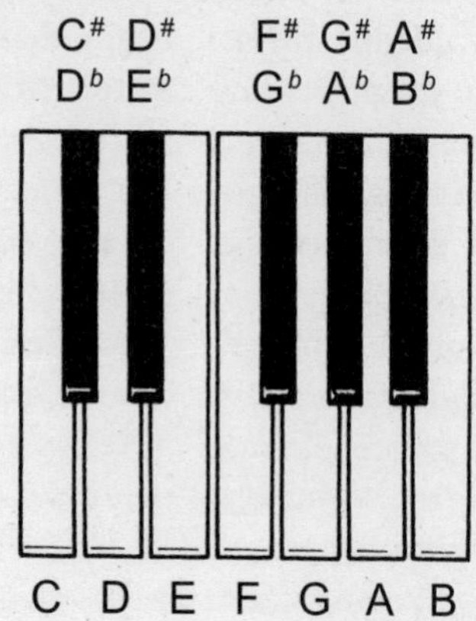

36. a)

37. a) Aristotle, from the *Poetics*; b) George Balanchine (1904–1983), Russian-American choreographer whose 1954 staging of *The Nutcracker* was the first full-length ballet that the New York City Ballet performed and which is said to have saved the company from financial disaster; c) Stéphane Mallarmé (1842–98), French poet and leading member of the Symbolist movement; d) St Basil (329–379), early Church Father who defended the orthodox faith against the heretical Arians; e) Plato, from the *Laws*; f) Isadora Duncan (*c.* 1877–1927), the American interpretive dancer whose work paved the way for modern expressive dance.

38. a) Soon after the First World War, the German artist and poet Kurt Schwitters (1887–1948) began to create compositions assembled from various everyday objects (such as train tickets, wooden spools, newspaper, string, cigarettes and postage stamps). Similarly, his poems were composites of newspaper headlines, advertising slogans and other printed ephemera. He referred to all of his artistic activities as *Merz,* a nonsense word derived from the second syllable of the word *Kommerz* (German: 'commerce').

39.

David Kaminsky: Danny Kaye
Charlton Heston: John Charles Carter
Demi Moore: Demetria Gene Guynes
Harry Houdini: Erik Weisz
Gene Wilder: Jerome Silberman
Meg Ryan: Margaret Hyra
Omar Sharif: Michael Shalhoub
Woody Allen: Allen Konigsberg

40. c), although all three other answers are among the top ten songs played at funerals. 'My Way' originated as a French song called 'Comme d'habitude' ('As Usual') by Claude François. The French version tells the story of a man whose marriage is ending due to the tedium of everyday life. While in France, the singer/songwriter Paul Anka discovered 'Comme d'habitude' and rewrote the lyrics so that the song features a man looking back fondly on a life he lived on his own terms. It became one of Frank Sinatra's signature songs when it was released in 1969.

41. a) *Birth of Venus* (1482–6) is one of the most famous paintings in the world. It was painted by Alessandro di Mariano Filipepi (1445–1510), known as Sandro Botticelli. It hangs in the Uffizi Gallery in Florence. b) *Young Girl in Green* by Tamara de Lempicka (1927), Musée National d'Art Moderne, Paris. When Lempicka died in 1980, her ashes were spread over the top of the volcano Popocatepetl, as per her wishes. c) *Fission* by Bridget Riley (1963). Riley burst on to the London art and cultural scene in the sixties with her illusionistic and abstract paintings which represent 'the pleasures of sight'. *Fission* is a classic example of Riley's work – a square covered in black dots that is rendered vertiginous by progressive warping of the circles and the compression of their spacing. It hangs in the MoMA in New York. d) *Café Terrace at Night* by Vincent Van Gogh (1888). The café depicted still exists in Arles, though today it is called Café van Gogh. This painting is in the Kröller-Müller Museum in Otterlo, Netherlands. e) *Girl with a Pearl Earring* by Johannes Vermeer (1665) is in the Mauritshuis Gallery in The Hague. f) *The Kiss* by Gustav Klimt was painted in 1907–8. Klimt had attempted to represent the subject of fulfillment before, but the embrace depicted here, in a womblike space, has come to be seen as the ultimate image of personal intimacy. It is in the Österreichische Galerie in Vienna.

42. a) The *Didaskalia* provides the names of the dramatists, the plays, the principal actors and the prizes awarded. Euripides is recorded as the author of ninety-two plays (of which only nineteen survive) but he won the first prize only four times, and once posthumously. Whether this was due to the high quality of the contemporary competition or Athenian hostility to his work is difficult to say . . . The crane carrying gods at the theatre of Dionysus did exist and is called the *mêchanê*.

43.

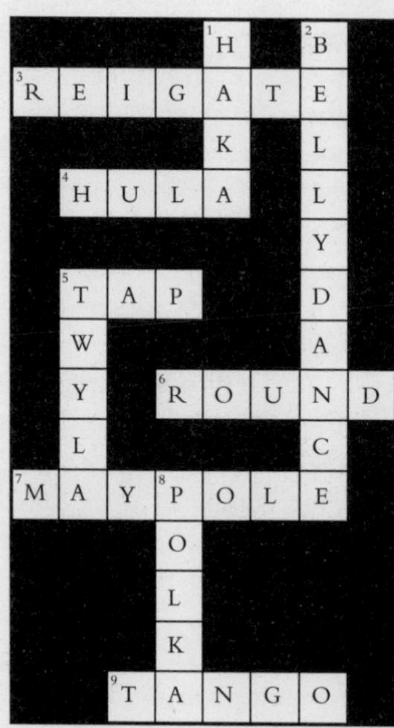

44. b) Quentin Tarantino is a huge fan of the Three Stooges, the American comedy team noted for violent, anarchic slapstick and comedy routines rooted in the burlesque tradition, but couldn't get the rights to show them in the movie. So while a Three Stooges film appears on screen, the Three Stooges themselves do not. Emil Sitka, the frequent Three Stooges co-star who does appear on screen, is credited as 'Hold hands you lovebirds'.

45. a) 'Silent Night'. The origin of the most famous Christmas carol of all time was a poem written in 1816 by Joseph Mohr, an Austrian priest. On Christmas Eve in 1818 in the small alpine village of Oberndorf it is reputed that the organ at St Nicholas Church had broken. Mohr had written a poem called 'Silent Night' ('Stille Nacht') and gave it a friend who composed the melody and finished the simple carol in time for Midnight Mass. b) 'Good King Wenceslas'. The words to this carol (in which there is no reference to the nativity) were written by John Mason Neale and published in 1853, but the music originates in Finland 300 years earlier. St Stephen's feast day was celebrated on 26 December, which is why this song is sung as a Christmas carol. c) 'The Holly and the Ivy'. The carol we are familiar with was first published by Cecil Sharp, though it is thought to have pagan origins and could therefore date back over 1000 years. The holly and the ivy have always been taken indoors during the winter, the hope being that the occupants would survive difficult conditions just like the hardy foliage. It is most unusual for a carol like 'The Holly and the Ivy' to have survived over the years especially during the stern protestant period of the seventeenth century. d) 'Away in a Manger'. Originally published in 1885 in a Lutheran Sunday school book, there is a widespread misconception that the lyrics of 'Away in a Manger' were written by Martin Luther himself. The author is unknown, though the music was composed by William J. Kirkpatrick in 1895.

46. c) Caravaggio had many encounters with the law. In 1600 he was accused of beating up a fellow painter, and the following year he wounded a soldier. In 1603 he was imprisoned on the complaint of another painter and released only through the intercession of the French ambassador. In April 1604 he was accused of throwing a plate of artichokes in the face of a waiter, and in October he was arrested for throwing stones at the Roman Guards. In May 1605 he was seized for misuse of arms, and on 29 July he had to flee Rome because he had wounded a man in defence of his mistress. Within a year, on 29 May 1606, during a furious brawl over a disputed score in a game of tennis in Rome, Caravaggio killed one Ranuccio Tomassoni.

47. a) False. This is, in fact, the definition of auteur theory which became popular in the 1950s. b) True. We say so-called New Wave because it was never a formal branch of film theory but rather a term used to describe the stylistic innovations of a particular group of French directors all working at about the same time. c) False. The term 'the male gaze' originated with the British academic Laura Mulvey in her 1975 essay 'Visual Pleasure and Narrative Cinema' (the meaning of it given in the question is correct, however). d) True. Some of Dziga's *kino-glaz* films include *Shagay, Sovyet!* (*Stride, Soviet!*), 1925, and *Tri pesni o Lenine* (*Three Songs of Lenin*), 1934.

48. b) The acclaimed stage, film and television actor Richard Griffiths stopped in the middle of his lines, fixed the offender with an icy stare and said, 'I am asking you to stand up, leave this auditorium and never, ever come back.' Other members of the audience applauded as the man left the theatre.

49. a) A stave (or 'staff'); b) clef; c) whole note; d) simple time; e) the length of each beat by indicating what kind of note receives one beat; f) measure; g) how many beats there are in a measure; h) volume; i) triad; j) major and minor; k) b-sharp; l) rest. A whole rest.

50. a) Paparazzo, played by Walter Santesso, is a commercial photographer and the film is credited for adding 'paparazzi' to the English language. The film also normalised the adjective 'Felliniesque', referring in part to the director's embrace of the surreal, to many film critics' lexicons.

PHYSICAL EDUCATION

Some people believe that sport is a way of sublimating the intrinsic urge to violence lodged deep in the psyche of all human beings. Others just enjoy watching people running around in shorts or whacking things with different shaped sticks. How you feel about sport is probably influenced by your earliest experiences of competitive exertion in P.E. classes at school. Whether you were sentenced to dragging yourself round the playing fields in freezing sleet, or got to prance about practising the ribbon dance in your rhythmic gymnastics lesson instead, involvement in sport probably instilled in you the values of fair play and introduced you to the satisfaction of pitting yourself against your fellow man with only your own muscles, and possibly some form of arcane equipment to rely upon. Whether you feel traumatised by your memory of the shameful defeat you endured in the egg and spoon race, or hobbled by your increasingly creaky knees, you can still enjoy the vicarious thrill of witnessing the glittering exploits of those heroes of track and field who pit themselves against each other and the elements in the pursuit of everlasting athletic glory.

1. Everyone loves a Renaissance man. We're all familiar with those clever souls who can sashay effortlessly from Science to the Arts but it's less usual to find those of clerical occupations also excelling themselves as physical specimens on the sports fields. Which internationally renowned playwright is the only such writer to appear in the hallowed pages of the *Wisden Cricketers' Almanac*?

a) Harold Pinter
b) Simon Gray
c) Samuel Beckett
d) Noël Coward

2. Who has knocked out more opponents than any other professional boxer?

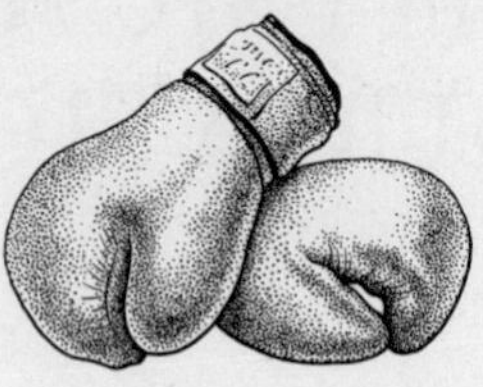

a) Muhammad Ali
b) Sugar Ray Robinson
c) Archie Moore
d) Marvin Hagler

3. There is precious little unsullied tradition in modern football these days, and this is reflected in the lucrative but deeply depressing phenomenon of selling naming rights to stadia. Arsenal changed their home from Highbury to the Emirates, while Bradford City once ran out at Valley Parade and now do so at the distinctly deflating Coral Windows Stadium. Some teams, however, have managed to retain ground names that evoke a little more of their roots – can you match the team with the football club?

a) Deepdale	Burnley
b) Huish Park	Rochdale
c) Moss Rose	Yeovil Town
d) Plainmoor	Southend United
e) Prenton Park	Bury
f) Spotland	Tranmere Rovers
g) Roots Hall	Macclesfield Town
h) Turf Moor	Preston North End
i) Gigg Lane	Torquay United

4. Sean FitzPatrick, John Kirwan, Jonah Lomu and Zin Zan Brook have all played for which awe-inspiring monochrome side?

a) The Australian rugby league
b) A USA basketball team
c) The New Zealand rugby union team
d) A Canadian ice hockey team

5. Which all-American game was invented in 1891 by Canadian James Naismith, who, being a practically minded PE teacher, wanted to devise a cheap, non-contact sport that could be played, with minimal adaptation, in existing gymnasiums (and so all year round), and with very little kit?

a) Baseball
b) Water polo
c) American football
d) Basketball

6. Nothing to do with the frequent smashed noses and mangled ears that are the least of rugby players' injuries these days, what is the significance in rugby of 'broken time'?

7. You'd be hard pressed to convince some people that there is more to sport than football. Happily, life is full of variety and different countries have very different beautiful games. Match the definitions of these international sports with their names:

a) Ritualised Brazilian combat dance much beloved of telly advertisers	Sumo
b) Team territorial wrestling game popular in India and across Asia	Pelota
c) Calf-carrying horseback sport popular in Central Asia, especially Afghanistan	Kabaddi
d) Rugby/football cross played by whey-cheeked aristocratic schoolboys	Ba' Game
e) Basque racket sport	Capoeira
f) Japanese wrestling for those of good girth	Buzkashi
g) Sophisticated version of keepie-uppies originating in Malaysia and popular throughout south-east Asia	Eton Wall Game
h) Mass participation football game involving whole towns in Scotland, most famously played by Orcadians in Kirkwall	Sepak Takraw

8. Gnarly dude Kelly Slater is the current world champion in which bodacious sport?

a) Ski jumping
b) Surfing
c) Snowboarding
d) Skateboarding

9. From 'Beefy' Botham to Eddie 'the Eagle' Edwards, and 'Psycho' Pearce to 'the Thorpedo', 'the Round Mound of Rebound' and QPR defender, 'One Size' Fitz Hall, sports fans love a good nickname. Snooker has some of the best. Which humorous handle was given to snooker legend Steve Davis:

a) The Whirlwind
b) The Essex Exocet
c) The Nugget
d) Mr Intensity

10. Who comes next in this sequence of illustrious recent football stars: Fabio Cannavaro, Kaka, Cristiano Ronaldo, Lionel Messi?

a) Steven Gerrard
b) Andres Iniesta
c) Lionel Messi
d) Mesut Ozil

11. Flashes of aggressive neon zipping up brutal gradients with piston-like limbs whirling, professional cyclists are an exciting spectacle to behold. Who is the only cyclist to win each of the three Grand Tour events (the Tour de France, the Giro d'Italia and the Vuelta a España) at least twice?

a) Eddy Merckx
b) Lance Armstrong
c) Miguel Indurain
d) Bernard Hinault

12. What exhausting honour is shared by tennis players John Isner and Nicolas Mahut?

a) Record number of doubles titles
b) Longest rally in tennis history
c) Longest match in tennis history
d) Record number of singles matches played against each other

13. Not just the second-best right arm in the cricketing business (according to the ICC rankings), spin-wizard Graeme Swann also has a winning way with a tune. What is the name of the band in which he is the lead singer?

a) Dr Comfort and the Lurid Revelations
b) Six and Out
c) The Big Bad Dread and the Bald Head
d) The Droitwich Spinners

14. The honourable pastime of darts is thought to have its origin as a form of archery practice that migrated into public drinking establishments. Which of these numbers in the modern game is the odd one out and why?

a) 159
b) 162
c) 166
d) 167

15. Who is the odd one out of the following list?

a) Kenny Dalglish
b) Ryan Giggs
c) Peter Shilton
d) Pat Jennings

16. The Irish are passionate about their national sports: hurling and Gaelic football are a key part of their proudly held cultural heritage, so much so that it is hard to find any area of Irish life which is untouched by the GAA (the Gaelic Athletic Association). Which of the following Irish politicians is the odd one out and why?

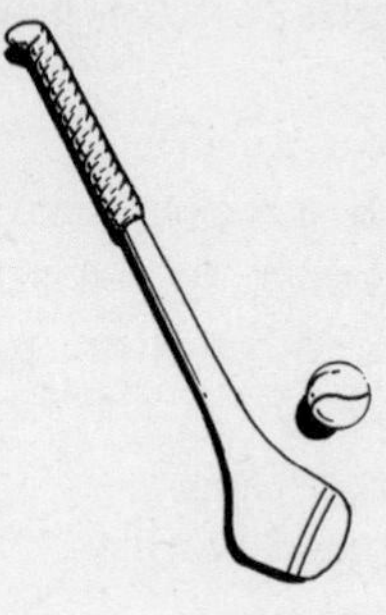

a) Jack Lynch
b) Dick Spring
c) Bertie Ahern
d) Seamus Mallon

17. We're sure that the German football team is endlessly entertained by being reminded of the two World Wars and one World Cup we have over on them, but when did Germany last win the said World Cup?

a) 1990
b) 1992
c) 1994
d) 1998

18. Cricket is a famously complicated game for the uninitiated, with even the field placings having their own intricate and arcane language. Can you find twelve of them hidden in the grid below?

G W Z O T M I D W I C K E T

S P O T Y I K M N C A L I E

X O Y S I L L Y M I D O N T

R I P J I K L A V B E N F T

U N G R A P O T N M I G S R

T T U W E R H D I K M O O F

E T Y F M H J P I O N N T Y

S E T Y I O M G L I S A T E

L D W E D N P U N I Q U E L

T O P X O N E L H U U K X A

P O N D F U L L G R A N T O

I B O G F E A Y E R R I R P

C B O U S L E R S G E C A B

L L O N D T Y A I N L Z C R

S K O O M T O D S A E Y O C

V L R I G B I P M X G Q V P

T H I R D M A N F R T I E A

D R O P I K D L I S E D R L

19. The first depictions of humans swimming appear in cave paintings from thousands of years ago. Nowadays it is a hairless, high-tech-swimsuit sport but the strokes remain familiar from those earliest pictograms. Who beat hirsute hunk Mark Spitz's record of winning seven gold medals at one Olympics, set at the 1972 games in Munich?

a) Ian Thorpe
b) Rebecca Adlington
c) Michael Phelps
d) Ryan Lochte

20. The Calcutta Cup, the Bledisloe Cup and the Webb Ellis Cup are all trophies in which sport?

a) Ruby Union
b) Cricket
c) Australian Rules Football
d) Squash

21. Didier Defago followed in the footsteps of equally wonderfully named greats like Pirmin Zurbriggen and Franz Klammer by winning gold in which event at the Vancouver Winter Olympics in 2010?

a) Speed skating
b) Luge
c) Men's downhill skiing
d) Men's figure skating

22. Rugby champions are not generally renowned for their svelte elegance but in fact these most tenacious and tough team players come in all shapes and sizes. Put the following men's rugby union players in descending weight order.

a) Sebastian Chabal (France)
b) Jonny Wilkinson (England)
c) John Hayes (Ireland)
d) Shane Williams (Wales)

23. Here is a bit of a soccer stumper for you: there are currently four English football clubs in the four top divisions whose names begin and end with the same letter of the alphabet. Can you name them?

24. Ah, the sweet smell of equine exertion, the fascinating discussions of the 'going', the windmilling tic-tac of the bookies, the pounds frittered away because you happen to like the colour of the jockey's silks or the name of the horse, and of course the hats. What can beat a day at the races? Which is the odd one out of the following famous English horse races:

a) St Leger
b) The Oaks
c) Cheltenham Gold Cup
d) The Derby

25. It is a beautifully ornate silver ewer, first won in 1851, and is the oldest trophy still competed for in any sport. For which salty sporting challenge is it awarded?

a) Swimming the English Channel
b) Swimming the Hellespont
c) The America's Cup in yachting
d) The Blue Riband for the fastest crossing of the Atlantic

26. In 1547 King James II of Scotland banned the playing of golf as he was worried it was distracting his subjects from the more useful practice of archery. Happily, nowadays golf no longer has to be played in secret, at risk of royal disapproval, and professional golfers can wear their silly trousers with pride. Put the following top players in descending order according to the number of majors they have won in their career.

a) Tiger Woods
b) Nick Faldo
c) Jack Nicklaus
d) Gary Player

27. The most gruelling of all running races, the marathon, is named after a famous battle in Ancient Greece in 490 BCE, where, according to legend, one of the swift-footed Athenian soldiers brought the news of victory against the Persians back to the capital by jogging the twenty-six miles from the battlefield to the capital in one go. Who is the current world record holder in the men's marathon?

a) Moses Kiptanui
b) Haile Gebrselassie
c) Brendan Foster
d) Said Aouita

28. Sports commentary is an eloquent art, requiring lightning-quick thinking, poetic turns of phrase and the ability to capture the atmosphere and tension of athletic endeavour in all its glory. Match these commentators with the sports they have done much to define:

a) Dan Maskell	Rugby League
b) Kenneth Wolstenholme	Wrestling
c) Harry Carpenter	Snooker
d) Ted Lowe	Rugby Union
e) David Coleman	Horse racing
f) Eddie Waring	Golf
g) Bill McLaren	Tennis
h) Peter Aliss	Motor racing
i) Kent Walton	Football
j) Peter O'Sullevan	Boxing
k) Brian Johnston	Athletics
l) Murray Walker	Cricket

29. Which ancient, regal game is also known as court tennis, royal tennis and jeu de paume?

a) Real tennis
b) Badminton
c) Table tennis
d) Croquet

30. For some it's just a frantically speeded-up version of the M25, for others it's the pinnacle of sporting entertainment. Motor racing is a big-money, high-tech, thrills and spills spectacular, and also extremely dangerous. Put the following competitors in ascending order of most driver's championships won:

a) Ayrton Senna
b) Michael Schumacher
c) Stirling Moss
d) Alain Prost

31. If you arrived at a bonspiel armed with a stone and a broom, which winter sport would you be about to take part in?

a) Ice hockey
b) Bobsleigh
c) Curling
d) Freestyle snowboarding

32. It will be to your advantage in working out the following puzzle if you love tennis. Decode the following anagrams to find twelve top players, past and present.

a) Sir Bob Creek
b) Alien Siesta
c) Conjoins Mr My
d) Biennial Elk Jig
e) Canoes Miles
f) Value Slim Wins
g) Meats as Prep
h) Area Lad Flan
i) Rave Lord
j) Fag Set Riff
k) Licks Jet Rims
l) Avian Ride Wig

33. Although much derided, wrestling is an internationally popular phenomenon with huge followings in Japan, Mexico and the USA in particular, as well as being beloved by British sports fans of a certain age for brightening up boring Saturday afternoons with larger-than-life characters and acrobatic antics. Which of the following is NOT a wrestling hold?

a) Boston Crab
b) Stretch Plum
c) Murakami Forklift
d) Half Nelson

34. Who is the all-time leading scorer in Premier League football?

a) Alan Shearer
b) Didier Drogba
c) Thierry Henry
d) Ruud van Nistelrooy

35. What is the significance of the number 766 in England's 2010 Ashes series victory in Australia?

a) It is the record-breaking highest first innings total set by England in the second test.
b) It is the number of runs conceded by Aussie fast bowler Mitchell Johnson in the series.
c) It is the number of different-coloured panama hats worn by Geoffrey Boycott in the commentary box.
d) It is the number of runs scored by Alistair Cook in the series.

36. If you add the number of players on a netball team to those on a rugby league team, to those on hockey team, then subtract the number of players on a lacrosse team, what figure are you left with?

a) 14
b) 18
c) 21
d) 28

37. Why do golf balls have dimples in them?

a) To grip the face of the club better.
b) Because they were originally covered in treated pig skin and the dimples replicate this pockmarked effect.
c) To make them easier to find in the grass as light hits the dimples.
d) They give the ball a steadier and longer flight.

38. What do these five footballers have in common: Bellini (1958), Mauro (1962), Carlos Alberto (1970), Dunga (1994) and Cafu (2002)?

39. Who owns the following sporting icons?

a) A.C. Milan
b) Rule of Law
c) The Oval
d) Muhammad Ali's 'Rumble in the Jungle' robe

40. Whether you go for the grit of the gridiron or the glamour and glitz of the half-time entertainment, American Football is the perfect place to punch the air with a giant foam hand in time to a Bon Jovi classic. Which of the following is NOT a position in an AFL or NFL team?

a) Wide receiver
b) Tight end
c) Wing attack
d) Cornerback

41. Which baseball team won the World Series in 2004, and why was it significant?

a) St Louis Cardinals
b) New York Yankees
c) Boston Red Sox
d) Baltimore Orioles

42. 'What you're loo-king at, is the mas-ter plan . . .' You wouldn't want your gardener taking out your appendix, or your solicitor fixing your plumbing. However, several sporting greats have felt it necessary to mount attacks on the pop charts. Match the following sporting artistes with their ill-advised forays into the world of music:

a) Glenn Hoddle and Chris Waddle	'Snooker Loopy'
b) Liverpool FC	'Diamond Lights'
c) Matchroom Mob with Chas 'n' Dave	'Fog on the Tyne'
d) New Order featuring John Barnes	'The Anfield Rap'
e) Lindisfarne featuring Gazza	'World in Motion'

43. It would be a dull world if all the football clubs in the UK were sensibly named Blahblah United or Whatsit FC. Thank goodness our footballing forefathers showed more imagination than this. In which British towns or cities are the following mysteriously-named clubs situated?

a) Aston Villa
b) Heart of Midlothian
c) Port Vale
d) Partick Thistle
e) Leyton Orient
f) Queen of the South
g) Tranmere Rovers
h) St Mirren

44. Who is the odd one out of these sports stars and why?

a) Jim Brown (American footballer)
b) O. J. Simpson (American footballer)
c) Vinnie Jones (footballer)
d) David Beckham (footballer)

45. A recurve, compound and a barebow are all types of what?

a) Leg fractures common in football players
b) Types of crown green bowling shots
c) Types of bow used in archery
d) Types of offensive manoeuvres in American football

46. At which Olympic Games did famous vegan Carl Lewis win four gold medals?

a) Munich 1972
b) Moscow 1980
c) Los Angeles 1984
d) Seoul 1988

47. In cycling's most prestigious event, the Tour de France, various jerseys are awarded for different feats as the race progresses. Can you match the discipline of the wearer with the jersey?

a) King of the mountains – the best climber in the higher sections of the race	Yellow
b) Best rider under twenty-five years old	Green
c) Overall race leader	White
d) Highest points total – points are awarded for various sprints	White with red polka dots

48. The following is a description of which hotly debated cricket law?

The striker is out in the circumstances set out below.

(a) The bowler delivers a ball, not being a No ball and (b) the ball, if it is not intercepted full pitch, pitches in line between wicket and wicket or on the off side of the striker's wicket and (c) the ball not having previously touched his bat, the striker intercepts the ball, either full pitch or after pitching, with any part of his person and (d) the point of impact, even if above the level of the bails, either (i) is between wicket and wicket or (ii) if the striker has made no genuine attempt to play the ball with his bat, is either between wicket and wicket or outside the line of the off stump and (e) but for the interception, the ball would have hit the wicket.

a) Leg before wicket
b) Caught behind
c) Duckworth Lewis method
d) Run out

49. Balestra, patinando, envelopment and appel are all manoeuvres in which Olympic sport?

a) Gymnastics
b) Figure skating
c) Fencing
d) Basketball

50. If marathons, duathlons, triathlons, quadrathlons, pentathlons and heptathlons are not enough for you, what you need is a good decathlon. Can you name the ten events that make up this gruelling Olympic competition?

PHYSICAL EDUCATION ANSWERS

1. c) Craggy-faced genius Samuel Beckett won the Nobel Prize in Literature in 1969 and is best known for his existentialist masterpiece *Waiting for Godot*. As a youth, Beckett was a keen cricketer and represented Dublin University in two first-class games against Northamptonshire, thus earning his place in Wisden. He scored 35 runs at an average of 8.75, and bowled 23 parsimonious overs conceding 64 runs without taking a wicket. Both Simon Gray and Harold Pinter were also cricket lovers; Pinter was first captain then chairman of the respected wandering club side, the Gaieties, while Gray waxed lyrical in his famous diaries about the wonder of Andrew Flintoff.

2. c) Ol' Mongoose, as he was known, finished with career stats of 220 bouts of which 131 were won by knock-out. His career spanned an incredible four decades in which he fought both Rocky Marciano and, in 1962, his one-time pupil Cassius Clay (who changed his name to Muhammad Ali in 1964), who defeated him in round four.

3.

a) Deepdale – Preston North End
b) Huish Park – Yeovil Town
c) Moss Rose – Macclesfield Town
d) Plainmoor – Torquay United
e) Prenton Park – Tranmere Rovers
f) Spotland – Rochdale
g) Roots Hall – Southend United
h) Turf Moor – Burnley
i) Gigg Lane – Bury

4. c) More usually known as the All Blacks of course.

5. d) Unusually for a new sport, Naismith very nearly got it all right first time – his first set of regulations were so well-considered that twelve of the thirteen still stand, with only the rule against dribbling relaxed in the modern game.

6. 'Broken time' was the term used for the hours lost to working men in the north of England while playing rugby for club and country. The loss of six shillings a week was not such a life-changing consideration for their upper-class counterparts who played and ran the game in the south, but for the men of Bradford, Wakefield and the other industrial towns whose players increasingly dominated the game, it was a serious business. The failure of the governing Rugby Football Union to agree to compensate players for broken time, in fierce protection of the amateur status of the game, eventually led to the schism between the RFU and the newly formed Northern Rugby Football Union in 1895, which would eventually become the Rugby League we know today. The loss of their competitive, brawny northern colleagues was felt immediately on the English national side – before the split the team had won thirty-four of its previous fifty-four games, but afterwards won just ten of the subsequent forty-nine games and didn't win the Home Nations Championship (forerunner of the Six Nations) for another fifteen years.

7.

a) Capoeira
b) Kabaddi
c) Buzkashi
d) Eton Wall Game
e) Pelota
f) Sumo
g) Sepak Takraw
h) Ba' Game

8. b) In fact, Slater could probably lay claim to being the most successful surfer of all time. He has been World Champion a record ten times and has won more career events than any other surfer in history.

9. c) Davis was christened the Nugget by his friends as he was such a reliable bet as a young player doing the rounds of the Essex snooker halls. The Whirlwind is Jimmy White, Mr Intensity is Peter Ebdon and the Essex Exocet is the nickname favoured by Ronnie O'Sullivan over the more common 'Rocket' sobriquet.

10. c) The list shows players who have won the prestigious Ballon d'Or (now the FIFA Ballon d'Or) for European Footballer of the Year since 2006. Messi won for the second year in a row in 2010. The first recipient of the award was Stanley Matthews in 1956 and only three players have won the award three times (Johan Cruyff, Michel Platini and Marco van Basten).

11. d) Hinault was known as 'le Blaireau' (the Badger) because of his tenacious pursuit of his prey. He learned his craft by riding the unforgiving hills of his native Brittany in all weathers. He is also one of very few top cyclists to be untainted by any doping scandals. The legendary Merckx won more Grand Tour events overall (eleven to Hinault's ten) but only won the Vuelta once.

12. c) Isner eventually won the match at Wimbledon in 2010, 6-4, 3-6, 6-7, 7-6, 70-68 (!), after an astonishing 183 games, played in eleven hours over three days.

13. a) Six and Out is the group in which Australian speed merchant Brett Lee plays bass, while Curtly Ambrose, erstwhile scourge of English batsmen generally and Michael Atherton in particular, plays bass in the Big Bad Dread and the Bald Head.

14. d) The other three totals are impossible to check out with only three darts. A player needs to finish on a double or bull's eye, so to close out a leg on 167 you'd need to hit treble 20, treble 19 followed by the bull. Good arrows!

15. b) The other three are the most capped players of the 'home' national football teams, Dalglish for Scotland (102 caps), Shilton for England (125) and Jennings for Northern Ireland (119). The most capped Welshman is in fact goalkeeper Neville Southall (92). Giggs played for Wales 64 times and retired from international football in 2007.

16. c) The others all played Gaelic games to a high standard before embarking on their political careers. Jack Lynch reached the pinnacle in both his sporting and political careers and is a genuine GAA legend. He represented Cork and Munster at hurling and football, winning five All-Ireland titles in the former and one in the latter, before going on to be Taoiseach from 1963 to 1973 and from 1977 to 1979.

17. a) In fact the team was still classified as West Germany in 1990 as the nation reeled from the recent fall of the Berlin Wall. You might notice that 1990 is considerably more recent than 1966, but still, there's no harm in reminding them of a defeat that took place coming up for half a century ago.

18. Fine Leg, Extra Cover, Third Man, Slip, Gully, Square Leg, Point, Silly Mid On, Mid Off, Long On, Long Stop, Mid Wicket.

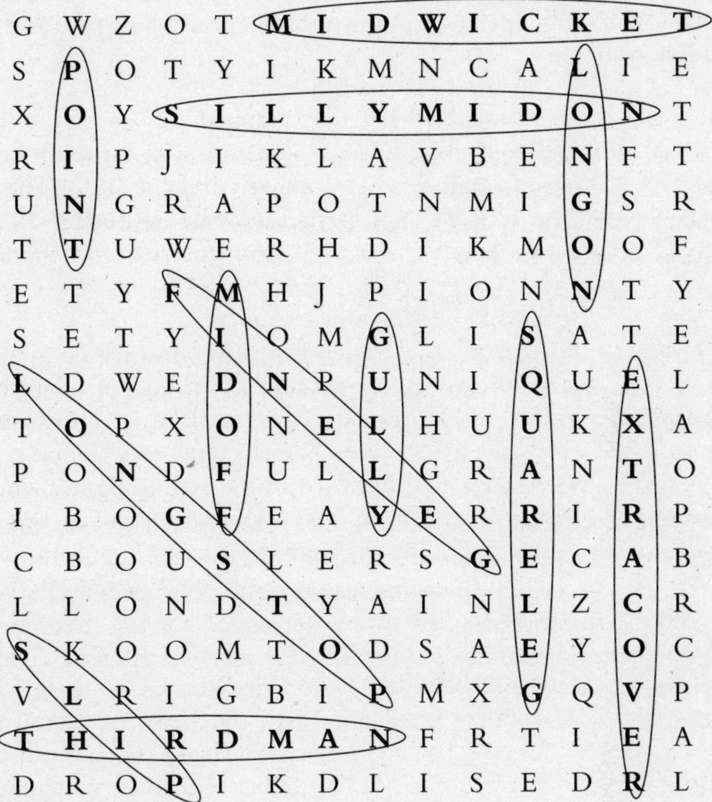

19. c) Phelps won eight gold medals in swimming at Beijing in 2008. He has won a total of sixteen Olympic medals, second only to the gymnast Larissa Latynina who won eighteen medals over three games.

20. a) The Calcutta Cup is contested by England and Scotland, and the Bledisloe Cup is contested between New Zealand and Australia. The Webb Ellis Cup is the rugby union World Cup trophy. It is named after William Webb Ellis, the schoolboy who, according to legend, invented the sport.

21. c) The amazing Alpine Abfahrtsläufer won this spectacular slide with a time of 1 minute 54.31, beating the silver medal-winner by a crucial 0.07 seconds. Defago became the oldest ever gold-medal winner of an Olympic men's downhill event at the grand old age of thirty-two.

22. c), a), b), d). Ireland's stalwart prop (also known as the Bull) weighs in at 282 lb (over 20 stone), Chabal, France's No. 8, weighs 252 lb, England's talismanic fly-half weighs 193 lb, while mercurial Welsh winger Williams weighs 169 lb.

23. Liverpool, Aston Villa, Charlton Athletic and Northampton Town. Score a bonus point if you managed to get all of these in under three minutes.

24. c) The Gold Cup is a national hunt event, with the course running over jumps. The other three are not just flat races, but are also three of the five 'classics' of the flat-racing season – the other two are the 1000 and 2000 Guineas. These last two were named for the prize-money the winners received. Now that we've gone decimal, the prize fund for both stands at over £375,000.

25. c)

26. c) 18; a) 14; d) 9; b) 6.

27. b) The Ethiopian completed the Berlin course in a staggering 2 hours, 3 minutes and 59 seconds in 2008. The women's world record is held by Paula Radcliffe. Fortunately, competitors these days tend to have happier fates than the original marathon runner, usually named as Pheidippides, who is said to have died of exhaustion immediately after delivering his joyful message.

28.

a) Tennis
b) Football
c) Boxing
d) Snooker
e) Athletics
f) Rugby League
g) Rugby Union
h) Golf
i) Wrestling
j) Horse racing
k) Cricket
l) Motor racing

29. a) Real tennis is thought to date back to the fifteenth century, and was famously much-loved by the young Henry VIII, before he clearly stopped working out and developed the rather less athletic figure of his middle age. It is still played widely today but much less than its Johnny-come-lately nineteenth-century cousin, lawn tennis.

30. c) 0; a) 3; d) 4; b) 5. Stirling Moss never won a driver's championship – by anyone's standards he was one of the all-time greats, but his career unfortunately overlapped with probably *the* all-time greatest, Juan Manuel Fangio, who won five driver's championships.

31. c) Curling is an ancient game whose precise origins are unclear though it has roots in several of the frostier parts of Northern Europe, even appearing in a painting by sixteenth-century Flemish master Pieter Bruegel.

32.

a) Boris Becker
b) Ilie Nastase
c) Jimmy Connors

d) Billie Jean King
e) Monica Seles
f) Venus Williams
g) Pete Sampras
h) Rafael Nadal
i) Rod Laver
j) Steffi Graf
k) Kim Clijsters
l) Virginia Wade

33. c) The Boston Crab and the Half Nelson are two of the most well-known and popular holds, while the Stretch Plum is named after Japanese women's wrestler Plum Mariko.

34. a) The Premier League has only existed since 1992, when it replaced the old First Division. Shearer scored 260 Premiership goals for three clubs: Southampton, Blackburn Rovers and his hometown team, Newcastle United.

35. d) Cook's batting was the bedrock of England's triumph. His total is the second-highest ever for an English batsman in an Ashes series, after Wally Hammond's 905 runs in 1928-9. Cook credits his choirboy past for instilling the necessary self-discipline to endure such epic episodes at the crease.

36. c) 21 (7 players on a netball team, 13 players on a rugby league team, 11 players on a hockey team and 10 players on a lacrosse team), which incidentally is the number of points required to win a game of badminton.

37. d) Golf balls were originally smooth but it was soon discovered that as they acquired nicks and dents with prolonged use, drag was reduced and the balls went further and performed generally better. This led to the development of intentionally dimpled balls.

38. They all had the honour of hoisting aloft the World Cup as captains of the Brazilian team. The brilliant Brazilians have won the World Cup five times – more than any other nation. World Cup victories can have a very stimulating effect, not just on national pride, but also on a country's economy: after its 1994 win Brazil saw a 5.9% increase in economic growth and after 2002 it saw a rise of 2.7% and the reversal of its recession.

39.

a) Silvio Berlusconi.
b) Sheikh Mohammed bin Rashid Al Maktoum, ruler of Dubai. His family's stables, Godolphin, own a host of winning steeds.
c) Prince Charles – The Oval is officially owned by the Duchy of Cornwall.
d) The US government – The Smithsonian's National Museum of American History has this robe as an exhibit.

40. c) Wing attack is a position in netball.

41. c) This was the first time the most famous of all baseball teams had won the World Series since 1918.

42.

a) 'Diamond Lights'
b) 'The Anfield Rap'
c) 'Snooker Loopy'
d) 'World in Motion'
e) 'Fog on the Tyne'

43.

a) Birmingham
b) Edinburgh
c) Stoke-on-Trent
d) Glasgow

e) London
f) Dumfries
g) Birkenhead
h) Paisley

44. d) The other three all went from sporting to film careers, with varying degrees of success. Jim Brown is widely regarded as one of the greats of NFL, and subsequently went on to star in a string of 'blaxploitation' films, as well as appearing among a star-studded cast in *The Dirty Dozen*. O. J. Simpson is probably best-known to moviegoers for his appearance in *Towering Inferno*, but after a murder, a car chase and a trial is now much more (in)famous than either American football or films could have made him. Soccer ruffian Vinnie Jones exploited his hard-man image to good effect with an appearance in *Lock, Stock and Two Smoking Barrels*. Beckham is still just about playing top-level football, but with his male-model good looks a future in film surely beckons. The closest he's come so far is appearing as the subject in Sam Taylor-Wood's video artwork, 'David', where he snoozes throughout.

45. c) The archery contest at the 2012 London Olympic games will be held on the hallowed turf of Lord's cricket ground.

46. c) Lewis won gold in the 100m, 200m, long jump and 4 x 100m relay, thus emulating Jesse Owens' famous achievement at the Berlin games in 1936. He wasn't a vegan at this stage in his career but switched to a vegetable-only diet in 1990.

47.
a) White with red polka dots
b) White
c) Yellow
d) Green

48. a) These days lbw appeals and dismissals have a new level of accuracy or contentiousness (depending on your point of view) as they can now be referred to a third, off-field umpire for review by video before a final decision is reached.

49. c) It may sound like gobbledegook to the uninitiated but a balestra is a short preparatory jump forward, a patinando is a step forward with a simultaneous rear-footed appel, envelopment is the controlling of an opponent's blade (the foible) by making a complete circle maintaining blade contact throughout, and an appel is the action of hitting the floor with the ball of the foot.

50. They are the 100m, 400m, 1500m, 110m hurdles, long jump, high jump, pole vault, shot put, discus and javelin. Phew! No wonder the winner of the gold medal in the decathlon is traditionally acknowledged as the world's greatest athlete.

ACKNOWLEDGEMENTS

We are very grateful to: Rosemary Davidson, Gemma Avery, Simon Rhodes, Rachel Cugnoni, Monique Corless, Jane Kirby, Tom Drake-Lee, Lucy Luck, Claire Wishaw, Roger Bratchell, Dan Franklin, Oliver Bebb and Chloe Johnson-Hill. Also to Christopher Wormell, Iree Pugh, John Garrett, Chris Lyon, Peter Ward and Lindsay Davies.

And special thanks to: Rosalind Porter, Rachel Salvidge and Jack Murphy.

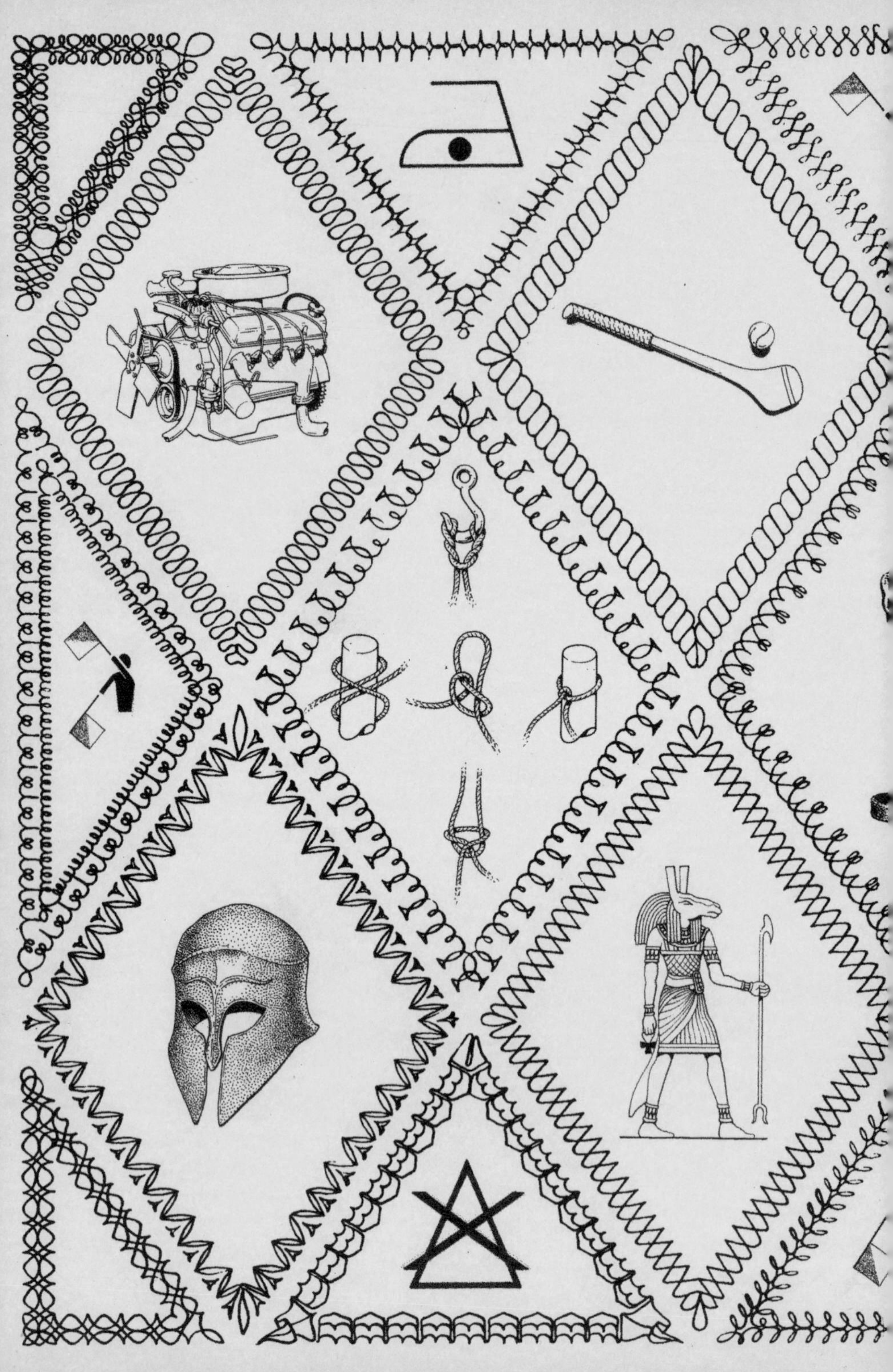